THE CRITICAL YEARS

The
Critical Years

Young Adults and the Search for Meaning, Faith, and Commitment

SHARON PARKS

HarperSanFrancisco

A Division of HarperCollins*Publishers*

Grateful acknowledgment is made for use of the following: "Take Something Like a Star" from *The Poetry of Robert Frost*, edited by Edward Connery Lathem. Copyright 1949, © 1969 by Holt, Rinehart and Winston. Copyright © 1977 by Lesley Frost Ballantine. Reprinted by permission of the Estate of Robert Frost and Henry Holt and Company. From *The Uncommitted: Alienated Youth in American Society*, by Kenneth Keniston. Copyright © 1965 by Kenneth Keniston. Reprinted by permission of Harcourt Brace Jovanovich, Inc. From *Youth and Dissent: The Rise of a New Opposition*, by Kenneth Keniston. Copyright © 1960, 1962, 1968, 1969, 1970, 1971 by Kenneth Keniston. Reprinted by permission of Harcourt Brace Jovanovich, Inc. From *Seduction of the Spirit* by Harvey Cox. Copyright © 1973 by Harvey Cox. Reprinted by permission of Simon and Schuster, Inc. and The Sterling Lord Agency, Inc.

continued on p. 247

FIRST HARPERCOLLINS PAPERBACK EDITION PUBLISHED IN 1991.

Library of Congress Cataloging-in-Publication Data

Parks, Sharon.
    The critical years : young adults and the search for meaning, faith, and commitment / Sharon Parks.
      p.   cm.
    Reprint. Originally published: San Francisco : Harper & Row, © 1986.
    Includes bibliographical references and index.
    ISBN 0–06–066488–6 (alk. paper)
    1. Young adults—Religious life.   I. Title.
[BV4529.2.P37   1991]
248.8'3—dc20   90–44659
                                            CIP

91 92 93 94 95 FAIR 10 9 8 7 6 5 4 3 2 1

This edition is printed on acid-free paper that meets the American National Standards Institute Z39.48 Standard.

Contents:

Acknowledgments   ix

Introduction   xii

1. The Elusiveness of Adulthood   1

2. Meaning-Making: An Activity of Faith   9

3. Developmental Theories: Insights into the Motion of Faith   28

4. The Journey Toward Mature Adult Faith: A Model   43

5. Young Adult Faith: Promise and Vulnerability   73

6. Imagination: The Power of Adult Faith   107

7. Higher Education: A Community of Imagination   133

8. Culture as Mentor   177

Appendix A   206

Appendix B   208

Notes   209

Index   238

For

Rick, Rob, and Wendy Evans
Matt, Josh, and Timmy Avery
Susie, Jeff, and Krista Hunt
and Timothy Hull
who will all be a part of our next generation of
young adults

Acknowledgments

This book is shaped, in part, by a conviction of the interdependence of all life—a relational principle to which the creation of this book itself bears witness. I am grateful to many persons and institutions who have directly and indirectly contributed to the formation of the thought and work presented in this volume.

Teachers and mentors who have shaped not only my work but my life and who thereby have been for me the sort of "professors" described in this book are Clarence Simpson, Marion Jenkins, David Dilworth, James Loder, Jacqueline Grennan Wexler, Marion Hackett, Richard P. Langford, Beverly Harrison, James W. Fowler, William R. Rogers, Richard R. Niebuhr, William G. Perry, and my parents, Emmett and Eloys Parks. In relation to this book, among these I must express particular appreciation to Jim Fowler. His initial work in faith development created the context for my doctoral work, and though he left Boston in my first year of study, he continued to serve as a primary advisor—an act of fidelity perhaps only those who have engaged in doctoral study can fully appreciate.

Faculty and administrators of Whitworth College, especially David Erb, Duncan Ferguson, Edward Lindaman, Shirlene Short, and David Winter, helped create the context in which the central ideas of this work and my energy for it initially found form. The Danforth Foundation and particularly Robert Rankin offered decisive encouragements, both financial and intellectual, in the initial stages of my study. The Chinook Learning Center and Community, co-directed by Fritz and Vivienne Hull, has most significantly nurtured and sustained the spirit and vision of this writing; Harvard University, particularly colleagues and students at the Divinity School, has fostered the ongoing discovery and discipline that have informed and refined this work.

My colleagues who form the Clinical-Developmental Institute—Robert Kegan, Gil Noam, Anne Colby, Ann Henderson, Laura Rogers, Alexandra Hewer, Michael Basseches, Robert Goodman, and Ann Higgins—provide the locus of conversation which has kept alive the intuition that the fundamental motion of personality is the evolution of the shared activity of meaning-making. It is our growing conviction that this understanding can make an essential contribution to the transformation both of persons and of cultures. Cheryl and Jim Keen and Jim and Roswitha Botkin, along with our friends at the International Center for Integrative Studies in New York, continue to inspire and confirm my conviction that educators have a primary contribution to make to the future of the global human family.

The actual writing of the book has required a host of others. Karen Thorkilsen, Linda Barnes, Larry Daloz, Glenn Jolley, John Mann, and Mary Moschella gave a quality of care to the formulation of this manuscript that reflected the quality and commitments of their own lives, and in so doing they provided the decisive affirmation and encouragement that made this book possible.

Others who read (and in some cases reread) portions of the manuscript and contributed both precision and support were Bill Perry, Sharon Bauer-Breakstone, Kristin Morrison, Robert Kegan, George Rupp, Susan McCaslin, Dwayne Huebner, Owen Thomas, Craig Dykstra, Donald Capps, J. Paul Balas, David Grainger, and my sister, Patricia Parks Evans.

Patricia McCallum, Deborah Haynes, and Woody Sheetz-Willard contributed their skill as research assistants. Margaret Studier not only worked wizardry with the word processors but also attended to content and editorial concerns, giving of her time and energy far beyond what was merely expected or required. John Loudon, my editor at Harper & Row, was consistently a source of competent support.

I am most deeply indebted to my students and other young adults who have trusted a portion of their lives with me and in so doing have required me to reconsider earlier theoretical assumptions and to reflect upon the shipwreck, gladness, and amazement of my own young adulthood. They have thereby invited me into more faithful theory building (theory is, more than we theorists find it easy to admit, at least in part "biography writ large").

Though I have acknowledged all of those named above, it still must be said that I have been dependent upon yet many other friends, family members, and colleagues who have believed in me and in the importance of this work. The writing of a book can be an onerous task; but it is also an occasion for recognizing that one's life is dependent upon and blessed by an infinite circle of relationships.

Sharon Parks

Cambridge, Massachusetts
The Feast of All Saints, 1985

Introduction

"There must be more to life than watching young people grow to a point in life when they realize there has to be more to life." This wry comment, which appeared in *The New York Times Magazine* a few years ago, succinctly raises the problem of meaning-making in adulthood, while implying that there is a "point in life" where that problem begins. This book holds that it is in young adulthood that a person begins self-consciously to reflect on the meaning of life itself. Young adulthood plays a critical role in the drama of human life. In the recognition of young adulthood as a crucial and "new" era in the human life cycle, much is at stake, not only for the individual, but for the culture as a whole. Young adulthood is the birthplace of adult vision and the power of on-going cultural renewal.

Young adults do many things—they go to school, seek adventure, prepare for a profession, explore and establish long-term relationships, become parents, serve "apprenticeships" in any number of occupations, become financially independent. But I wish to point here to the primary significance of the young adult era, which is not located in any of these tasks per se. The power and vulnerability of young adulthood lie in the experience of the dissolution and recomposition of the meaning of self and world and its challenges to faith. To become a young adult in faith is to discover the limits of one's assumptions about how "life will always be"—and to recompose a meaningful sense of self and world on the other side of that discovery. Yet the quality of that recomposition depends on the leadership of adult culture, as mediated through both individuals and institutions.

The institution of preference for young adults in American

culture is higher education. For some eighteen years, and in varying roles (residence director, director of student activities, instructor, chaplain, teaching fellow, scholar, and professor), I have studied with, taught, and counseled young adults in college and university settings. I was on a major university campus during the turbulence of the late sixties and early seventies. I saw then the power of young adult energy to sway a society (and wondered at the apparent disappearance of that energy once the Vietnam War ended and the television cameras had departed from campus).

During these years my scholarship has been primarily in the fields of developmental psychology, theology, and education. Insights drawn from these disciplines have served as useful interpreters of the young adults I was teaching. At the same time, young adults themselves prompted me to notice that even some of these "disciplined" interpretations of young adulthood have been misleading. The theories defined young adulthood as "prolonged adolescence," a merely "transitional" time, a period of "idealism" soon to be outgrown. The theories implied that young adulthood ends, or should end, with the granting of a college degree. The actual lives of the young adults I knew said otherwise.

My experience with young adults called into question my assumptions about human development, educational practice, and the character of human faith. I began to listen yet more carefully to young adults and to compare what I heard with some of the theories by which they have been interpreted. With my colleagues David Erb and Timothy Tiemans, I conducted a pilot study that tentatively confirmed my hunches and enlarged my questions. I then left my role as faculty member and administrator, moved across the country, and resumed full-time study to re-examine the working assumptions of my profession.

I remember those first weeks vividly. Although I had been a member of a college faculty for several years, when I arrived at Harvard University to begin doctoral work, those freshman feelings intruded all over again. In the first week my department gathered for a potluck supper. Ordinarily I try to practice what I call "the ministry of connections"—helping people in new situations to feel at home by introducing them to others. Yet, as I stood there, shifting from foot to foot, trying to look poised, I felt that whoever might have served such a role on my behalf had not come that evening. I was relieved when we could at last go through the line and get a plate of food—it gave me something to do. Then, seated by the fireplace, plate on knees, I was further rescued by my adviser, who came and sat nearby; we had met earlier in the week and therefore presumably had some natural basis for further conversation.

Then he did a wonderful thing for me. He proceeded to comment on the experience he was having that September as his eldest child went off to college for the first time. Being a parent and sending a child on to higher education was, he was discovering, quite different from being a professor and receiving students sent by other parents. This disclosure was a gift to me, because I could slip out of my role of "anxious freshman" and back into my role of chaplain, reassuring an anxious parent on the opening day of school.

I found myself saying to him, "Well, don't worry. Whatever you are most afraid will happen to him, won't. It will be something else." (How I presumed to know that and why I was audacious enough to say it, I'm still not sure.) But he quickly responded by saying, "Good. I've already decided what would be the worst thing that could happen to him." Immediately curious, I asked him what that would be. He replied, "I think the worst thing that could happen to him would be to have the time come when he would feel it was no longer possible to make meaning."

I had heard many anxious parents on the opening day of school, but I had never heard any parent express that concern (though perhaps the concerns I had heard tell me something about how parents make meaning). In any case, we can recognize that this sensitive professor and father had named something at the very core of his son's existence; for we human beings seem unable to survive, and certainly cannot thrive, unless we can make meaning.[1] We need to be able to make some sort of sense out of things; we seek pattern, order, coherence, and relation in the disparate elements of our experience. We must discover fitting connections between things. When we perceive life as only fragmented, we suffer confusion, distress, stagnation, or despair.

It has been said that the function of an organism is to organize, and that what the human organism organizes is meaning.[2] This capacity and demand for meaning is what I invite the reader to associate with the word *faith*. For most of us, this represents a shift from the usual connotations of the word *faith*. Faith is often linked exclusively to belief, particularly religious belief. But faith goes far beyond religious belief, parochially understood. Faith is more adequately recognized as the activity of seeking and composing meaning in the most comprehensive dimensions of our experience. Faith is a broad, generic human phenomenon. To be human is to dwell in faith, to dwell in one's meaning—one's conviction of the ultimate character of truth, of self, of world, of cosmos (whether that meaning be strong or fragile, expressed in religious terms or secular).

Thus, this father's concern that his son's meaning-making might prove vulnerable in the context of higher education was not inappropriate. It is hard enough to make meaning, to compose a faith, within the complexity of the contemporary world, but it is especially difficult to do so in the institution charged with teaching the value of critical reflection upon life in that world. Some would argue that meaning-making is not the business of higher education, that its proper task is the discovery and teaching of empirical truth, and that issues of meaning are more appropriately dealt with elsewhere in the culture.

Yet the culture itself has not always made this assumption. At the beginning of the story of American higher education, the founding of Harvard College, we find the following statement of its purpose:

After God had carried us safe to *New England* and wee had our houses, provided necessaries for our livelihood, rear'd convenient places for God's worship and settled the Government: One of the next things we longed for, and looked after was to advance *Learning* and perpetuate it to Posterity: dreading to leave an illiterate Ministry to the Churches, when our present Ministers shall lie in the Dust.[3]

This is to say that, for our forebears, learning and faith were integral to each other. Moreover, both were at stake in the establishment of higher education. The little college, which was at once a divinity school and the seed of one of the world's finest universities, was charged with preparing people who could responsibly nurture human faith for future generations.

With this in mind, I propose to examine the place of young adulthood and the role of higher education in the pilgrimage toward a critical and mature adult faith—a faith adequate to ground both an adult life and a more humane and life-giving culture. I will do so by drawing upon the insights of developmental psychology (Piaget, Erikson, Kohlberg, Gilligan, Perry, Kegan, Keniston), linking that discipline with insights from the study of religion and theology. This work will both stand within and critically elaborate upon the emerging interdisciplinary study of faith development best represented by the work of James Fowler. I will hypothesize a stage between Fowler's stages three and four—a stage between a conventionally assumed faith and a critically appropriated adult faith. In addition I will draw attention to a matter of some concern within the field: the relationship between structure and content. Though developmental theorists to date have concentrated on describing the formal structures of each stage of the human journey, careful consideration must also be given to the formative power of the images (content) these structures hold.

This is to suggest that every subject in the curriculum of higher education potentially contributes to the formation of young adult faith. This also suggests that faculty and others directly related to the life of the young adult inevitably have an influential role, upon which the young adult appropriately depends. Finally, I will propose that not only higher education but also the culture it serves play a mentoring role in the formation of each new generation of young adults.

Today's young adults must make meaning in the midst of an intensifying personal and global complexity and awareness of an expanding universe. Both younger and older adults stand on a new frontier in the history of human meaning-making, in the history of human faith. In reconsidering the character and formation of young adult faith and the power of higher education to determine its quality, we may recognize again that faith—the meaning-making that shapes a culture and its future—is of critical concern in higher education and wherever young adults search for a faith to live by.

1. The Elusiveness of Adulthood

When does adulthood begin? The response of North American culture to this question is increasingly ambiguous. Accordingly, the threshold of adulthood has become equally elusive. Chronological age does not seem to serve as a consistent indicator, and the "rites of passage" are various—obtaining a driver's license or a social security card, sexual experimentation, graduation from high school, graduation from college, establishment of a residence apart from family of origin, marriage, becoming financially independent, becoming a parent, becoming eligible to enter the military. Each of these serves to some degree as a cultural indicator of "adulthood," yet even the ages established by law for some of these varies from sixteen to twenty-one and are not uniform from one jurisdiction to another. Further, conventional wisdom often asserts, "You may be twenty-one, but . . . !"

For many working-class young people, graduation from high school and/or going to work full-time has been regarded as sufficient. For those placed on the margin of the economy, receiving one's own welfare check has sometimes marked a "coming of age." In the case of women, marriage and/or giving birth to a child has rendered one an adult—or has conferred as much adulthood as the culture has been willing to grant to women. But for all those who have claimed the American Dream as their own, whether wealthy or poor, male or female, it has been assumed that initiation into adulthood could surely be accomplished by completing four years of college by roughly the age of twenty-two.

Indeed, those responsible for undergraduate education generally have had at least some awareness of having a role in the formation of adulthood. Whether intuitively or more self-consciously informed by developmental theories, faculty, student personnel administrators, parents, and others have perceived the sponsorship of development into adulthood as a task of the college. The underlying assumption of liberal higher education at its best has been that during the college years the student moves from an uncritical dependence upon prevailing conventional, family, and peer group authority to a critically aware sense of responsibility for self and world. All concerned have assumed that this developmental achievement is facilitated by the cultivation of critical thought, the acquisition of knowledge, and the preparation of the student for a suitable career—and have further recognized, to varying degrees, the value of establishing relationships during the college years that form the basis for meaningful (and/or useful) networks of association through adulthood.

But these assumptions no longer hold up as well as they may have in the past. Parents find themselves surprised and dismayed when, for a variety of reasons, their children seem to need to move back home after college; parents ponder whether and for how long it is appropriate for them to provide financial support for children twenty-five and older. Professors are frustrated by the unsettledness of their graduate students. Corporation planners are puzzled by the fluidity of young adult goals. Young mothers, with partners who do not yet seem ready to be fathers, have few guidelines for determining what they may ask, claim, demand. And many young adults themselves wonder if they will ever find what they really want to be and do. All are bewildered when the sort of self-confidence, commitment, and stability that are associated with adulthood are not as evident as they had expected. On the other hand, college juniors and seniors, graduate students, and others making their way into the world of adult work often clearly demonstrate their ability to carry significant responsiblity for self and world (including the competence to critique both) and thereby distinguish themselves from adolescents.

Religious communities have traditionally provided rituals to mark the passage into adulthood. But religious communities also now participate in (and contribute to) the bewilderment about what adulthood is and when it begins. Traditionally, becoming adult in faith has been marked by rites of initiation—bar or bat mitzvah, confirmation, or membership—typically in the early teenage years. There is a growing recognition, however, that although these rites (rooted in ancient puberty rites) do appropriately mark a new era in the journey toward adulthood, the young teenager in the contemporary world is not yet crossing the threshold into full adult religious commitment. Indeed, in practice, many faith communities make the informal assumption that young people will tend to leave the faith community some time after such confirmation rites but will return "when they have children"—read, "when they are adults." It is being observed, however, that young adults do not necessarily return as expected, and if they do, they do so at a later age than has been assumed.[1]

Even when adulthood is presumed instead to be marked by the rites of marriage and vocation (ordination, etc.), the puzzle about adulthood is not resolved—though these rites typically occur at a later point in the life span. The religious community may, on the one hand, be uncomfortable with young adult couples choosing to live together instead of marry, but it is equally uncomfortable with separation and divorce arising from the perception that "we just weren't ready to make that commitment." With a frequency that used to be unthinkable, ordination or other religious vows, which likewise have tended to be regarded as "forever," are also being brought under review on the basis of a feeling that one was "too young to really know."

This puzzle about the threshold of adulthood also surfaces in the literature of developmental psychology. Those seeking to describe this developmental era have used such terms as *prolonged adolescence*, *moratorium*, *regression* and *equilibrated transitional*.[2] These inventive, awkward terms (some of which contradict fundamental tenets of developmental psychologies) should, by their very awkwardness, alert us to the presence of discrepant data[3] that our prevailing myths of human development do not adequately account for.

Indeed, developmental theorists do not agree about when "adolescence" ends and "adulthood" begins. There is general agreement that adolescence begins with puberty, but there is little agreement about where adolescence ends. Douglas Kimmel, cataloguing some of the discrepancies among biological, chronological, social, and perceived age, notes that "there is a growing emphasis on the age of eighteen as a socially defined turning point in the life cycle that, in many ways, marks the beginning of adulthood in a social and legal sense."[4] He also notes, however, that Buhler would place "adulthood" at twenty-five, and that Jung perceived "youth" to extend from puberty to the ages of thirty-five to forty. José Ortega y Gasset's "conception of generations in the history of society and in the life cycle identifies the ages of fifteen to thirty as 'youth.' "[5] As developmental psychology has found its way into common usage, many people perceive, to their discomfort, that apparently adolescence ends only with one's mid-life crisis!

In this maze of contradictory cultural signals, it is difficult to have a clear sense of what to expect of either oneself or of others as "adults." Even an indicator such as "becoming established" no longer seems useful, when professional education may extend into the early thirties, when it is becoming common to change careers several times in one's lifetime, when marriages are difficult to sustain, when childbearing may be postponed until one's thirties, and when "personal development" is sometimes neglected in favor of "career development" (or the reverse).

Questions about the meaning of adulthood, maturity, and responsibility also arise, at least in significant measure, from the extension of the life span and from a need on the part of a postindustrial, technological, and increasingly complex culture both for a delay of entry into the work force and for a high degree of education and training. It is no wonder, therefore, that the developmental puzzles concerning "adulthood" intensify in the context of higher education. Undergraduates, graduate students, and faculty alike are directly affected by the educational needs of a postindustrial culture and by an awareness of the increase in information and of the finitude of all knowledge. Young intellectuals in particular suffer the awareness of always standing on a new threshold of knowledge, continually being prodded to revise their perceptions of self and world and their apprehension of truth. The elusiveness of adulthood is further compounded by the financial dependence typically required for the pursuit of higher education, an often frustrating dependence in a culture that prizes economic achievement as a mark of adulthood. Although all this may to some degree have plagued university students in every age, today it is exacerbated by an awareness of dramatic shifts in patterns of life and thought, particularly the awareness of living on a "shrinking planet," which seems to render the world both more complex and more fragile. If "adulthood" connotes a confident and secure sense of self in relationship to one's world, adulthood is difficult to achieve in a cultural climate marked by change in every dimension of knowledge.

So, we may ask, who is an adult in the context of higher education? Everyone who registers for Physics 101? The seventeen-year-old male? The thirty-six-year-old mother who has never learned to drive a car and who has decided to finish her baccalaureate degree? The twenty-nine-year-old assistant professor who teaches the course? The person who at twenty-seven has just transferred into a third master's program? The forty-four-year-old professor and the twenty-seven-year-old graduate student who are having an affair? A parent in his twenty-sixth year of life and third year of college who defensively maintains a fundamentalist worldview that cannot be critically engaged from any perspective? The student who at the age of twenty has been permanently crippled in a car accident and who writes an eloquent honors thesis on the subject of hope? The twenty-three-year-old woman who has just joined a new religious cult? The twenty-four-year-olds who live off campus and have just furnished their apartment with furniture "lifted" from the campus dormitory? The eighteen-year-old freshman woman who is deciding whether or not to have an abortion? The twenty-one-year-old who is taking a year away from studies to work for peace? The promising twenty-nine-year-old scientist who has just been caught falsifying research data? The doctoral students who are protesting the university's investment policies? And furthermore, if these are adults, are they mature adults?

I suggest that the hesitancy or ambivalence we may feel in making such judgments reflects our growing awareness that the process of human growth and maturity is not tied exclusively either to chronological age or to biological maturation. Becoming an adult is a process that is neither sufficiently recognized by our cultural norms nor adequately comprehended by our life span psychologies. Developmental psychologies have given limited address to adulthood. Fascinated and preoccupied with the dynamics of development in childhood and adolescence, theorists of developmental psychology have only begun to focus on adulthood.[6] Thus the term *late adolescence* is appropriated most frequently to name the experience of the process of seeking a fitting relationship between self and world—a somewhat pejorative naming of a sense of "movement toward" rather than "arrival at" that place called adulthood.

Embedded in this question of the threshold of adulthood are two other important questions: The first is, What is adulthood? I suggest that adulthood is a way of making meaning. To be an adult is (1) to be aware of one's own composing of reality, (2) to participate self-consciously in an ongoing dialogue toward truth, and (3) to be able to sustain a capacity to respond—to take responsibility for seeing and reweaving (in the activity of one's every day) a fitting pattern of relationships between the disparate elements of self and world.

The second question is, When does it become incumbent

upon established adult culture to recognize a person as a responsible participant in adult meaning-making—as a worthy and essential contributor to adulthood's care for life itself? When is it time to give to a younger person the respect and trust due another adult? Older adults may become weary (if not irritated or angry) to hear that one more university somewhere on the globe has been closed because of student protests against a government. Management personnel, whatever the institutional context, tend to be resistant to disrupting pressure from their juniors. Some parents tend to want to see their adult children as children—or at least as still dependent upon parental authority and competence. But correspondingly, established adult culture feels at least a mild uneasiness when its younger adults seem passive, oriented to absolute security, and bereft of idealism.

This question becomes most focused in the awareness that the quality of future leadership, and, indeed, the quality of the future itself, will shortly depend upon those who are now young adults. What fosters the readiness and the capacity to receive and enhance the heritage of a civilization, particularly in an era of unprecedented change?

These puzzles that converge in the question of the threshold of adulthood take on particular significance in the context of higher education. Issues of adulthood are a matter of consequence for educators as well as for other policymakers. Embedded within assumptions regarding adult maturity are deeper issues pertaining to the development of wisdom, courage, integrity, freedom, and fidelity—values associated with the best of the intellectual life and essential to the quality of all life. These issues determine educational assumptions and goals and shape the conditions of accountability for both students and faculty; they are concerns that appropriately belong at the center of life in the academy. Further, as we shall see, not only the academy but the culture itself finds its orientation in its vision of adulthood—its vision of future maturity.

Thus, an examination of the dynamics of adult meaning-making in its most comprehensive dimensions—the formation, loss, and recovery of faith itself—provides one important perspective from which to reconsider the present assumptions about young adulthood held by both the academy and the culture. This is to suggest that to contemplate the significance of young adult experience encourages us to re-examine our own assumptions about adulthood and our own capacity to live meaningful adult lives. When our understanding of the development of adult meaning-making is deepened, our understanding of the relationship of student, academy, and culture in their shared engagement with truth may be recomposed.

2. Meaning-Making: An Activity of Faith

How is the capacity to compose mature forms of meaning developed in adult life? To reflect on this question is to wonder about the character and dynamics of adult faith, yet we do not readily recognize that meaning-making is unavoidably associated with faith. The word *faith* itself has become problematic, specifically so in relation to higher education.

For some, *faith* is a strong and positive word with a venerable history. For others, contemporary personal and cultural ambivalence about its connotations makes it a powerful but negative word. For many others, faith has become a matter of indifference, an obsolete or otherwise irrelevant category. If recognized as a part of human life—even an important part—it is, nevertheless, seen as *only* a part, and considered separable from other important elements of life, such as career, relationships, political commitments, economic life, and so on. Many regard faith as a private matter divorced from the public sphere and, therefore, something one may choose or not choose to incorporate into one's particular life-style. Knowing another's faith is not necessarily considered important to knowing the person or to discerning how he or she may be expected to make choices. At the same time, there are others (particularly some who have a specific and intensely held set of religious beliefs) who assume and assert that the character of faith is such that a given faith (theirs) fully interprets and may be arbitrarily imposed upon all experience (theirs *and* others'). Finally, common to many understandings of the word *faith* is the assumption that faith is something relatively static. The word *faith* is not conventionally used to connote something that undergoes change, transformation, or development.

Yet it is a central conviction of the perspective being offered here that faith is integral to all human life, that it is a human universal, that it conditions both personal and corporate behavior, that its particular forms (expression in language, ritual practice, and so on) are always finite, and that it is a dynamic phenomenon that undergoes transformation across the whole life span, including the period of adulthood. Therefore, if we are better to understand young adult faith, we must attend to a prior examination of the phenomenon of faith itself.

We may begin to examine the phenomenon of faith by reconsidering the word *faith*—but not as a mere exercise in etymology. If we are to recognize faith in the experience of the young adult and in relation to the institution of higher education, the word *faith* must be emancipated from its too facile equation with religion and belief and reconnected with trust, meaning, and truth.

FAITH AND BELIEF

In contemporary English usage the word *faith* is used only as a noun, is strongly associated with religion, and is frequently used synonymously with *belief*.[1] This has not always been so. But since it has become so, if faith is to be recognized as a universal human phenomenon and integral to the concerns of both young adults and higher education, it must provisionally be distinguished from both *religion* and *belief*.

Wilfred Cantwell Smith, a historian of religion, has engaged in careful study of the words *faith* and *belief*, and his work has substantially informed faith development theory. He has shown that, since in English the word *faith* is used only as a noun, "to believe" was chosen as the verb form to express the noun-concept "faith." This was not inappropriate, for in earlier centuries "the Anglo-Saxon-derived word 'believe' in its various forms meant pretty much what its exact counterpart in German, *belieben*, still means today: namely, 'to hold dear, to prize.' It signified to love, . . . to give allegiance, to be loyal to; to value highly." The Latin *credo*, meaning, literally, "I set my heart," was translated "I believe," and thus was not a mistranslation.[2] "To believe" connoted an essential human activity involving the whole person.

In modern times, however, the word *belief* has shifted so as to no longer connote an essential human capacity and activity. Smith traces three important shifts in the use of *believe*, which together have altered its meaning.

The first shift is from the personal to the impersonal. A personally felt object receiving one's love and allegiance is replaced by an impersonal proposition. Believing in a person shifts to believing what a person says. Religiously, belief shifts from a sense of relationship with Being to a mere intellectual assent to an abstract proposition or dogma. Many persons thus assume that if someone should inquire about their "faith," an appropriate response would pertain to religious affiliation or perhaps to whether or not they affirm a particular body of dogma.

The second shift, also in the direction of the impersonal, is a change in the subject of the verb. The dominant usage, "I believe" or "believe me," has shifted primarily to the third person, "she believes" or "they believe" (p. 52).

The third shift pertains to the relationship of belief to knowledge. "Belief" did once serve as "the name given to that further step of giving one's heart to what one's mind knows to be true" (p. 61), or the sense of trust that adds something to knowledge, "designating the difference between knowing inertly and knowing responsively" (p. 65). In modern usage, however, *belief* increasingly connotes a lack of trust and confidence: "Do you really think that is so?" "Well, he believes so." Therefore, believing, which formerly denoted a relationship of the self to truth, is now typically a matter of someone else's affirmation of a proposition that is not necessarily true.

As a result, *belief* has come to suggest an exclusively propositional or cognitive enterprise. Further, it connotes mere opinion—or even the dubious and the false—rather than matters of truth, reality, and ultimate importance. When the word *faith* is used synonymously with *belief*, it takes on these same connotations. As a consequence, these static, impersonal, objective, propositional, cognitive connotations separate faith from the personal, subjective, affective, visceral, and passional dimensions of being and knowing. Alternatively, the association of *faith* with that which is dubious links faith with "irrational knowledge" and consigns it to the private, emotional sphere, divorced both from public life and from the life of the mind.

That the meanings of the words *faith* and *belief* have so shifted is of critical importance to contemporary Western culture. This shift participates in a post-Enlightenment reorientation of our relationship to knowledge, affecting our most cherished institutions and assumptions—and specifically our assumptions about faith, religion, and belief. Christianity has been the prevailing religion in the Western world, and Christianity has, in Smith's view, fallen into the modern "heresy" of requiring "belief" as the primary evidence of faith (p. 78). Faith, a more fundamental dynamic than belief, has been obscured. When *belief* has become mere intellectual assent to abstract propositions and when specific religious propositions have become meaningless, impersonal, or at least dubious to a large number of Western, post-Enlightenment people, by synonymous usage *faith* has come to be equally meaningless.

Therefore, if we are to recover a more adequate understanding of human faith in the context of present cultural experience, we must be clear that when we use the word *faith* we are speaking of something quite other than *belief* in its dominant contemporary usage. Faith is not simply a set of beliefs that religious people have; it is something that all human beings do.

This distinction becomes particularly important when we focus our attention on the dynamics of faith in the context of higher education. Higher education is committed to the apprehension of truth. To seek truth requires rigorous examination of one's most elemental assumptions. In this process it is common for both faculty and students to perceive an earlier experience of faith or religious belief—an earlier way of making sense and of perceiving truth—as now "outgrown" or otherwise irrelevant. And, indeed, if faith is understood as static, fixed, and inextricably bound to a particular language, community, and/or worldview, it must be discarded as obsolete if the integrity of ongoing intellectual life is to be maintained. A richer perception of the phenomenon of faith, however, enables us to recognize that the recomposing of truth as it occurs within the context of higher education may indeed necessitate a change in or abandonment of a particular set of "beliefs"—and yet be important to the task of "faith."

Any attempt to recover a generic understanding of the word *faith* capable of illuminating essential human capacities and commitments—including the commitment to truth—is bound to encounter skepticism. Yet in modern life skepticism itself may be closely related to faith. Skepticism may serve as an alternative to despair arising from a sense of the irretrievable loss of a once-shared trust in a universe of meaning—however that was defined. For many people today, a thin veneer of public sophistication masks a private, lonely anguish that neither the rational mind nor economic sufficiency can resolve. While it may have been easier in an earlier time to assume that transcendent meaning exists beyond "knowledge" (understood in a narrowly positivist sense), in our time we have become at once scientifically informed, philosophically relativistic, and disillusioned. But the possibility of a worthy faith has not been dismissed from the deepest intuitions of the human spirit. A renewed definition of the word *faith*, set in dialogue with insights from developmental psychology and theories of imagination, responds to this intuition and directs our attention toward a richer perception of the character of human knowing, acting, and being.

FAITH: A MATTER OF MEANING

Though *faith* has become problematic, the importance of "meaning" has not. Modern people can more easily recognize that the seeking and defending of meaning pervades all of human life. Meaning-making is the activity of seeking pattern, order, form, and significance. To be human is to seek coherence and correspondence in the disparate elements of existence. To be human is to want to make sense out of things. To be human is to want to be oriented to one's surroundings. To be human is to seek to understand the fitting connections between things. To be human is to desire relationship.

It is in the activity of finding and being found by meaning that we as modern persons come closest to recognizing our participation in the life of faith. It is this activity of composing and being composed by meaning, then, that I invite the reader to associate with the word *faith*.

We are helped to perceive faith in this way by the thought of William F. Lynch, who recognizes faith as "the most elemental force in human nature."[3] This primal force courses through human life as an assumption and demand for order, pattern, and relation. Lynch invites us to imagine faith as coming into force "as soon as promises begin to be made to it"[4]—that is, at the very dawn of human existence, in the womb. (Although he uses this image only as a metaphor, prenatal psychology now suggests that it may indeed be more than metaphor.)[5] We only can imagine that we come to our first consciousness in a rudimentary sense of dependable pattern, wholeness, and relation—a sense of an ultimate environment that intends our good; we awaken to life as a primal force of promise. Then, in the experience we call birth, we undergo what must seem like utter chaos: sound louder than ever before, light, touch, breathing for the first time. The task of the infant is then the struggle to regain—to compose—that which was promised at the dawn of existence, a felt sense or conviction of trustworthy pattern and relation.[6] Erik Erikson has identified an infant's first task as the establishment of basic trust;[7] however, as I am describing the process, the first task of a human being is the *re*-establishment of basic trust.

But we know that though the infant may re-establish connection, relation, and trust, this is a task not accomplished alone, and neither is it accomplished once and for all. Over and over again life will require the encounter with the unexpected. Again and again, we undergo the loss of our most cherished patterns of meaning and anchors of trust as we discover their insufficiency. Mature faith knows that the forms of faith are finite—but the promise is kept.

This patterning and repatterning activity of meaning-making occurs in every aspect of human life. The mind does not passively receive the world, but rather acts upon every object and every experience to compose it. Every act of perception is an ordering activity. For example, when we perceive a tree, we compose it, organizing its various parts into a whole—branches, leaves, trunk, roots, textures, colors, height, breadth, and whatever we may know of the intricate systems by which it is nourished or threatened through the seasons of its existence. Each of us, though we may encounter the same tree, perceives (composes) a different one.

It is much the same with our experience of a handshake. We compose a perception of warmth or sincerity or aloofness or strength or ambivalence or mere social custom according to the way another grips (or fails to grip) our hand. This perception is ordered by our history, our mood in the moment, our knowledge of the other person, and a whole host of other elements in our environment. Each of us may shake hands with the same person, but each of us composes a different perception of that person.

We compose the discrete elements of our every day, such as trees and handshakes, into an overall pattern that orients us and grounds us. We cannot accomplish even the proverbial task of getting out of bed each morning without some sense of the relative relationship of coffee pot, shower, breakfast—whatever constitutes our ritual of initiation into a new day. We need to make a distinction here, however. Though it may be important to acknowledge that there are times when getting up in the morning is, indeed, an act of heroic proportions, nevertheless the primary concern here is not with meaning-making activity at the level of the discrete and mundane. Rather, the focus here is upon the capacity of human beings to know and to live at a more than mundane level, to compose a sense of the whole of life, not only of a discrete part.

The meaning-making that constitutes what we are calling adulthood is a self-aware composing and maintaining of pattern, order, and significance in the most comprehensive dimensions of our awareness. In other words, whenever we organize our sense of a particular object, series of activities, or institution, we are also compelled to compose our sense of its place in the whole of existence. We speak of this activity as composing a "world." But even "world" becomes a provincial concept as our awareness of "cosmos" increases. This is to say that all human beings must compose and dwell in some conviction of what is *ultimately* true. Human beings self-consciously or unselfconsciously compose a sense of the ultimate character of reality. (It should be noted that higher education is a primary institution from which the culture expects assistance with this task.)

The word *faith* as I am using it primarily denotes the activity of composing meaning in the most comprehensive dimensions of our awareness. Thus, to speak of faith is to point toward the meaning-making that frames, colors, and relativizes the activity of the everyday (i.e., the activity of the everyday is lived in relation to and dependent upon a comprehensive frame of meaning). To attend to faith is to be concerned with the questions so familiar to those who grieve and to others who suffer meaninglessness: "Why should I get out of bed in the morning?" "What is the purpose of my existence and the existence of others?" "Does anything really matter?" "What can I depend upon?" "Are we ultimately alone?" "What can be trusted as real, and what is my relationship to that?" "What is the ultimate character of the cosmos in which I dwell?"

James Fowler, building on the thought of both Wilfred Smith and H. Richard Niebuhr, speaks of faith as the activity of "intuiting life as a whole" or as the composing of an "ultimate environment." He also describes faith as "triadic," in that faith is a felt sense of relation between (1) self and (2) other as conditioned by loyalty to (3) a center of power and value.[8] He thereby points toward the relational character of faith and toward the necessity of composing a sense of the whole—of self, world, and "God." All human action is conditioned by a felt sense of "how life really is (or ought to be)," "how things really are," or "what has ultimate value."

Until this point we have spoken of faith without speaking of "God" per se. In the dynamic activity of composing the meaning of life, the pattern we ultimately depend upon for our existence functions as "God" for us. Or, we may say that whatever is at the center, *whatever* serves as the centering, unifying "linchpin" of our pattern of meaning—that center functions as "God" for us. H. Richard Niebuhr wrote that when we perceive faith as dependence on a value center and as loyalty to a cause, then "when we speak of 'gods' we mean the gods of faith, namely such value centers and causes."[9] Using Tillich's familiar concept, we might see whatever is of "ultimate concern" to people as that which acts as the center, or "God," of their ultimate meaning frame. This perspective suggests that most persons are in this sense "theists." When seeing in this way, we begin to recognize that many more people than perhaps we had imagined are people of "faith." "To deny the reality of a supernatural being called God is one thing; to live without confidence in some center of value and without loyalty to a cause is another."[10]

Yet we also begin to recognize that, for many, contemporary life is characterized by "polytheism." Using the images of pattern and center that we have been employing here in conjunction with the thought of H. Richard Niebuhr, polytheism is the composing or creating of several patterns of meaning (perhaps often experienced as "arenas" of meaning), each with its own center, or "god." From this perspective, polytheistic faith is the product composed by those who have "intuited life as a whole" but have only been able to compose such "wholes" as they can. For example, many people yearn for a sense of deep integration in their lives, but experience even the worlds of home and work as composed of separate patterns of meaning and oriented to differing values, expectations, loyalties, and affections.[11]

Alternatively, other people construe a single pattern of meaning around a single cause or center, such as their particular institution, political goal, study, project, or personal relationship, but do not seem able to relate such a center to any larger frame of meaning. Niebuhr describes this form of faith as "henotheism." The boundaries of their world are inclusive, because they are tightly drawn. The "center" they rely on to give ultimate meaning to the world they compose, however, is not adequate to unify the complexity, the variety, and the tragic elements of human experience; therefore, their henotheistic faith is vulnerable to competing centering images and to any significant shift in the conditions of personal or cultural life. This form of faith is similar to the "cramping faith of blind and fanatical particularlism," which Smith describes as "narrow faith."[12] Henotheistic faith may take the form of love for a child or of commitment to artistic achievement, scientific inquiry, a political dream, a business venture, and so forth. The question is not whether these are worthy and valuable forms of engagement with life. The question is, Do self, world, and "God" collapse when the child dies, or a permanently injured hand can no longer play a musical instrument, or the funding for the laboratory dries up, or one is defeated in an election, or the business enterprise ends in failure? Is there a pattern of meaning, a faith, that can survive the defeat of its finite manifestations?

H. Richard Niebuhr's discussion of polytheistic and henotheistic faith moves next to what he terms "radical monotheism." Whereas polytheism "depends for its meaning on many centers and gives its partial loyalties to many interests,"[13] and henotheism centers in a god who is "one among many possible gods," radical monotheism is the composing of a pattern of meaning centered in the "One beyond all the many," by which Niebuhr means confidence in and loyalty to a center of power and value adequate to all the ongoing conditions of the experiences of persons and their communities.[14]

I would note, however, that Niebuhr's imagery emphasizes the transcendent character of faith, at the expense of its immanent character. It is important to recognize that when we speak of "God" as the anchoring pattern of the whole of life, we speak of that which not only transcends us (is *beyond* us) but also permeates our very existence (exists *within* and *among* us). To describe "God" as the gift of faith is to seek to name that which is both transcendent and immanent, both ultimate and intimate.[15]

FAITH AS TRUTH AND TRUST

When the activity of faith is recognized in these comprehensive dimensions, we begin to perceive that truth and trust are at stake in the composing of faith. A worthy faith must bear the test of lived experience in the real world. It is in the ongoing dialogue between self and world, between community and lived reality, that a robust pattern of faith takes form. Faith must stand up under the test of the truth of lived experience.

But human beings not only must compose a sense of what is ultimately true, they must finally also depend upon the ultimacy they find or are found by. Here it must be noted that, given this generic sense of faith, it may be said that some (even many) compose an ultimate sense of "mis-trust," a conviction of a universe of, say, randomness. For them, randomness is what is most true and most "trusted." They have faith that this is how the world really is. Therefore, it must also be acknowledged that the word *faith* has been (and still is) reserved primarily for the composing of meaning which affirms a pattern of trustworthy ultimacy, though its character may be complex, dynamic, and variously described.[16] This raises a question for many people who take for granted that faith always has to do with "God" as they have been taught to think about "God" by their religious tradition. For them to speak in more general terms of faith and trust without necessarily referring to "God" as previously conceived seems confusing, if not beside the point. We must, therefore, explore further the intimate relationship between faith and trust and truth.

This relationship is reflected in Wilfred Cantwell Smith's study of the notion of faith across cultures, specifically in his discussion of the Hindu *sraddha*. The word *sraddha* permeates Hindu literature but has received little systematic commentary in Hindu scholarship because it is assumed in all religious sensibility. Smith perceives that it can be called an Indian concept of "faith." *Sraddha* "is a compound of two words, *srad* (or *srat*), heart, and *dha*, to put."[17] *Sraddha* "means placing one's heart on" (p. 62). Smith observes that India has said that "the religious life, whatever its form, begins . . . with faith; and faith, in its turn, is one's finding within that life (one's being found by) something to which one gives one's heart" (p. 62).

Sraddha in itself leaves unspecified the object of faith. It can be recognized, however, that one gives one's heart by initiative and/or response only to that which one "sees" as adequate, trustworthy, and promising. Indeed, Smith notes the Hindu insight that "in fact, the universe and human beings were created in such a way that faith is the intrinsically appropriate human orientation towards what is true and right and real, its absence or opposite (*asraddha*, unfaith, disinterest) being apportioned similarly as the proper human attitude to what is false and awry. The Creator, 'observing two forms, differentiated them as Truth and Wrong; he then established faithlessness (or: lack of interest) for Wrong, faith for Truth.' "[18] "Faithing" is the impulse or force toward, and the putting one's heart upon, that which one trusts as true; it is a convictional knowing and trusting in the pattern one "sees" as real.

"Faithing," in other words, is the composing of the heart's resting place.

FAITH AS ACT

Faith—one's conviction of the ultimate character and meaning of existence—is the resting place of the heart and the orienting guide of the mind. Faith forms, centers, and anchors integrity. Therefore, faith determines action; faith is manifest in act (and, as we shall see, faith is constituted by act). When we recognize faith as the composing of what is true and trustworthy at the level of ultimacy, we recognize that faith is intimately related to doing. We human beings act in accordance with what we really trust—in contrast to what we may merely acclaim.[19] We act according to our actual, most powerful centers of trust (or mis-trust). Thus our acts, powered by a deeper faith, often belie what we say—or even think—we believe. Our actions will be consistent with our verbal affirmations only if these affirmations reflect our real convictions about ultimate meaning and are not superseded by unspoken commitments, loyalties, and fears oriented to other (and actual) ultimate centers of power, value, and affection. Our "faith" is "done." Faith makes itself public in acts of decision, obedience, and courage.[20]

Thus, we may recognize faith in many manifestations: as the primal force of promise, as our everyday activity of meaning-making that is both ultimate and intimate, and as act. But faith is also a suffering.

FAITH AS A SUFFERING

We may think of faith, then, as the laying of the warp of a tapestry, upon which the rest of the particular threads of life find their place. We might also imagine this activity as the weaving of an overarching "canopy of significance" that embraces, orders, and relativizes all of our knowing and being.

Both metaphors recognize faith as both infinitely *transcendent* in character and simultaneously profoundly *immanent*. This is essential, because faith, as noted earlier, is a composing activity that at once reaches infinitely beyond and infinitely within the particulars of existence.

The metaphor of the canopy was made accessible to many cultures through the play *Fiddler on the Roof*. When the second daughter chooses to follow her revolutionary lover into Siberia, her father, waiting with her for the train, acknowledges that they do not know when they will see each other again. Then his daughter gives him a special gift. She responds by saying, "I promise you I will be married under the canopy." This is a gift to her father, for in the Jewish wedding the canopy represents not only the home that is formed by that union but also the whole household of Israel. She is promising her father that the fabric of meaning into which he has woven his life will be sustained and will transcend both miles and ideology. Later, we see his canopy stretched to its limits—and perhaps rewoven beyond its limits—when his youngest daughter chooses not to be married under the canopy.

Particularly because much of contemporary life finds its meanings in forms that are not perceived as traditionally religious, we are often unaware that we too have woven a canopy of significance—a faith that we hold and are held by—until people we value do not choose to affirm that upon which we discover our sense of life has ultimately depended. For many, an awareness of the weavings that have ordered personal and corporate life emerges only in the suffering of the unraveling or rending of those weavings that held a personal and/or a public trust.

The experience of betrayal confronts us with the inescapable force of faith. Faith as a primal, elemental force of promise permeating the whole of life is manifest most treacherously in faith betrayed. William Lynch sees in Medea the "dark side" of the primal, elemental character of faith. Medea has been "terrible" in her fidelity to Jason the Argonaut. In fidelity she follows him everywhere and gives up everything. When he abandons her for Creusa, the princess of Corinth, Medea says she made a mistake when she "trusted the words of a Greek." She then murders her own children and Creusa, demonstrating the limitless fury that floods the vacuum created by faith's disappearance, thereby revealing the power of this primal force "transformed into one of its dark forms."[21]

This should not surprise us. There is in most societies a legal distinction between "crimes of passion" and other crimes. We may think of such tragic moments as arising when the very fabric and center of one's meaning, one's sense of wholeness and connection, is violated, broken, shattered. The promise is broken. Faith erupts into fury. These are the Furies of whom the poets speak, the Furies who rage in witness to the world as it "ought to be." They are the expression of the pain of the betrayal of life itself.[22]

This is a dimension of what Richard R. Niebuhr recognizes when he asserts that any attempt to rethink and reappropriate the category of faith in relation to contemporary life is insufficient without a recognition of faith as a "suffering" as well as a virtue of reasoning and willing.[23] By "suffering" he means, in part, "undergoing," and he is thus recognizing not only the suffering of fury just described but also the suffering of doubt, of being overwhelmed, of drifting, of struggle, of yearning, and of despair (all of which may be a significant part of the young adult faith experience).

During my own graduate study, it happened that the professor I most frequently heard applauded was this same Richard R. Niebuhr. The reasons were not immediately obvious, since he does not seek to capture the student imagination either with entertaining anecdotes or with a lecture style designed to dazzle by the aesthetic of its systematic outline. Rather, when he lectures it is as though he has generously allowed others to be present to his own contemplation. As he reflects on the material for the day, he may pause and look out the window, waiting for the word to come that will fittingly name what he is coming to see and understand. When the word does come, it seems to be the right word. And when applause breaks out at the end of the class, it is perhaps because we are grateful for the naming of the intuitions that dwell in the deepest currents of our being.

When Professor Niebuhr reflects on human faith, he does so, in part, with the metaphors of "shipwreck, gladness, and amazement."[24] These metaphors connote the subjective, affective, dynamic, and transformative nature of faith experience. Since to suffer is "to undergo" and "to be totally affected," when people undergo the unraveling of what has held their world together, inevitably, to either a greater or lesser degree, there is suffering. When we must even question, let alone suffer the collapse of, our sense of self, world, and "God," our whole being aches or is disoriented or is bewildered or feels empty—drained of those rich connections that create significance and delight and purpose.

It may feel something like shipwreck. To undergo shipwreck is to be threatened in a most total and primary way. Shipwreck is the coming apart of what has served as shelter and protection and has held and carried one where one wanted to go—the collapse of a structure that once promised trustworthiness. Likewise, when we undergo the shipwreck of meaning at the level of faith, we feel threatened at the very core of our existence.

"Shipwreck" may be precipitated by events such as the loss of a relationship, violence to one's property, the collapse of a career venture, physical illness or injury, the defeat of a cause, a fateful moral choice that irrevocably reorders one's life, betrayal by a community or government, or the discovery that an intellectual construct is inadequate. These experiences may suddenly rip apart our fabric of life, or they may more slowly but surely dissolve the meanings that have served as the home of the soul.

When we do survive shipwreck—when we do wash up on a new shore—there is gladness, the gladness of relief and restoration. It is a gladness that pervades one's whole being;

there is a new sense of vitality, be it quiet or exuberant. Usually, however, there is more than relief and restoration: there is transformation. We discover something different beyond the loss. Rarely are we able to replace, to completely recompose, what was before. The loss of an earlier meaning is irretrievable and must be grieved and mourned. But the gladness is the discovery that life continues to unfold with meaning, with connections of significance and delight. We rarely experience this as a matter simply of our own making. As that primal, elemental force of promise stirs again within us, we often experience it also as a force acting upon us, carrying us, sometimes against our resistance, into a new meaning, a new faith, a new ultimacy.

This gladness is experienced, in part, as a new knowing. And though sometimes this knowing comes at the price of real tragedy, which even the new knowing does not necessarily justify, we typically would not wish to return to not knowing that which we have come to see on the other side of shipwreck. We do not want to live in a less adequate truth, a less robust sense of reality, an insufficient wisdom. There is a deeply felt gladness in an enlarged knowing and being and capacity to act. (This is not to say that diminishment is not also possible— yet even the experience of diminishment may potentially lead to a more adequate perception of the reality that human beings are continually both enlarged and diminished in the course of ongoing lived experience.)[25]

Along with gladness, there is also amazement. The power of the feeling of shipwreck is located precisely in one's inability to immediately sense the promise of anything beyond the breakup of what has been secure and trustworthy. Until our meaning-making has become very mature, in the midst of shipwreck there is little or no confidence of meaningful survival. The first time we are self-consciously aware that faith itself has been shattered is, after all, the first time: How could we know that even this might be survived? Even if we accept the dissolution of our self, world, and "God" with steely and sophisticated courage, we may expect nothing more. The possibility of "more" has hitherto not been a part of our experience. Then, we are met by the surprise of new meaning. We are amazed. Passover is the celebration of amazement. Easter is what happens to us when we look back and say, "I survived that?!"[26]

The metaphors of shipwreck, gladness, and amazement point toward the dynamic, transformative character of faith. This is to recover *faith* as a verb, a powerful activity that can be provisionally distinguished from static notions of both religion and belief. Faith is a dynamic, composing, multi-faceted activity. Faith is an active dialogue with promise.[27] The motion of shipwreck, gladness, and amazement describes, not only the primary crises of meaning that punctuate the story of our lives, but also the rocking, flowing, tumbling motion of our every day—as we dwell in a continual dialectic between fear and trust, hope and hopelessness, power and powerlessness, doubt and confidence, alienation and belonging.

The power and motion these metaphors grasp includes, but is not limited to, mere cognitive activity. Yes, faith is intimately related to knowledge; yet it is also prior to knowledge in any formal sense. The faith of the infant, for example, is composed by a rudimentary cognition that relies on and composes meaning through sensory, affective modes of knowing. Trust (or mis-trust) is grounded in the affection that informs cognition. So it is with adults. A trustworthy ultimacy is composed by feelings as well as thoughts, by being touched as well as by intellectual persuasion. Faith is affective as well as cognitive in character. This is to say that affect has an ordering power.[28]

To suffer shipwreck, gladness, and amazement on the journey of faith is to suffer the relinquishment of the pattern of ultimacy one has seen, known, felt, and acted upon. Therefore, even as the word *faith* is recovered as a verb, it remains also a noun. We journey from faith to faith. Faith is a composing and a composition. Faith is not only the act of setting one's heart, it is also what one sets one's heart upon. When we say people have a strong faith, we mean both (1) they confidently engage in the activity of faith in their ongoing meaning-making, trusting, and acting and (2) they have found the pattern of shipwreck, gladness, and amazement to be true and trustworthy—and they hold it dear, they believe. They dwell in an awareness of an intricate, intimate pattern of life that holds at the level of ultimacy. Their faith is manifest as trust, knowledge, value, and emotion—permeating every facet of existence.

Mature adult faith composes meaning in a self-conscious engagement in the repeated shipwreck and repatterning of one's perceptions of the fabric of life, the dynamic shifting of the assumed connections between persons, things, ideas, events, symbols, the natural order, the social order, space, and time. The suffering of adult faith is the learning how to hold on and when to let go of the perceptions, patterns, and relationships that one experiences as partaking in ultimate value and truth.[29]

It is a particular form of "shipwreck" that sets in motion the emergence of young adult faith.

3. Developmental Theories: Insights into the Motion of Faith

Dorothy Day was born in Brooklyn in 1897 into a lower-middle-class family. Even as a young girl, she hoped to become a writer of "such books that thousands upon thousands of readers would be convinced of the injustice of things as they were." She was baptized in the Episcopal church, but after childhood her interest in religion faded. "In its stead, she embraced a new faith in the ideals of the social and political radicals whose promise to change the world . . . seemed the most sensible response to social conditions." Throughout her twenties she pursued her dream of becoming a writer, immersed herself in the visions of socialists and anarchists, at times lived the rootless bohemian life, journeyed through powerful but finally unhappy love affairs, and at the age of thirty, upon the birth of a daughter, joined the Roman Catholic church. Her radical friends were dismayed, but, for Dorothy, becoming a Catholic was a deepening of her political convictions. Her attraction to the Gospels lay precisely in their proclamation of God's indwelling presence in the world and in their vision of liberation, community, solidarity, wholeness, and holiness—a vision faithful to, yet surpassing, what a political vision alone could provide.

Then, in 1932, after five years of further struggle and puzzlement over the purpose of her life, she and Peter Maurin envisioned what became the Catholic Worker Movement—a network of people committed to seeing Jesus in the life of the poor. Her commitment continued to take her to picket lines, to jail—and to her typewriter, where she did, indeed, write about injustice, but also about the mysterious depths of love.

She chose voluntary poverty (which she clearly distinguished from the destitution imposed upon the poor by the structures of injustice), living that life in such a way that it could be said that what she believed, wrote, and lived were one. She practiced also "the duty of delight," dwelling in a freedom that comes from the clear sense that one has nothing left to lose. Her relentless and tenacious witness to the importance of working for a "society where it is easier for people to be good" made her a troubling figure, confounding both the hierarchy of her church and the FBI. Though eventually she was revered and honored, she resisted being called a saint, insisting to the end of her life in 1980 that, "I don't want to be dismissed that easily."[1]

Frederick Law Olmsted, born in 1822, at the age of four suffered the death of his mother. His father sent him to private schools run by clergymen, where he developed a distaste for religion. He found solace wandering in the countryside, the silent happiness of which his father and stepmother had introduced him to at an early age. After finishing his basic schooling, he went to sea—and to scurvy. His life between the ages of twenty-four and twenty-six was described by his biographer in a chapter entitled "Scattered Enthusiasms." The scatteredness of his pursuits (including several romantic attachments) may be explained in part by factors that prevented him from settling easily into one of the more usual occupations of his day. He lacked the robust health of a seaman, the sensibilities of a merchant, and the schooling of a scholar.[2] But his wide-ranging interests began to find some measure of focus in farming, though the intellectual dimension of these interests took him to Yale for one term of study.

At Yale, an encounter with religion led to a "conversion," but not to the church. "He already had a fixed aversion to sectarianism and dogmatic Christianity. The thought that truth was the exclusive possession of any group whatever and that all outsiders—Carlyle, Jefferson, Voltaire, Socrates, his tirelessly good and loving father—were destined to eternal torment outraged justice and common sense; and his sense of his relationship to his fellowmen precluded his identifying himself with the elect and the rest of humanity with the damned" (p. 43).

He tried writing for a while. Writing on behalf of the Richmond County Agricultural Society, he expressed his passion for using scientific knowledge to improve the breeding of livestock, for awakening a sensibility to the beautiful, for increasing the profit of labor, and for promoting moral and intellectual improvement, "instructing us in the language of Nature" (p. 63). A trip to England enlarged his vision and deepened his despair of realizing it. But as his brother observed, "There was a certain obscure coherence behind Fred's successive enthusiasms: he was feeling his way toward his place in the world" (p. 50).

That place in the world was found in the vocation of bringing the countryside into the cities. His compassion for humanity called for the creation of beauty in the city, and his reverence for the integrity of nature required him to work with nature on its own terms. His commitments became manifest in the creation of Central Park in New York and the Emerald Necklace in Boston. He also involved himself in the plight of soldiers during the Civil War, and he maintained a concern throughout his life for projects that involved volunteers or provided jobs for the unemployed—projects that could guide the public mind into a social climate conducive to the beautiful and the healthful. He believed that as civilization evolved, his influence could ultimately triumph.

In both of these lives we observe the motion of faith. Each composes and recomposes what is ultimate, what is trustworthy, what is promised. Each tells a story of a pilgrimage from assumed ways of seeing, knowing, acting, and trusting, through curiosity, bewilderment, and dissolution toward a larger generosity, a deeper trust, a finer wisdom. Both pilgrims learn the peril and promise of commitment and cultivate the capacity to sustain commitment to truth and to service.

We can observe the lives of others who also grow older, move through various transitions, change. They may be able to reflect critically on self and world; but we do not seek them out for their wisdom; we cannot count on them to be compassionate toward all. We sense in them that fear—if it does not triumph—continually wrestles to a draw in the struggle with trust. They have commitments, but these commitments embrace limited spheres and do not beckon them to service beyond the boundaries of their own familiar immediate experience. Yet these same people, along with Dorothy Day and Frederick Law Olmsted, are all people of faith. They all construe some sense of ultimate meaning that shapes their thinking and feeling and action. So how are we to understand the differences between them?

I am persuaded that insights from the discipline of developmental psychology can assist us in deepening our understanding of the ongoing motion of human faith. When faith is recognized, in part, as the continual activity of composing meaning, it is possible to hear a resonance between the experience of faith and the insights of developmental psychology.

Though *psychology* is generally defined as the study of the mind or the self, the etymology of the word suggests that, at its heart, psychology is the study of the soul.[3] *Soul* refers to the animating essence, principle, or cause of an individual life. *Development* connotes a process of unfolding, revealing, maturing, differentiating, growing, expanding, evolving, elaborating. Developmental psychology may be thought of as the study of the ongoing revealing and elaborating of the animating essence of a human life—the unfolding and maturing of the soul.

We turn then to a short survey of some key developmental theorists. This will lay the necessary groundwork for the model of the young adult's journey toward mature faith that I shall propose in chapter 4.

DEVELOPMENTAL THEORISTS

Developmental psychology is a relatively young discipline. It has arisen from two primary dynamics in our culture. First, the average life expectancy has been extended, and consequently our interest in the journey of the self across time has been enlarged. Second, as we seem to be living in a time of profound change, we have an intensified need to understand how the self and the human community live through the dynamics of transition and transformation. These dynamics have created a receptiveness on our part to the study of developmental psychology, as we must recompose stories, myths, and theories by which to make meaning of our experience.

Developmental psychology has two primary grandfathers[4]—Erik Erikson and Jean Piaget. Erik Erikson's theoretical perspective is rooted in the psychoanalytic tradition and has extended Sigmund and Anna Freud's developmental notions so as to "move from the world of forces and energies to the world of meanings, possibilities, genuine development and ethical realities."[5] His perspective retains a strong biological and psychosexual orientation, while at the same time he attempts to account for the role of social institutions that human development both gives rise to and is dependent upon. He describes eight stages of development across the life span. Each stage is characterized by a primary developmental task, and the resolution of each task, or crisis, creates the foundation for all future ego strengths (virtues) and weaknesses. The eight stages he describes are each identified by their primary task: basic trust vs. basic mistrust, autonomy vs. shame and doubt, initiative vs. guilt, industry vs. inferiority, identity vs. role confusion, intimacy vs. isolation, generativity vs. stagnation, ego integrity vs. despair.[6] Each of these developmental stages is tied to biological maturation; thus, people go through these stages "ready or not" as biological changes inevitably unfold across a lifetime. His understanding of the formation of identity moves beyond an exclusive focus on the earliest period of life to suggest the significance of the entire life span, and his attention to the social dimension of development offers a rich understanding of the significance of the interdependence or "cogwheeling" of the generations.

That so many people recognize their experience in his description of development attests to the enormous intuitive power of Erikson's theory. It has substantively influenced educators and clinicians and has served as a primary contributor to the present cultural circumstance in which people tend to think in terms of stages: in common discourse now we are apt to hear something like, "He's just going through a stage."

Jean Piaget is the grandfather of constructive-developmental psychology. His theoretical work is rooted in the intellectual tradition of Immanuel Kant, James Mark Baldwin, George Herbert Mead, and John Dewey. Originally a biologist (and at the age of sixteen an expert on mollusks), Piaget became a genetic epistemologist whose fascination with the logic behind the "wrong" responses children made to IQ tests led to powerful insights into human development.

Piaget took with radical seriousness Kant's recognition that the human mind acts upon its world to compose it, and he extended Kant's insight.[7] Piaget has helped us to see that, not only do we human beings compose our world, we also develop in our capacity to do so. Through careful and elegant observation, Piaget discerned that human beings, in interaction with the environment, develop increasingly complex structures (or capacities) to receive, compose, and know their world.

He observed, for example, that infants know their world through performing certain sensorimotor operations by means of which they can relate to the environment, but infants cannot "hold in the mind" the rattle they can hold in their hand—out of sight is literally out of mind. Toddlers, by contrast, can hold an image in mind but cannot coordinate images—cannot, for example, put items in sequence—neither can they distinguish between dream and waking reality. School-age children, however, achieve the competence by which they are liberated from a world in which all images float free, as they develop the capacity for "concrete operations"—the capacity for ordering and categorizing the world of empirical reality. The concrete-operational child, however, does not have the capacity for abstract thought. It is the adolescent who may develop "formal operations," or the capacity to transcend the concrete world of literal objects and actual experience. Piaget's understanding of formal operational thought is often described as the capacity to think about thinking. One may now think propositionally, hypothetically, inferentially, and symbolically. Possibility is no longer a subset of concrete reality. Reality becomes a subset of possibility, as formal operations make it possible to "spin out an 'overall plan' of which any concrete event . . . is but an instance. Put most simply . . . 'what is' [becomes] just one instance of 'what might be.' "[8]

We are still discovering the implications of Piaget's insight, which insists, we remind ourselves, that the development of underlying structures or capacities of thought actually conditions a person's capacity to know reality. Knowing is a matter of structure as well as of specific content. Children of nine who use concrete operations to receive and compose their world simply cannot know, cannot make meaning, in the same way that may be possible for a fifteen-year-old. Consequently, such life events as achievement or defeat in school or athletics or the divorce or death of one's parents are grasped and known quite differently in different eras of development. The child of nine typically dwells in a concrete-literal world of direct cause and effect, whereas the adolescent may dwell in an expanded and more complex world. Their meaning and reality are composed differently, and thus terror and comfort may take different forms for the child than they do for the adolescent.[9]

We must remind ourselves, too, that development takes time.[10] Piaget described development of these structures (or stages) as a complex, evolving process of balancing and rebalancing, of assimilation and accommodation. By the term *assimilation*, he describes those times when, in the interactions between person and environment, the person receives an image (e.g., object, symbol, concept, or event) from the environment and is able to grasp it by means of his or her previously composed structures of knowing. That is, the image is assimilated. By the term *accommodation*, he describes those times when the present structures are not adequate to receive and make sense of the image and the structures must change—requiring accommodation. Human beings seek an equilibrated (balanced) state between assimilation and accommodation. When we are only assimilating, we eventually become bored. When too much accommodation is required of us, we become stressed. Piaget described development as an evolving movement from equilibrium through disequilibrium toward a new equilibrium.

We are well aware of such a process whenever we move to a new and unfamiliar setting, particularly if we find ourselves in a new culture. Customs that have become matters of assimilation for us—such as how food will be packaged, prepared, and eaten—become matters of accommodation as we are required to recompose our concepts and habits. This accommodation takes time, particularly if we must change our appetites, giving up types of food that we associate with our own well-being, delight, and sense of home and "rightness." We may eventually learn to depend upon and even relish those foods that are initially unfamiliar or distasteful. But we will, at least for a time, continue to choose familiar foods when possible (assimilation) and only over time gain an appreciation for new tastes and habits (accommodation). Here in the dialectic between cultures, and at the level of basic physical nourishment, we experience development as it always presents itself—in the tension between self-preservation and self-transformation.

As Piaget has observed it, the development of the capacity for complex thought (that is, the development of cognition) requires the same sort of interaction over time between person and environment. Piaget's vision of development, unlike Erikson's developmental theory, regards biological maturation as a necessary but not sufficient condition. Piaget's constructive-developmental vision is dependent, not only upon biological maturation, but also upon a sponsoring environment. Just as one is not apt to change one's eating habits except as conditions in one's environment require it, the development of cognition depends upon the environment. We develop the capacity—the structure—to think with increasing complexity only if the situations we encounter present us with the need or the challenge to do so. This means that individual persons do not necessarily undergo the development Piaget describes, because structural development is dependent upon the character of the interaction with the environment.

Though Piaget recognized that cognition and affect cannot be separated, and that knowing arises from an interaction between and dependent upon both the person and the environment, he focused his attention on the development of cognition in the individual child. As a consequence, Piaget, Piagetians, and their constructive-developmental stage theories are, not inappropriately, perceived as being only about childhood, cognition, the individual, concepts (or knowing), stages, and the discontinuities in human development (what is new and changed in the person). As important as these dimensions of human being and becoming are, however, they neglect other dimensions that are also integral to the journey of the soul—adulthood, emotion, the social, existence (or being), process, and the continuities in development (what in the person persists through time).

Robert Kegan, a constructive-developmental psychologist in the Piagetian tradition, asserts that these "neglects" are "actually unitary, that they are all the result of a single truncation in the attention of the paradigm."[11] That is to say, all of these seeming neglects in the Piagetian perception of development may be addressed if we return to Piaget's central insight: development arises in the interaction between the person and his or her environment, between self and world.

Kegan, therefore, invites us to return our attention to the study of the interaction between self and other. Kegan affirms that the self–other or subject–object differentiation and relation is indeed one of the most significant, robust, and universal phenomena to be found in nature, but that its significance is obscured by the failure to recognize the motion, or the interaction, that gives rise to it. He calls this motion "meaning-constructive evolutionary activity," by which he refers to "something that is more than biology, philosophy, psychology, sociology, or theology, but is that which all of these, in their different ways, have studied. .... the restless creative motion of life itself" (p. 407). He means that individual persons are not their stages of development but are a motion, within which stages of development are merely moments of dynamic stability.

Kegan has extended Piaget's insight by focusing less on the stages Piaget describes and more on the interaction by which stages are composed—the interaction between the person and the environment, between self and other, self and world, self and truth. He asserts that the *motion* of such interactions, recognized by Piaget as essential for the development of cognition, is a larger conception. This larger conception—the motion of the self–other relation—is a dynamic central to the formation, not only of cognition, but of personality. Kegan has pushed Piaget's theory of cognition to a theory of ego—or, better, a theory of the self in motion. He has done so by recognizing that the activity of cognition is but one actor in a larger drama—the composing of meaning. This larger drama includes both the affective and the social, and the continuities as well as the discontinuities of development. It includes being, or the ontological, as well as concept, or the epistemological. It has everything to do with adulthood, as well as with childhood.

Kegan is moved by the dignity and the "astonishingly intimate activity" of a person's laboring, struggling, and delighting in making sense. The heart of life as revealed in this drama is not a static structure—a stage or series of stages. It is a motion in which what one is subject to continually evolves so as to become object. Growth involves a process of emergence from embeddedness (the assumed truth of one's perceptions and conceptions), a process of creating a new object from a former subjectivity.[12] Kegan is suggesting that another way of thinking about this motion of development is to recognize that the person is always both an individual and an "embeddual," meaning that we are embedded in our perceptions until we can distinguish between our perceptions of the other and the other itself. Hence, an important step into a more mature adulthood is the evolution from "I *am* my relationships" to "I *have* relationships (and cherish and wrestle with and despair over and delight in and depend upon them, but am no longer so fused with them or embedded in them)."

As Kegan describes the evolution of the self–other relation, each new equilibrium or balance (stage) is an evolutionary truce in the ego's understanding of the truth of both the differentiation and the relation of subject and object. Though Kegan's version of the drama of development tends, nevertheless, to tell a story of the evolving self in which the evolving other plays only a supporting role, his perspective restores motion to development and helps to redirect the attention of developmental psychologists toward a renewed awareness that truth is composed in the self–other relation. Truth is a relational phenomenon. Kegan's perspective thus begins to modify the sharp distinctions between subject and object composed by the Western mind. The self–other motion that Kegan perceives as underlying the composing and sustaining of truth requires the recognition that finally a person remains, if not "subject to," at least "in relation to" that which one may also "take as object."

It is Carol Gilligan, however, who most powerfully retells the story of human development in relational rather than in more individualistic terms.[13] Taking seriously the voices of women as they compose moral judgments, she and her associates describe an evolving understanding of moral choice in a world in which "all things being equal never are." This journey unfolds in a language—a voice—that seeks to give adequate expression to the reality of evolving relation and responsibility. This "voice" (expressive of both male and female experience, but tending to be more salient in the expression of women) contrasts with the juridical voice of differentiation and rights that had been identified in Kohlberg's earlier study of moral reasoning in males.[14] The voice Gilligan has identified focuses, not upon the differentiation of subject from object, but upon the *relation* that orients subject to object, self to truth.

Gilligan clarifies the distinctions between these two voices with the example of two young children playing together and wanting to play different games. The girl said, "Let's play next-door neighbors." "I want to play pirates," the boy replied. "Okay," said the girl, "then you can be the pirate that lives next door." The children might have resolved the dilemma by the fair solution (Kohlberg) of taking turns and playing each game for an equal period; this solution would honor the rights of each child and keep the identity and truth of each child intact, while providing opportunity for each child to experience the other's imaginative world. But, asserts Gilligan, "The inclusive solution, in contrast, transforms both games through their combination: the neighbor game is changed by the presence of a pirate living next door; the pirate game is changed by bringing the pirate into a neighborhood." The inclusive-relational solution creates not only a new game but a new image of self, a new relation, and a new truth.[15]

In the developmental theories of Erikson, Piaget, Kegan, and Gilligan, we begin to hear echoes of the dynamics of faith—a process of maturation, of making sense, of composing meaning, of ordering relation, and an activity that transforms being, knowing, and doing. Indeed, Kegan has affirmed that to incorporate a dynamic notion of faith into the constructive-developmental insight is not to add something at the periphery of the developmental perspective, but to speak from its heart.[16] For when constructive-developmental theory moves beyond a focus on stages to a focus on the motion that gives rise to the stages, it moves "into the very experiences and phenomena that have been a feature of . . . faith communities and individuals, as long as persons have given expression to the reality of being alive. Any developmental framework, taken as a whole, should be a kind of attention to the human dance—the changing form through time in space. The constructive-developmental perspective has not yet found a way to do justice to what Whitehead called the ultimate reality of the universe—its motion. Much less has it recognized the religious dimension of our relation to this reality, what Buber spoke of both as an inevitable lifelong tension between the I-Thou and the I-It, and as the sacredness of the everyday. Yet of greater magnitude than this neglect is the potential of the same framework to reflect this very motion . . . and to do it honor.''[17]

James Fowler, a theologian, ethicist, and developmental psychologist, is the person who has most comprehensively and effectively pioneered the interdisciplinary study of the relationship between developmental psychologies and faith.[18] Influenced by both Erikson and Piaget and also by Kohlberg, Fowler and his associates have developed an interviewing method that assists us in listening to the story of a person's journey in faith. Informed by theological and psychological perspectives and by the patterns that began to emerge from the analysis of hundreds of life stories, Fowler has enunciated a conceptual framework by which to interpret the development of faith and has described six stages in faith (see appendix A). Five of these stages are based on empirical research data, and a sixth stage is constructed by inference from biographies and from developmental and theological perspectives.

Fowler has identified seven aspects of the capacity for faith that develop in a manner analogous to Piaget's form of cognition: form of logic (modified Piaget), perspective taking (modified Selman), form of moral judgment (modified Kohlberg), bounds of social awareness, locus of authority, form of world coherence, and symbolic function. These seven aspects may be thought of as girders for each stage structure. It is through the confluence and development of these aspects that faith is restructured in the direction of greater adequacy.

Although, like that of other Piagetians, Fowler's work has

had a cognitive and stage-structure bias, he has also recognized the power of affect and symbol in human development. Furthermore, he has not only forged the linkages between psychological development and human faith but has also contributed significantly to the extension of constructive-developmental insights into adulthood. Our consideration of the particular character of young adult faith will build upon and critically refine and elaborate Fowler's work, particularly attending to the relation between cognition and affect, the role of imagination, and a re-examination of the dynamics he has described as transitional between the third and fourth stages of his scheme (i.e., the shift from assumed, conventional faith to a critical, self-aware faith).

A theorist who is crucial to this re-examination of Fowler's third and fourth stages is William G. Perry. Perry is the theoretician who, with his colleagues, has made the most informing study of intellectual and ethical development in the context of higher education. His study is characterized by an unusual quality of careful listening and by a sensitivity of interpretation that serves as a worthy guide for all researchers willing to value the integrity of human experience more than theoretical tidiness. He frequently repeats one of his favorite axioms: "The person is always larger than the theory."

As described in his book *Forms of Intellectual and Ethical Development in the College Years: A Scheme*, he has, with elegant simplicity, identified nine positions or forms of composing truth through which human beings make their way as natural epistemologists (coping with the questions of how we know) in the context of higher education.[19]

In the chapter that follows, I will draw on insights from each of these developmental theorists in order to compose a descriptive model by which we may better understand important dynamics in the journey of faith in adulthood. This model will enable us to re-examine the life stories of persons such as Dorothy Day and Frederick Law Olmsted so as to foster a deepened respect, not only for their final accomplishments, but for the process by which they were achieved. Especially, we may be prepared to recognize the critical place of young adulthood, that period when Dorothy was a wandering political radical and Frederick seemed to be lost and depressed in his scattered enthusiasms—and when each was on a journey toward a mature adult faith.

Faith—the activity of seeking, composing, and being composed by a meaning both ultimate and intimate—cannot, of course, be reduced to psychological processes, but the recognition and understanding of such processes can enhance our appreciation and respect for what concerns human beings most intimately and ultimately.[20]

4. The Journey Toward Mature Adult Faith: A Model

I have studied many times
The marble which was chiseled for me—
A boat with a furled sail at rest in a harbor.
In truth it pictures not my destination
But my life.
For love was offered me and I shrank from its disillusionment;
Sorrow knocked at my door, but I was afraid;
Ambition called to me, but I dreaded the chances.
And now I know that we must lift the sail
And catch the winds of destiny
Wherever they drive the boat.
To put meaning in one's life may end in madness,
But life without meaning is the torture
Of restlessness and vague desire—
It is a boat longing for the sea and yet afraid.

— EDGAR LEE MASTERS
Spoon River Anthology, "George Gray"

The journey of faith can take us to new vistas of knowing, to deepened realms of trust, and to ever-widening circles of belonging. I wish to describe some of the perils and promises of this experience as it may occur in adulthood by tracing three discrete strands[1] of development: form of cognition, form of dependence, and form of community. Woven together, these strands form a descriptive model of the journey of faith in adulthood that is strong without being unnecessarily complex. This model is anchored in a description of intellectual development because it is this dimension of young adult development that is most unambiguously the focus of higher education. The primary purposes of the model, however, are, first, to enable us to see the intimate relationship between cognitive development and the development of affect, community, and faith and, second, to set forth a picture of the broad contours of the path of adult faith. In the following chapter we will focus on the place of young adulthood.

FORM OF COGNITION

As noted earlier, William Perry, during his years as a master listener, counselor, and teacher at Harvard's Bureau of Study Counsel, accompanied a good many students as they made their way as natural epistemologists coping with the puzzles of life in the context of higher education. Further, he and his associates have listened systematically to yet more students in order to confirm and better understand their emerging intuitions of a discernable pattern of development. They have identified nine positions, and their variants, through which persons seem to make their way.[2] I have collapsed, modified, and extended these into four positions.

Form of Cognition	Authority-bound Dualistic	→	Unqualified relativism	→	Commit-ment in relativism	→	Convictional commitment

AUTHORITY-BOUND AND DUALISTIC

The first form of knowing Perry identifies is oriented to Authority and is dualistic in character. In this form of knowing, what a person really trusts, knows, and believes is finally based on some Authority "out there." Such Authority may take the form of a particular person or group, or it may take the more diffused but subtly powerful form of a person's conventional ethos: media, that is, films, television, newspapers, magazines, books, journals; culturally affirmed roles and personalities, such as parents, government officials, religious leaders, recognized artists and popular entertainers; and custom, that is, expected conventions of thought, feeling, and behavior. These various authorities are confirmed by the stories, myths, and symbols that hold the meanings of a people and their institutions.

When persons compose their sense of truth in this form, they may assert deeply felt and strong opinion but, if they are asked to reveal the basis for their knowing, eventually they will reveal their uncritical, assumed trust in a source of authority located outside the self. In some way regarded as self-evident, this Authority is presumed to have access to Truth. This form of knowing may be characterized as "Authority-bound" (not Perry's term), in that this form of authority functions in an all-powerful, determinative manner; the person cannot "stand outside of it" or otherwise have any critical leverage upon it. The person's knowing is inextricably bound up with the power of the trusted Authority.

This form of knowing also tends to be "dualistic." People who compose self, world, and "God" in this form can make clear divisions between what is true and untrue, right and wrong, "we" and "they." There is little or no tolerance for ambiguity. It is important to note, however, that *what* such persons hold absolute certainty about—the "content" of their sense of truth—will vary from person to person, though they share the same cognitive structure. Thus, even though the "structure" of this form of knowing is quite rigid, the "content" that is known so absolutely may itself be seemingly fluid. The language of "relativism," for example, is now commonplace enough to be part of the conventional ethos. Yet this Authority-bound and dualistic way of knowing may still be heard in declarations like "It is totally wrong for anyone to think that truth isn't merely relative," or "You *must* be tolerant."

In this form of knowing, even the truth of the self is composed by the authority of others. The power of that Authority is revealed in these words of a college senior reflecting on the changes he experienced in his college years:[3]

Some of the main things I can think of are like in high school everybody said, "Oh, you're tall, you must play basketball." So I translated it, "You *must* play basketball." I just hated basketball, but I turned out every year anyway (laugh). So finally . . . I said, "Hey, I'm tired of that. I don't want to." And I sort of stepped out of the role of being the tall sports figure and into just being myself. I liked that a lot more.

Another senior, reflecting on how he felt after his first exam of his freshman year, reveals the way in which the Authority-bound form of knowing is determined by authority outside the self. The values and criteria of others have the power to shape one's sense of self.

In terms of studying, I didn't know how I would stand in a class. Like I remember the first test I took was in History and Culture of the Orient. I didn't know at all what I would get on the test . . . anything from a C to an A. I didn't think I had flunked because I had studied for it, but I didn't know quite how I stood. And I got the test back and I got an A. And that seemed to set a precedent, you know, what goals I set for myself. It's kinda strange. I look back, if I'd gotten maybe a B or a C on that test I might have . . . set lower standards for myself.

A key insight from a constructive-developmental perspective, however, is the recognition that this uncritical, Authority-bound, and dualistic form of knowing is characteristic, not only of children and adolescents, but also of some persons throughout the whole of biological adulthood. From a constructive-developmental point of view, development of cognition beyond this Authority-bound form of knowing does not inevitably occur.

Some who go to college or university arrive with this mode of composing meaning very much intact; for others this form of knowing, this form of faith, has already begun to dissolve.[4] In either case, the journey that follows (for which higher education at its best has been a primary sponsor) is the journey from this uncritical form of certainty to another kind of knowing.

A transformation of Authority-bound knowing typically occurs in the discomfort of finding that established patterns of thinking do not accommodate lived experience. For example, while taking notes from several different yet trusted professors, a student may begin to recognize that one professor's point of view seriously conflicts with another professor's. The student will then either compartmentalize them, place them in some hierarchy of value,[5] or begin to recognize the validity of competing points of view that cannot easily be reconciled into simple either-or forms of true and untrue, good and evil. For a time the student may trust that there is still a "right" answer that some Authority has or will surely discover, since the existence of such a right answer cannot be in question. But the cataclysmic shift occurs in the revolutionary moment when the relative character of *all* knowledge becomes the only "truth."

UNQUALIFIED RELATIVISM

Now the student can no longer avoid the awareness both that the human mind acts upon its world to compose it (rather than simply receiving it "as it is") and that all knowledge is relative, meaning that all knowledge is conditioned by the particularity of the relation or context in which it is composed. This requires the student to recognize that the most trusted adults and the most venerable disciplines of knowledge (even the natural sciences) must each compose reality in a pluralistic and relativized world, now perceived as a universe in which every perception leads to a different "truth," and, therefore, every opinion and judgment may be as worthy as another. This form of knowing is Perry's "position 5," and in its most robust form it might appropriately be termed "unqualified relativism."[6]

This shift may occur gradually or abruptly in the context of ongoing lived experience. It may be precipitated by a "lead from the head," as when a person is intentionally introduced to competing perspectives in a stimulating seminar. Authority-bound and dualistic thinking, however, is not besieged only in the seminar room; it may also come unraveled outside the classroom. Wherever one undergoes experience that does not fit the assumptions of one's conventional world, there is an invitation to begin to recognize the relative character of all knowing and to develop critical thinking. Sometimes the reordering of meaning is initiated in forming or losing relationships. For instance, in the pluralistic setting of a typical college or university (or in the military or in prison or in moving to a new place), a person is apt to associate with someone he or she had always defined as "they." When it is discovered that "they" neither fit the stereotypes nor can be assimilated as a mere "exception" into an assumed system of meaning, the dualistic world of "we" and "they" begins to decline in power, and the Authority by which it was composed is called under review. For a time, a person may cope by saying things like, "I have my truth; you have your truth; they have their truth. It doesn't matter what you think, as long as you are sincere." "The Truth" seems to become one truth among many. But this sort of statement discloses, on one hand, the hope that absolute certainty still dwells somewhere (in this case in sincerity), while, on the other hand, it reveals a sort of bravado that serves as a defense against the increasing awareness that conventional certainty just isn't holding well at all. Doubt is deepened when someone points out that both Martin Luther King, Jr. and devotees of Adolf Hitler were in a sense "sincere."

Likewise, a person may be involved in a romance, or some other close association, that is assumed to be trustworthy because it fits the myths that the person holds about life and how it will be. Under these conditions, when "the" romantic relationship or "the" career opportunity collapses, the person suffers, not only the obvious loss, but also the shipwreck of self, world, and "God,"—the truth of life itself betrayed.

The balance or the pattern of subject and object shifts. The person is no longer "subject to" the assumptions of his or her conventional world; these assumptions may now be held as possible points of view among others—"objects" of reflection.

This new balance may offer some new power and freedom, but it is achieved at the cost of an earlier certainty. Perry expresses the experience as it may be felt from the "inside":

Soon I may begin to miss those tablets in the sky. If this [one possible interpretation among others] defines the truth for term papers, how about people? Principalities? Powers? How about the Deity . . . ? And if this can be true of my image of the Deity, who then will cleanse my soul? And my enemies? Are they not *wholly* in the wrong?

I apprehend all too poignantly now that in the most fateful decisions of my life I will be the only person with a first-hand view of the really relevant data, and only part of it at that. Who will save me then from that "wrong decision" I have been told not to make lest I "regret-it-all-my-life"? Will no one tell me if I am right? Can I never be sure? Am I alone?

Perry then observes:

It is not for nothing that the undergraduate turns metaphysician.[7]

A position of unqualified relativism is, however, difficult to sustain over time. One discovers that there is a difference between just any opinion and an opinion that is grounded in careful and thoughtful observation and reflection. One may move into a more qualified relativism, increasingly aware that discriminations can be made between arguments based on such principles as internal coherence, the systematic relation of an argument to its own assumptions, external data, and so forth. But the dilemma remains: If thinking doesn't bring us to certainty, why think?[8] The answer usually comes from the imperative of ongoing life.

COMMITMENT IN RELATIVISM

Certainty may be impossible, but choices must be made that have consequences for oneself and those one loves. Particularly in relation to issues of moral choice, a person may begin to look for a place to stand, a way of composing truth more adequate to lived reality than other possibilities are. This search for a place to stand is the search for a place Perry terms *commitment in relativism*.

To form commitment in relativism is to begin to take self-conscious responsibility for one's own knowing. One now joins with other adults in discerning what is adequate, worthy, valuable—while aware of the finite nature of all judgments. Fowler speaks of this form of knowing as the composing of an "explicit system" because the person has shifted from a form of world coherence that is "tacit" in its character and assumptions to a form of world coherence that is formed in a desire to make explicit the meaning of life as best one may. As we shall see, it is this movement that is most characteristic of the young adult in the university years.

CONVICTIONAL COMMITMENT

Fowler describes the development of yet another form of knowing on the other side of commitment in relativism. With Fowler, I believe that typically it does not emerge until well after the ordinary college years, indeed, not until after midlife. It is a place I wish to term *convictional commitment*. It seems to me that this form of knowing was expressed by Carl Jung in a film made near the end of his life. The interviewer asked, "Do you believe in God?" Jung immediately responded, "No." I happened to watch this film with a large university audience, mostly undergraduate, and many spontaneously laughed, assuming, "Of course Jung was too sophisticated to believe in God." Jung, however, continued his response, saying, "I don't have to believe in God, I know God." This time, no one laughed.

Jung exemplified a strength of knowing that is quite other than the Authority-bound, dualistic knowing described earlier. Aware that all knowledge is relative, he knew that what he knew on any given day could be radically altered by something he might learn the next day. Yet he embodied a deep conviction of truth—the sort of knowing that we recognize as wisdom. This wisdom is also reflected in a statement of Oliver Wendell Holmes, who is reported to have said: "I do not give a fig for the simplicity on this side of complexity. But I would give my life for the simplicity on the other side of complexity."[9] Mature wisdom manifests the simplicity on the other side of complexity. Mature wisdom is not an escape from, but an engagement with, complexity and mystery. Our response to this form of knowing is not necessarily agreement, but it does arrest our attention and compel our respect. Such knowing does not put us off the way Authority-bound and dualistic knowing may; rather, we seek it out, or sense that we are sought by it.

Convictional commitment corresponds with Fowler's fifth stage, which he has described as "multi-systemic" in contrast to either the tacit or the explicit forms of world coherence characteristic of earlier places in the epistemological journey (see appendix A). This form of knowing represents a "second naïveté" (Ricoeur)[10] that, without abandoning the centered authority of the self and a disciplined fidelity to truth, has a new capacity to hear the truth of another. This form of knowing "resists forced syntheses or reductionist interpretations and is prepared to live with ambiguity, mystery, wonder, and apparent irrationalities" (p. 81).

Cognitive development, as I have described it here, moves from Authority-bound, dualistic, and tacitly held forms of cognition through the development of intellectual thought (the capacity and desire to reflect critically upon the relationship of thought to value and action) toward responsible and convictional commitments. Observed in a distanced fashion from the outside, it may appear to describe a cognitive development of the mind, occurring independently from the affective, emotional life of the person. As experienced from the inside, however, this is decidedly not the case.

When a person undergoes the transformation of his or her sense of truth and reorders "how things really are," such a repatterning of life may involve feelings of curiosity, awe, fascination, delight, satisfaction, exuberance, and joy. But inevitably there is also some degree of challenge, threat, bewilderment, confusion, frustration, fear, loss, emptiness, or other suffering.

There is some element of the "shipwreck" described earlier. This suffering dimension and its relationship to cognitive-intellectual development is focused in an account given to William Perry by a young woman about her experience in a physics class. There was, she said, a particular apparatus that appeared to revolve in a circle; however, when the light cast upon it was changed, it then appeared instead to be oscillating. This change in perception, which occurred with only the flick of a light switch, catalyzed her recognition of the relative character of all perception. She concluded her telling of the incident, which had happened many months earlier, by remarking that in the midst of the experience her physics professor had been very helpful to her. When asked how, she said, "Well, now that I think about it, I realize that he didn't say anything; but the way he looked at me, I knew that he knew what I had lost."

To undergo the loss of assumed certainty, to have to reorder what can be trusted as true and real at the level of one's ultimacy, involves emotion as well as cognition. Cognition and affect are intimately woven together in the fabric of knowing. To travel along the epistemological journey that Piaget, Perry, and Fowler describe is to be affected and moved. Kegan has stated it nicely: "A change in how we are composed may be experienced as a change in our own composure."[11] This is to say that there is development in affective life also, for the evolution of meaning is simultaneously a consequence of evolving cognitive power and the ongoing experience of being affected in interaction with one's world. The experience of the motion of life is manifest as emotion—even if constrained by the conventions of "reasonableness" within the academy or some other social context. Indeed, all our deepest emotions may originate in the felt experience of continual meaning-making activity, the experience of our participation in the motion of life itself.[12]

In other words, if, as Piaget observed, the discovery of knowledge occurs in an interaction between self and world, then, since the self represents an intimate relation between body, mind, and heart,[13] developments in intellectual awareness are one with a reordering of feelings and relationships. Relation, power, and vulnerability are dynamically repatterned with every insight. The splitting of the atom, for example, is reordering our relationship to the earth and to each other, enlarging our power and our vulnerability, and fundamentally changing those matters that ultimately concern us. We have been affected. Whether we cope by means of psychic numbing[14] or a resolute engagement with the potential terror which has become our daily reality, we are moved and feel a new wave of emotion upon us. Our concern with the "balance of powers" between nations reflects our personal sense of being moved "off balance." Our inner sense of a dependable balance of trust and vulnerability has precariously shifted. Within this motion we are recomposing our sense of what is ultimately dependable (or our sense of "God"), as we begin to live with a new awareness that more depends upon us than we had previously supposed. We are moved to recompose more interdependent and, therefore, more dependable patterns of knowing and being.

Since it is apparent that the dynamic of dependence is integral to the relation within which cognition develops, I turn now to a consideration of the forms of dependence, an affective strand of development in the weaving of mature faith.[15]

FORM OF DEPENDENCE

Dependence is a manifestation of relationship. Dependence is an inevitable dimension of the power of the relation of self and other. To depend is to be "held by" or "subject to," but it is also "to hold" (as object). A focus on cognition gives us access to how a person *thinks* in her or his composing of meaning at the level of faith. A focus on dependence gives us access to what a person *feels*. For holding, being held, depending and being depended upon at the level of ultimacy (even in the conceptual dimension, even in adulthood) touches the core of the self so profoundly that emotions such as confidence, fear, vulnerability, and strength are inevitably evoked—emotions that undergo transformation and development. Humans are always and necessarily interdependent beings, but the form, experience, and awareness of dependence changes. I propose, therefore, that we add "form of dependence" as a strand of adult development.

Form of Cognition	Authority-bound Dualistic (tacit)	→	Unqualified relativism	→	Commit-ment in relativism (explicit)	→	Convictional commitment (paradoxical)
Form of Dependence	Dependent/Counter dependent			→	Inner-dependent	→	Inter-dependent

DEPENDENCE

At the time of Authority-bound knowing, it follows logically that a person's sense of world is dependent upon an uncritically assumed Authority (though, particularly in adulthood, this may take subtle forms that mask the profound dependence that is, in fact, in place). A person may be able to give a variety of logical reasons for holding a particular position or point of view but, if pressed, will eventually reveal an unexamined trust in some form of Authority that that person is held by. The self quite literally hangs in a balance of self and other in which the self is uncritically dependent upon an authoritative other outside the self.[16] Feelings of assurance, rightness, hope, fear, loyalty, disdain, or alarm can be determined by Authority—whether in the voice of Walter Cronkite, the Pope, a government official, a person's "always there and always right" parent, a minister, a spouse, or others who serve individually or collectively as trusted mediators of Truth.

Kegan quite fittingly names this era in development "interpersonal," for here a person's sense of truth depends upon his or her relational and affectional ties. Fowler, with equal fittingness, names this era (stage three) "conventional," for here the person uncritically accepts the conventions of group and societal norms. The boundaries of the group may be rather narrowly drawn, as in the case of a "conventional" cult or club member, or more broadly construed, as in the case of a "conventional" Democrat, Republican, Protestant, Roman Catholic, marine, hippie, yuppie, activist, or Hell's Angel. In each instance, the person's sense of reality and what is fitting and true is dependent upon a sense of felt relationship to an ethos of assumed Authority.

COUNTERDEPENDENCE

A person's feelings will continue to be shaped by this assumed Authority until the day when there is the yearning (or the absolute necessity) to explore and test truth for oneself. This may occur in the midst of the utter shipwreck of the truth one has depended upon (in which it may be accompanied by feelings of devastation, betrayal, bewilderment, or the like), or it may emerge as a manifestation of just a restlessness arising as a sort of readiness for more being. In the latter instance, it is as though a strength has been established which can now "push away from the dock" of that which has been sure moorage, to move out into the deep waters of exploring for oneself what is true and trustworthy. Initially, however, this move is essentially another form of dependence, since this pushing away from the dock takes the form of counterdependence.[17]

Counterdependence is the move, in opposition to Authority, that provides momentum for the passage into the unknown. It is a dimension of the earlier dependence, because Authority is still in control in that the person can push against the pattern that is, but is not yet able to create a new one. Here, the "I" dwells in negative tension with every "truth." One is dependent upon moving apart, dependent upon creating some distance. Indeed, the very need for distance merely obscures continuing participation in a relation that is still (and in most instances will continue to be) quite powerful.[18]

This move can occur in relatively nontraumatic forms if the

person is in an environment of wise parents, sponsoring teachers, or others who consciously encourage or nurture it. Little "pushing against" is necessary, because one is encouraged to explore and is supported in doing so. However, when this motion is not understood and when the bond of relation has been particularly good and trustworthy, the person may have to push against the dock with greater force if a new relationship is to take form. In contrast, people with the least experience of positive trust may suffer counterdependence over an extended period of time, for relationships of negative tension may feel most fitting or truthful when one has had little experience of knowing a worthy truth grounded in positive relationship.

In any case, this may be a complicated time for parents, teachers, administrators, or students (or spouses trying to repattern their marriage bond). For example, when a student moves in the opposite direction from Authority, Authority may recognize this and may suggest the opposite of what is really intended. Clever students figure this out, however, and any real meeting or collaboration becomes quite impossible for everyone, even when the forms of this distancing motion are subtle rather than overt. (This is particularly the case when Authority resists the now necessary recomposing of the relationship and becomes authoritarian.) Frustrations abound as earlier forms of communication seem to dissolve and alternative patterns of relationship have not yet taken form (and cannot as long as connection feels like a return to earlier patterns of dependence).

Yet, in time, a person may begin to recompose Authority and recognize that, indeed, Authority doesn't hold ultimate truth or power. The counterdependent pilgrim is compelled, therefore, to begin to look less toward resisting Authority and more toward the self as an act of responsibility in relation to self, world, and truth. The person begins to move toward inner-dependence.

INNER-DEPENDENCE

The term *inner-dependence* is used here to signify something different from independence. Western culture places an extraordinary value on individuality and autonomy—a sort of independence that implies, not only strength of self, but also the utter absence of a fundamental recognition of the adult's need for affectional relation with others. The presumed needs of industrial societies have conspired with Freud's insights so as to cast suspicion on all forms of dependence. Dependence is regarded as infantile, particularly those forms of dependence that have religious justification. Partaking in the same industrial and Enlightenment influence, Protestant religious faith has simultaneously fostered a cultural ethos in which the individual conscience and independent action tend to have ultimate value. Yet, as William Rogers observes, "while there is solid conviction as well as psychological wisdom in both religious and general cultural manifestations of independence, the excess of such claims easily leads us to the suspicion that they may betray more underlying anxiety about forms of dependence."[19] Not all forms of dependence are appropriately equated solely with weakness, immaturity, or a dynamic of regression to infantile relationships. Dependence also points toward the relational dimension of all being, a dimension neglected to the impoverishment of our cultural myths and our over-individualized lives.

Inner-dependence, in contrast to the common associations we make with notions of independence or autonomy, is not intended to connote a "standing all by oneself." Rather, the motion into inner-dependence occurs when one is able to self-consciously include the self within the arena of authority. In other words, other sources of authority may still hold credible power, but now one can recognize and value also the authority of the self. Carol Gilligan's study suggests a corresponding motion in the dimension of care. People (especially women) who have previously tended to extend care almost exclusively to others to the neglect of the self (because only others had the authority to claim care) can now extend care also to the self (who now also has the authority to claim care).

Responsibility to authority outside the self is thereby relativized (but not demolished). With the term *inner-dependence*, then, I wish to signify, not a negation of the essential relatedness upon which all human life depends, but a new consciousness of the authority of the inner life of the self in the composing of truth and of choice. A person begins to listen within, with a new respect and trust for the truth of his or her "own insides." That is, the person begins to listen and be responsive to the self as a source of authority and as an object of care. Again, this does not mean that sources of insight outside the self or the claims of others for care necessarily become irrelevant; it does mean, however, that the self takes conscious responsibility for adjudicating competing claims for truth and care.

In this movement of the soul, there emerges the possibility of a new quality of correspondence between inner and outer realities—and the potential for new bonds of relation between self and world. There is sometimes also a new vulnerability that comes with a heightened awareness of the discrepancies between the claims of the self and the capacity of the social structures of one's world to respond to those claims. Before a new relation between self and world is created, the claims of each may threaten the other.

After inner-dependence is established and the trustworthiness of the inner self is confirmed, there seems to be yet another movement toward the further enlargement of trust and conviction of promise. This movement again expands the arena of authority and of care.

INTERDEPENDENCE

In the mid-life period, a person may simply move through a transition from the first half of his or her life to the second half. (It is my sense that "mid-life" occurs at different times for different persons, because it is determined by one's own inner sense that one has probably lived half of one's life. The future is no longer infinitely revisable. One's sense of "life-time" becomes more focused. This is a transition in conscious-ness, usually marked by physical changes as well.) But transitions can be occasions for transformation. The transfor-mative potential of the mid-life transition lies in the strength of the inner-dependent self. For only when one has become strong enough can the "deep self" emerge to be re-known as a resource for the further repatterning of truth and faith.[20]

The "deep self" is composed of those buried dimensions of oneself—particularly the sufferings of childhood, the unre-solved issues of adolescence, and, as we shall see, the most luminous dreams and hopes of young adulthood. This deep self may now surface to be healed, to be realized, or at least to be known and lived with nondefensively. This movement may be resisted, but, if allowed, it may lead not only to a deeper knowing and trust of the self but also to a more pro-found awareness of one's relatedness to others.

This transformation constitutes another qualitative shift in the balance of vulnerability, trust, and faith. Now more at home with the limitations and strengths of the self, one can be more at home with the truth embedded in the strengths and limitations of others. A person's locus of primary trust now resides neither in the assumed authority of another nor in the courageously claimed authority of the inner self. Rather, trust is now centered in the meeting of self and other, recognizing the strength and finitude of each and the promise of the truth that emerges in relation. This trust is the self-conscious expres-sion of interdependence.

When meaning-making moves into an interdependent form, it is not the fact of interdependence that is new. As we are beginning to recognize more adequately, from infancy through adulthood a person is always interdependent, always depend-ent in varying ways upon faithful relationships with others. What is new, however, is one's awareness of the depth and pervasiveness of the interrelatedness of all of life. One now may become increasingly angered and saddened by assertions of truth that exclude the authority of the experience of others. A dean, for example, may earlier have been tolerant of shared inquiry and decision making, and even have affirmed the notion ideologically—all the while silently harboring a sense that his or her inner synthesis of experience, knowledge, and intuition would more efficiently achieve an adequate enough "truth." Now, however, he or she perceives dialogue to be not merely politically expedient, but essential. Yet one brings to that dialogue the strength of one's own capacity to author truth—a strength to which one now is no longer subject, but that one can now hold as object in dialogue with others to whom one can now listen with new attention. The person can depend upon others without fear of losing the power of the self. When this motion occurs within the marriage relation a yet more profound intimacy becomes possible, for the person not only is a self, but can hold even that self as object to be given to another. This is to say that the person now participates in a freedom allowing both weakness and strength, needing and giving, tenderness and assertiveness—without anxiety that in the recognition and even enlargement of the other the self will be diminished.

A person who has composed and is composed by this form of dependence—interdependence—comfortably dwells in the truth that the needs of nurturance, affection, and belonging extend throughout life and into every domain of being, both public and private. Interdependence can now be profoundly "owned" at the affective level. The person now most trusts the truth that emerges in the dialectic, or, better, in the communion between self and other, self and world, self and "God." The person can recognize and know with the whole self the truth of the interdependence that we are. This knowing involves the feelings of delight, wonder, freedom—and often a deep sense of the tragic arising from the capacity to see what others cannot or will not.

Attention to the development of dependence gives us some

access to the ebb and flow of the feelings of trust, constraint, threat, fear, confidence, and communion. These are feelings rooted in inner experience. But the motion of affective life and its development emerges neither in a merely private inner world nor in abstract reflections upon relationship but only in the frustrations and transformations of relationships lived out in the everyday. The importance of relationship brings us to reflect upon a third strand of development, form of community.

FORM OF COMMUNITY

One of the distortions of most psychological models is that their attention to the particular and inner experience of the individual obscures the power of social dynamics in the shaping of personal reality. The reifications of the disciplines of psychology and sociology reflect the split in modern thought between subject and object, private and public, and do not serve to cultivate the strength of understanding required to interpret a world increasingly requiring our recognition of the interdependence of all of life.[21]

A potential (but yet unrealized) strength of the Piagetian paradigm is its conviction that human becoming absolutely depends upon the quality of the interaction between the person and his or her environment.[22] The human being does not compose meaning all alone. The individual person is not the sole actor in the drama of human development. Just as the infant is dependent upon others for the confirmation of a universe of care and promise, even so is everyone throughout life dependent upon a *network of belonging*. Every person needs a psychological "home." This home is constituted by the patterns of connection and interaction between the person and his or her environment. The composing of ultimate meaning is determined, in part, by our relationship with "those who count."[23] Faith as a patterning, connective, relational activity is embodied, not in the individual alone, but in the social fabric of life.

Networks of belonging may take the form of an obviously

present and easy to identify circle of relationships, membership in which confirms identity and security. In other instances, the network of belonging may be scattered geographically or otherwise dispersed among arenas of involvement and may include people both living and dead. For example, one may live in a strong sense of association with a historical figure one has never met, but who serves as a touchstone for one's life and values. Or one may live and work far from colleagues who share one's vision and commitments and yet be able to sustain committed action, even when criticized in the immediate situation, because of the felt linkage with others who confirm one's very being. Even those who choose the life of solitude dwell in a dependence upon others who have formed and confirmed the self.

The power of the network of belonging is two-fold. First, the security it offers bestows the gift of freedom to grow and become. Second, every network of belonging has composed norms and boundaries that one cannot cross and still belong. The network of belonging is simultaneously a freedom and a constraint.[24] Thus social norms may manifest a collective wisdom that protects and nourishes the individual, but the same social norms may also distort and/or in time unnecessarily limit the promise of human life. Transformations in the meaning of the self, therefore, not only occur in the interaction with the social world, but may require a mutual recomposing.

It is this awareness that has prompted Dwayne Huebner to insist that the most worthy point of any developmental theory lies not in its capacity simply to diagnose an individual; rather, developmental theorists find their most fitting vocation in enabling us to respond to the question, What do the developing person and his or her community now mean to each other?[25] This is to say that the story of human development is also the story of the transformation in a person's experience of the meaning of community. Thus an understanding of adult development depends upon attention to forms of community.

Form of Cognition	Authority-bound Dualistic (tacit)	→ Unqualified relativism	→ Commitment in relativism (explicit)	→ Convictional commitment (paradoxical)
Form of Dependence	Dependent/Counter dependent	→	Inner-dependent	→ Inter dependent
Form of Community	Conventional	→ Diffuse	→ Self-selected class or group	→ Open to "others"

We never outgrow our need for others, but what others mean to us undergoes transformation. It is precisely at the point of becoming adult, however, that the form and role of community in our lives may become confused. Due to both the domination of the notion of independence in our understanding of adult psychology and the corresponding cultural perception that dependence is infantile, we are apt to feel uncomfortable if our need for community is strong.

The importance and the power of the social milieu has been somewhat more adequately acknowledged in psychological descriptions of children and adolescents. It is recognized that children are profoundly affected by parents, families, chums, and school groups; "peer groups" are well factored into the story of adolescent development. But when the mark of psychological adulthood is "autonomy," and maturity is measured in terms of degrees of "individuation," the ongoing and essential role of community in adult life becomes obscured.

The communion features of the psyche remain in focus, however, if we remember that the motion of meaning-making is located in the oscillation between "two great yearnings" of human beings: the yearning to be distinct—to exercise one's own action in the world, to stand alone, to differentiate the self from the other—and the yearning for connection, inclusion, belonging, relation, intimacy, and communion.[26] The current revisioning of constructive-developmental theory does well in reminding us that every new equilibrium "represents a kind of temporary compromise between the move toward differentiation and the move toward integration; every developmental era is a new solution to this universal tension" (pp. 412, 413).

CONVENTIONAL COMMUNITY

Fowler, building on the insights of Robert Selman[27] has attended to this social aspect of faith by describing the development of the "bounds of social awareness." At Fowler's stage three (typically, the era of adolescence and often beyond), the composing of self and world is located within and dependent upon "membership in a group or groups characterized primarily by face-to-face relationships."[28] These groupings are "conventional" because they conform to class norms and interests and are "ascriptive," meaning that one belongs because one is located by birth or other circumstance in that assumed context. Such groups and their prevailing ethos tend to "be defined by any one or some combination of the following: ethnic-familial ties, social-class norms, regional perspectives and loyalties, religious system, technoscientific ethos, peer values and pressures, and sex role stereotypes" (p. 63).

This boundary of social awareness is drawn so as to include only "those like us." People from out-groups may be appreciated as individuals for virtues and qualities determined by the values and norms of the in-group (pp. 63, 64). This form of community corresponds to the Authority-bound and dualistic form of cognition, in which Authority defines "we" and "they."

DIFFUSE COMMUNITY

But as one begins to want to know for oneself, often it is precisely this social ordering that is brought under examination. An experience of "other" that is contradictory to previous assumptions may recompose one's perceptions of the social order.

In the initial relinquishing of the assumed norms of relationship and the expanding of the boundaries of the social horizon, the form of community may become diffuse. An expansive, exploratory, experimental, and tentative character may predominate, for when any one truth or perspective is as good as another, there is some corresponding sense that any sort of relationship may be as good as any other. This is not to say that relationships become a matter of indifference. Quite the contrary may be the case when the person, now feeling a bit "at sea," has both a new freedom to explore the horizon of life and a new vulnerability to the potential power of every possible relationship. Rather, it is to say that when unqualified relativism prevails, the sustaining of any particular relationship becomes problematic. Ironically, however, the person awash in the sea of unqualified relativism may be sustained, nevertheless, only by the subjective experience of the importance of human connectedness, which may become "the spar we cling to" when the shipwreck of certainty dumps us into a seemingly meaningless world.

It is thus that people are typically dependent upon community for the formation of commitment within relativism, a community that will both represent and confirm a new pattern of knowing and being. Fowler describes the new social constellation that emerges at this time as a "self-selected class or group."

SELF-SELECTED GROUP

I became aware of the power of these dynamics to shape and reshape forms of community when I was teaching in a liberal arts college that encouraged off-campus study, particularly during its month long mini-term in January. With another colleague, I led a group of students to San Francisco, where they studied "the city" for a month. As an instructor in religion and a chaplain, I noted with interest that some students who had little or nothing to do with religion on campus were exploring the cathedrals in San Francisco as well as particular religious communities. They were also at times asking questions about religion, in contrast to their behavior on campus. At first, I assumed that this was simply because of a change in environment—that is, there were more cathedrals and more religious diversity in San Francisco. Only later did I recognize another dynamic at play with us in San Francisco—a change in the students' network of belonging.

On campus, students tended to choose patterns of affiliation based partly on their religious orientation. Once these were established, significant deviation was a threat to belonging. This meant that, for some, religion was "out of bounds" and, for others, "required." But when they were in a new social constellation, new questions and new behavior became possible.

We had expected that when students returned to campus those who had not traveled would benefit from association with those who had. We discovered, however, that the travelers tended to form new patterns of affiliation. They formed community—a self-selected group—with those who had also traveled and with whom they could confirm a new perception of the world.[29]

The "self-selected class or group" not only confirms the adult's new world of meaning that is composed on the other side of critical awareness, it also confirms a particular form of meaning. Even the most "cosmopolitan and liberal of mind" often discover, upon making a close examination of their own network of belonging, that at least initially, "those who count" are "of like mind"—though they may represent an expansion of previously held boundaries of ethnicity, class, geography, and so on. For example, one's network of belonging may be constituted by those who, though diverse in many respects, nevertheless hold similar political, religious, and philosophical views and values.

COMMUNITY OPEN TO OTHERS

Fowler's description of the evolution of the bounds of social awareness finds its most profound implication in the last stage he describes, a picture of mature faith manifest in a commitment to inclusive community marked by justice and love. But it is Ronald Marstin, building on the work of Fowler, who has most forcefully elaborated the essential linkages between the development of faith and the development of the capacity to move beyond provincial perceptions and conventional forms of community.

In his book, *Beyond Our Tribal Gods*, Marstin is not shy about acknowledging that implicit in developmental theory is the assumption that each succeeding stage is "better" in that each succeeding stage can account for more.[30] Each stage offers the capacity to handle greater complexity and thereby to be more inclusive. Marstin's boldness comes, not from an indifferent or arrogant elitism, but from a commitment to social justice. He sees clearly that not only is complex perspective taking essential to adequate moral reasoning (Kohlberg and Selman) but the character of one's composition of the whole of reality (one's faith) will condition what one finds tolerable and intolerable. He recognizes that the press to compose a fitting meaning in its most comprehensive dimensions becomes the press toward both truth and justice. Most fundamentally, he underscores the Piagetian insight that human beings develop "because we *need* to." We recompose meaning when we encounter the "other" in such a way that "we are left with no other choice, short of blocking out what we can no longer block out with any honesty. If we pass to a new way of interpreting the world, it is because the new way can account for things that the old way no longer could. We are now able to acknowledge considerations previously ignored, to account better for all the facts, to embrace a wider range of perspectives. We couldn't have reached the new stage without having first passed through the former stage. But the new one is not simply different; it is better" (p. 34). Development creates the capacity to embrace a more adequate truth and an expanded community.

Marstin celebrates the promise for human life inherent in a person's ongoing encounter with a world inhabited by other selves with their own needs, an encounter continually requiring the recomposing of what is true for the self in relationship to a world of others. As he does so, he shows that the process of cognitive development will surely require a relativizing of the tribal gods—one will be required to recognize the limitations of one's provincial ultimacy. But he is sobered by the recognition that, for many, leaving tribal gods appears to lead only to a new set of tribal gods. This is the case when people settle into a self-selected class or group that offers an easy ecumenism and the leisure to experiment, and shapes a private truth—while the earth remains sick (p. 44). This is to say that a "critically aware" movement to a "self selected class or group" may not necessarily represent an advance in inclusiveness. "Those of critical but like mind" may even represent a diminished concern for others, if critical awareness leads only to the formation of a network of belonging marked by cynicism and/or an ideology marked by exclusion (two conditions to which the young adult is particularly vulnerable).

Marstin quite rightly and compellingly sees two things: First, the content—the ideas and images that cognitive structures hold—is as important as the structures themselves (a matter we will take up in chapter 6) and, second, that yet another transformation in community is required for a faith that is mature in love and justice. When the conversation with "otherness" is sustained, when one continues to bump up against those who are different, the inner-dependent self begins to find a more adequate truth in a dialectic with the "other" both within and without. A yearning for community (not just association) with those who are profoundly other than oneself emerges.[31] The form of a person's community is transformed into a more profound inclusiveness, because it is truer. Ongoing meaning-making necessarily comes to challenge the system that protects some while neglecting others. "Issues of social justice are essentially about who is to be cared for and who neglected, who is to be included in our community of concern and who excluded, whose point of view is to be taken seriously and whose ignored. As faith grows, it challenges all the established [assumed and conventional] answers to these questions."[32]

This challenge becomes embodied in a form of community

that recognizes the "other" as "other." In the Fowler data, this form of community appears to be composed in the post-mid-life period. Perhaps this is because this capacity, not only to participate in, but to demand and create inclusiveness is nurtured, in part, by the capacity to include the "otherness" within.

Gordon Allport described the character of a faith that embodies convictional commitment, interdependence, and the creating and maintaining of a community that is genuinely open to others:

Maturity is never merely a matter of age, but one of development. A mature sentiment has a way of handling doubt, of realizing . . . that personal commitment is possible even without absolute certainty, that a person can be half-sure without being half-hearted.

The mature religious sentiment is dynamic in its desire to be truly comprehensive; it is not called upon only in fear, sorrow, and mystical moments; it saturates one's life. It joins a person's religion, which is deeply solitary, to social living.[33]

*   *   *   *

A MODEL

When we weave these three strands of development together, we are able to see some of the interrelated dynamics that shape the journey toward mature faith. The strands of cognition and dependence in their mutual resonance may assist us in recognizing that how we think about what concerns us ultimately and how we feel in the most intimate elements of our lives are dynamically interdependent. The strand of community begins to reveal that this telling of the journey toward mature faith represents a potential not necessarily realized in adult life; for the development of faith is a communal process dependent, not only upon the capacities and yearnings of the self, but also upon teachers, friends, mentors, colleagues, and neighbors who together form the social context that nourishes and enhances or diminishes and blocks the cultivation of the life of faith.

Form of Cognition	Authority-bound Dualistic (tacit)	→ Unqualified relativism	→ Commitment in relativism (explicit)	→ Convictional commitment (paradoxical)
Form of Dependence	Dependent/Counter dependent	→	Inner-dependent	→ Inter-dependent
Form of Community	Conventional	→ Diffuse	→ Self-selected class or group	→ Open to "other"
Forms of Faith	Egypt God as Parent	→ Wilderness The Far Country	→ Spirit Within	Promised Land Many members, one body

This model portrays a motion by which we may journey from Authority-bound forms of meaning-making anchored in conventional assumed community through the wilderness of counterdependence and unqualified relativism to a committed, inner-dependent mode of composing meaning, affirmed by a self-selected class or group. This model, furthermore, challenges the provincial character of much of adult faith by requiring attention to the possibility of further movement toward a yet more mature faith, marked by an engaged wisdom that manifests a conviction of interdependence and seeks communion with those who are profoundly other than the self.

Since the purpose of this model drawn with the tools of social science is to describe something true about the journey of faith in adult experience, we should also be able to find some resonance between this model and the ancient tales of our people. If the model illumines something that is true, we should be able to hear it echoed in the traditions of human faith. And we do. What is described here seems to correspond with the story in the Hebrew Scriptures of a movement from Egypt (initially a place of salvation, which becomes a bondage ill fitted to the promise of life) through a wilderness to a promised land.

This model also suggests that if a person's sense of ultimacy is recomposed in these modes, then the experience of God would also undergo transformation. Differing images of God might be more resonant at one place in the journey than another. For example, in the language of the Christian Scriptures, at the time of Authority-bound and dependent faith, one might know and experience God primarily as the loving parent or good shepherd "who cares for me and guides me"; the journey into unqualified relativism might be felt as a journey into the "far country" and away from God the Parent; a more inner-dependent commitment might be expressed in the imagery of the Spirit within; and interdependent, convictional commitment may have been something of what Saint Paul attempted to describe in the imagery of "many members . . . one body."[34]

Looking briefly at Eastern traditions, we may note that Confucian teaching holds the conviction that all human beings have the heart-mind that cannot bear to see the suffering of another, but that this feeling-knowing can be lost unless cultivated by an education that is a learning to be human.[35] Hindu wisdom has recognized stages of life in the imagery of a journey from apprentice (the dependent one), to householder (the responsible one), to seeker of spiritual truth (the wise one). The Buddhist vision begins in a story of a young person who went forth and found wisdom only on the other side of an encounter with suffering. Indeed, virtually all religious traditions have some story of pilgrimage.

The voice of faith, in this instance drawing on Christian imagery, perhaps captures the heart of the model of faith that has been offered here, saying:

Our greatest truths are but half-truths. Think not to settle down forever in any truth, but use it as a tent in which to pass a summer's night, but build no house for it or it will become your tomb. When you first become aware of its insufficiency, and descry some counter-truth looming up in the distance, then weep not, but rejoice: it is the voice of the Christ saying, "Take up your bed and walk."[36]

With this model to serve us as a broad framework describing the motion of adult faith, we are now prepared to focus on the experience of young adult faith and its significance in the formation of mature adult faith.

5. Young Adult Faith: Promise and Vulnerability

In the previous chapter I outlined a model by which to describe the journey toward mature adult faith. In terms of the college or university student it suggests a path from the assumed, conventional, tacit knowing of the adolescent to a critically aware adult faith, with some sort of transition, wilderness, or at least "sophomore slump" in between. As noted earlier, this three-part process has been essentially the pattern assumed by those in higher education responsible for accompanying the adolescent-becoming-adult. Four years of college could, it was also presumed, essentially provide the necessary time and sponsorship to complete what we would here describe as the journey from Authority-bound and dualistic faith to a commitment in relativism anchored in inner-dependence.

Constructive-developmental theories have in large measure shared these assumptions. Fowler's theory of faith development has described a movement from "Synthetic-Conventional" faith (stage 3) to "Individuative-Reflective" faith (stage 4) and the place in between as "transitional." Likewise, Kegan's description of the evolving self has described an evolution from the "Interpersonal Self" (stage 3) to the "Institutional Self" (stage 4), and again, the place in between as "transitional." Kohlberg described the evolution of moral judgment as a movement from conventional moral judgments (stages 3 and 4) to principled moral reasoning (stages 5 and 6), but he was not altogether able to account for the moral reasoning of students in their twenties, who, after having once achieved principled reasoning, seemed to find it inadequate and/or seemed to "regress."[1]

After my colleagues and I had composed the essential outlines of the model described in the last chapter, there was, in my ongoing teaching and counseling, a good deal I still could not account for either. It was helpful to be able to recognize and appreciate the loss of conventional thought, the nature of counterdependence, the struggle for inner-dependence, and the dynamics of community in the formation of students' faith experience. But additional puzzles emerged and evoked further questions. Where in these schemes could we locate the threshold of adulthood? At what point was it important to recognize that students had become responsible adults, and by what criteria? And what sort of time frame might be expected for the journey from adolescence into adulthood? If "stage four" was the constructive-developmental psychologist's answer to the search for adulthood, why didn't "stage four," or an equilibrated commitment to self, world, and "God," take form by the senior year? And if it did, why didn't it stay intact? Could I adequately describe what appeared as extended transition in terms of "prolonged adolescence" or "moratorium"?

Continuing to teach undergraduates first compelled me to notice how yet more complex were the dynamics of emerging adult faith. I observed that students who seemed quite strong in their junior year (inner-dependent?) often seemed more fragile in their senior year, and that they reflected a subtle, but surprisingly persistent, dependence on authority outside the self in their early alumni years. Never having wanted to be a professor who cultivated a cadre of dependent followers, I delighted in offering the well-timed push from the nest that would enable students to discover their own wings and soar away. Why, then, did the long distance phone calls come in every so many months "just to touch base"? And why, though obviously distinctly different, were they faintly reminiscent of the way a two-year-old goes off exploring, returning periodically to touch in with the parent in order to go off again? And why (after I had returned to studies myself) were two former students sitting at my breakfast table, delaying their scheduled departure? Both had moved through the ups and downs of undergraduate years, had differentiated themselves from their families, had developed critical thought, and had demonstrated a confident sense of direction upon graduation. One was now enrolled in a prestigious graduate program; the other was going abroad for travel and study—and both were surely about to miss the train. It was my sense that each was now less than confident (less committed?) and perhaps dependent in some way I didn't quite understand upon the security, affirmation, and haven I represented. I took them to the train myself and returned, bewildered, to resume my study.

These puzzling dynamics continued to confront me as I began to teach at the graduate level and perceived rather sophisticated graduate students as still engaged in recomposing a place to stand on the other side of the dissolution of their inherited, conventional faith. As they sat in my office and talked about the issues and struggles that confronted them, the strength, suffering, richness, and compelling integrity of their meaning-making simply could not be adequately described by the adjectives *adolescent*, *transitional*, or *arrested*, or by the notion of *moratorium*. I began to listen more carefully to both students and theorists and "found," embedded in the place called transition, an evolutionary truce—a distinct form of composing meaning, a recognizable stage. I began to see more clearly the power, promise, and vulnerability of the young adult soul.

IDENTITY: THE THRESHOLD OF ADULTHOOD

Returning to the question of where we might locate the threshold of adult faith, and informed by the thought of Erikson, I propose that the achievement of "identity" marks the threshold of adulthood. Adolescence, says Erikson, is "the last stage of childhood."[2] He also makes the statement that "identity" has a "claim to recognition as the adolescent ego's most important accomplishment" (p. 211). It seems appropriate that the achievement of the central accomplishment of adolescence—identity—marks the completion of adolescence and the threshold of adulthood. But what do we mean by "identity"? Erikson uses the term *identity* primarily to denote the "self-identity" that emerges as the adolescent successfully integrates differing role images and possibilities into a single ensemble of roles that secures social recognition.

Adolescence begins with puberty and the potential for formal operational thought—the capacity for symbolic and abstract thought. Formal operational thought also makes possible the capacity for third-person perspective taking—the ability to hold both one's own perceptions and the perceptions of another at the same time. Initially this new capacity leads to a new (and often painful) self-consciousness, as the adolescent can for the first time experience the self as perceived through the eyes of others. The adolescent lives under the tyranny of the "they." The task of adolescence is the development of a self that has the strength to counter the tyranny of the "they" and to mediate between the powerful images reflected in the adolescent's house of mirrors. This new strength is the power of "identity."[3] Cultivating this strength, and doing so in such a way as to achieve recognition in the social world, is, in Erikson's view, the achievement of adolescence. Whether or not the achievement of both identity and social recognition is fully accomplished at the end of adolescence is increasingly problematic, as we shall discuss shortly. But what may be achieved in adolescence is what Erikson points to as the hallmark of identity: a self-aware self. The self composed in the crisis of "identity vs. role diffusion"[4] is not only self-conscious but has enough ego strength to recognize that the self has power over the becoming of the self. As a person becomes aware of this power, there is a corresponding new quality of responsibility for the composing of self in relationship to other. There is now the awareness that there are other selves and other worlds one could compose. This new awareness of responsibility for self and world corresponds with the diminishment of an assumed, conventional, Authority-bound form of knowing. This self-conscious, critical awareness is an enormous achievement. This frequently takes the form of a person's being conscious of taking responsibility for choices that differ from those that conventional authority would choose, but of doing so not merely for the sake of difference (as would be the case in counterdependence).[5]

This is not to say that the critically aware postadolescent necessarily speaks of "composing a self." Rather, there is a deeper sense of choice and frequently some acceptance of struggle and its importance. A student we will name Bev, while describing her sense of movement to a new place on the other side of an assumed world, said:

> I guess I'd struggle . . . I'd give myself the freedom to struggle; then when I was done with a particular struggle and saw how I grew from it, that was really exciting for me and because of that . . . it was less threatening to me when other people would struggle with things— people that were really close. It wasn't like, oh, no—what's gonna happen? It was like oh, yeah, this is part of . . . it's part of growing so it's O.K. for them.[6]

It is significant for our purpose to note also that in Erikson's view the corresponding virtue developed with identity is "fidelity." This suggests the development of a new capacity "to set one's heart." I propose, then, that the threshold of young adulthood is marked by the capacity to take self-aware responsibility for choosing the path of one's own fidelity. A consequence of this awareness is the recognition that one even must take responsibility for the faith one lives by. This is sometimes a chilling recognition. Faith can now have a doubt of itself; it is no longer the simple adoption of the convictions of another. One becomes a young adult in faith when one begins to take self-conscious responsibility for one's own knowing, becoming, and moral action—even at the level of ultimate meaning-making. This moment in the journey of faith does not typically occur until at least the age of seventeen,[7] though for many people it emerges much later—or never.

When this new self-aware, critical, yet struggling strength does emerge, I am persuaded that it is an adult strength and marks the threshold of adult faith. But most of our prevailing assumptions and theoretical formulations have not been able to help us perceive and sponsor the particular character and integrity of young adult faith; as a consequence, we have perhaps also failed to comprehend messages of yearning, hope, and promise upon which the whole human family finally depends.

YOUNG ADULT FAITH

Kenneth Keniston is the theorist who has been most articulate in inviting attention to the emergence of a "new" post-adolescent stage in the human life span. Transcending the reifications of philosophy, sociology, and psychology, he works with a rich appreciation of the dynamic, shifting interaction between culture and person that shapes patterns of growth. He recognizes that "psychological development results from a complex interplay of constitutional givens (including the rates and phases of biological maturation) and the changing familial, social, educational, economic, and political conditions that constitute the matrix in which [people] develop. Human development can be obstructed by the absence of the necessary matrix, just as it can be stimulated by other kinds of environments. Some social and historical conditions demonstrably slow, retard or block development, while others stimulate, speed and encourage it. A prolongation and extension of development, then, including the emergence of 'new' stages of life, can result from altered social, economic and historical conditions."[8] His analysis requires a recognition of the power of the social component in the developmental process, the power of the other in the interaction that constitutes the self–other relation.

Keniston asserts that just as major transformations in American society after the Civil War effected such real change in human experience that "adolescence" emerged as a recognizable stage in human development, the same magnitude of change has subsequently occurred, "creating" yet another recognizable stage in the human life cycle. Among the changes he cites are the shift in the percentage of students who finish high school and begin college; an acceleration of social change, "a rate of social change so rapid that it threatens to make obsolete all institutions, values, methodologies and technologies within the lifetime of each generation; a technology that has created not only prosperity and longevity, but power to destroy the planet, whether through warfare or violation of nature's balance; a world of extraordinarily complex social organization, instantaneous communication and constant revolution" (p. 5).

He confirms the observation that, indeed, many young people are not adequately described as either adolescent or adult. For "the twenty-four-year-old seeker, political activist, or graduate student often turns out to have been *through* a period of adolescent rebellion ten years before, to be all too formed in his or her views, to have a stable [equilibrated] sense of self, and to be much further along in psychological development than his or her fourteen-year-old high school brother or sister" (p. 6). Yet Keniston also notes a significant contrast between such young persons and some other postadolescents whose place in society is settled—who, for example, are married, have become parents, and are fully committed to an occupation.

As he then describes the characteristics of this new "stage" in development, I am persuaded that he is alerting us to a particular form of postadolescent meaning-making; attention to this form of meaning illumines and clarifies the journey into adulthood and informs our understanding of the development of faith. We can begin to hypothesize that within Fowler's fourth stage, "Individuative-Reflective" faith, there are actually two separate, identifiable stages.[9]

The persons described by Keniston have achieved a self-aware self, individuated from family; this new self, however, is, as yet, "over-against" society or "the world as it is." The new self is not yet a full participant in what is perceived as the "adult world." The new self is aware of its emerging identity, values, and integrity as distinguished from societal (and conventional) norms that the power of self-conscious, critical reflection can now relativize. The self-aware self described by Keniston is able to "sense who he or she is and thus to recognize the possibility of conflict and disparity between his or her emerging selfhood and his or her social order."[10] What this postadolescent has not yet accomplished, however, is a fitting relationship between the promise of the new power of the emerging self and the power of the social world. Keniston, therefore, characterizes this postadolescent-not-yet-adult as not having "settled the questions whose answers once defined adulthood: questions of relationship to the existing society; questions of vocation; questions of social role and life style" (p. 6).

Erikson described the formation of self-identity as an adolescent task that includes both the achievement of self-awareness and the achievement of an effective social role. Keniston's insight, on the other hand, suggests that, though in earlier historical eras these two tasks may have been achieved simultaneously, now the composing of a self that is effective in society may occur in two steps. The self-aware self may come to birth in an encounter with the issues of effectiveness in society—as an issue. But the task of integrating the critically aware self with integrity into society, in a way that is both effective and satisfying, may now represent a second developmental task on the other side of the emergence of critical thought and inner-dependence. The task of the new, self-aware self is to reconcile and accommodate the two poles of self and society.

As noted earlier, this phenomenon has been described under such rubrics as "extended adolescence"—certainly a pejorative description at best and, as we are beginning to see, inaccurate. As Keniston states, "For, while some young men and women are indeed victims of the psychological malady of 'stretched

adolescence,' many others are less impelled by juvenile gran-
diosity than by rather accurate analysis of the perils and injustices of the world in which they live" (p. 6). This postadolescent
period is marked by a critical awareness of self and world; its
task is to discern a fitting relationship between self and society.

This new awareness of self and a corresponding new awareness of the relationship of self and world is expressed by Ernie
Boyer, Jr., who, when he was a young man of nineteen, left
the strong and sheltered harbors of his good upbringing and
lived out our nautical metaphor—he went to sea. In the journal he kept as a sailor and later printed on an antique press,
he wrote:

I often imagine myself skippering a small sloop, out on deck in the
dark hours of morning while the small crew sleeps below. I would
feel the ship beneath me slipping through the water, feel the sails
above me tugging against the breeze, and dream until I fell asleep
only to dream more deeply. As the wind shifted I would awaken,
check the compass, and readjust the sails to put us back on course.
Then I would wait for the sun to rise.

Always when I watch the sea . . . I think of the times when I would
have to fight it. I realize now, after seeing the height of these waves
and feeling the power of this wind, that sailing is the living of a
deadly balance. At times these forces would carry and caress me. But
there would be other times when forces would rise and tilt the balance
against me. Then I would be struggling for my life. I might win once
or twice—I might—but if I did it would be the sea's mercy more than
my skill that had saved me. I have seen the sea; I have watched its
moods, and I know: it has power as absolute as death itself, and no
man rides above it as long as he would like.

But everything would be so simple, life in its bare energy or death,
none of these squalid shades in between. I long for this life of the
sailor.[11]

Boyer expresses the postadolescent longing for a simpler
world now lost, the consciousness of both a new power and a
new vulnerability, the awareness of composing a balance between self and world, a participation in a relationship with

powerful forces impinging upon and transcending the self, and the encounter with ambiguity—"these squalid shades in between."

In "these squalid shades in between" is embedded the dynamic that most strikingly illuminates our concerns: the dynamic Keniston has observed as the *"pervasive ambivalence* [of this stage] toward *both* self and society."[12] Although in this period it is marked by the promise of a new self and world, nevertheless, the character of one's relationship to both self and world tends to be ambivalent.

Now it becomes apparent why this place in the journey of faith has been difficult for developmental theorists to recognize as other than merely transitional. The ambivalence characteristic of this stage may easily be confused with the dynamics of transition. But ambivalence, wariness, exploration, and tentativeness are the warp and woof of the tapestry of faith woven in the young adult era. It is the dynamic of ambivalence that has confounded the capacity of the developmental perspective to recognize a "dynamic stability," or stage, in this postadolescent place prior to a fully equilibrated "stage four"—the self-authoring, institutional, individuated adult stages described by Kegan and Fowler. A return to the particular strands of development described earlier may assist us in recognizing the integrity, stability, and structural power of this ambivalence.

William Perry's nuanced description of intellectual development perhaps comes closest to recognizing this period of ambivalence as a place in its own right. He identifies several positions within the discovery of relativism and the necessity of commitment. These he names "commitment foreseen," "initial commitment," "orientation in implications of commitment," and "developing commitments."[13] This suggests that commitment initially takes the form of a tentative or what I term *probing commitment*. One explores possible forms of truth and their fittingness to one's experience of self and world. Both the content of commitment and one's personal style of address to commitment are sorted out only over time. Thus, "commitments" formed on the other side of the encounter

with the relativized character of self and world may initially
last for two weeks, a term, or perhaps several years (a phenomenon that frustrates faculty and others hoping for commitments to departments and programs). In any case, as we shall
see, in this developmental moment, even deeply felt affirmations have a tenuous, exploratory, and divided quality—again
expressed in the voice of the sailor (during a second voyage):

What can I do? All day I have flitted from one book to another,
from one impulse, one dream to another, never mustering the resolution or sustaining the inclination to follow through my intentions.
There is so much I want to do, must do, not just today, but with my
life, with what time I have left. Not a second can be wasted. . . .

I try for too much. I try for nothing less than a mastery of the
world aesthetically, intellectually, and physically. To do this I need not
only a momentous strength, but a divided self; for each of these three
is incompatible with the other, and I must be a butcher, severing
myself into three segments to be used only one at a time while the
others are shelved and forgotten. What if I am too long with one?
Will the other two die? After spending some extra time with philosophy my aesthetic impulse is harder to revive, and my physical impulse is all but dead. It worries me.

It seems intolerably difficult to remain dedicated to all three of
these responses to the world. And yet three is a very small number,
and life has so many more aspects, those which many would say are
its most valuable and rewarding, all of which I have renounced. I am
a man very much alone. The scope of my choices is both infinite and
far too narrow. What is the remedy? There must be a solution, but I
thought and thought about it until that too has become frustrating.
Too much to ever be accomplished, too little for an adequate life, this
is my dilemma. What shall I do?[14]

Here Boyer expresses what Keniston describes as the "divided self" and the "wary probe" of both self and world. This
ambivalent and wary searching is qualitatively different from
adolescent experimentation in search of self-definition. The
probing of the postadolescent is a serious exploration of the
adult world (which the adolescent, in contrast, receives uncritically), through which society's "vulnerability, strength, integrity, and possibilities are assayed." A corresponding self-probing

tests the strength, vulnerability, and capacity of the self to withstand or use what society will make, ask, and allow.[15]

This period of *probing commitment* is the first of the two eras within the single place earlier described simply as commitment within relativism. I wish, therefore, to make a distinction between this probing commitment and what I term the *tested commitment* of the adult. Sometimes through a crisis in experimentation, and sometimes more gently over time, a point comes at which one can no longer be described as so divided, nor as simply exploring one's worldview, marriage, career commitment, life-style, or faith. One's form of knowing and being takes on a tested quality, a sense of fittingness, that one is willing to make one's peace with and to affirm (although not uncritically). In this period, which I term *tested commitment*, the self is not only "self-aware" but also more profoundly "self-reflective" and has the quality of centeredness—in marked contrast to the ambivalence or dividedness of the earlier period.

We are now ready to recompose our understanding of the strand of cognitive development as follows:

	Adolescent		Young Adult	Adult		Mature Adult
Form of Cognition	Authority-bound	→ Unqualified relativism	→ Probing commitment	→ Tested commitment	→ Convictional commitment

Evidence of Keniston's notion that altered social conditions may only reveal "new" stages, present but less recognized in earlier historical eras, is found in Howard Brinton's analysis of Quaker journals from the seventeenth, eighteenth, and nineteenth centuries. He has identified phases in the faith journey of Quakers that seem to corroborate the pattern described here. The first two phases are "childhood piety" and "youthful frivolity" (when Quaker young people want to dance and have fancy clothes). Brinton then describes a postadolescent period that he terms the "divided self." During this period, the young person struggles between Quaker values and alternative values in the wider culture. This period of division is resolved in the choice to be at one, centered in the image of the "inner light" and the adoption of Quaker ways.[16]

Keniston terms this probing, postadolescent period *youth*. However, since *youth* is a term that generally applies to young people across a large portion of the life span, including adolescence and sometimes childhood, I wish to term this early period of postadolescent probing commitment *young adult*.[17] I am suggesting that *adult* connotes one's having achieved the composition of the self-aware self, with its attendant responsibility *for* the self. The qualifier *young* connotes the appropriate exploratory, wary, tentative, and dependent quality that stands at the threshold of adulthood. This "young" quality points us once again to the strand of development we have described as form of dependence.

FORM OF DEPENDENCE

It was, of course, the young adult's form of dependence that first confounded my assumptions regarding the process of human development in the context of higher education. Issues of trust, need, confidence, and relation did not resolve neatly into inner-dependence by the end of the college experience. At the same time, most juniors and seniors were certainly taking more self-aware responsibility for their composing of self, world, and "God" than could freshmen and sophomores. The movement from dependent faith to inner-dependent faith seemed to be more complex and extended than theories of the development of autonomy implied.

Fowler has identified the "locus of authority" as a crucial aspect of faith development (see appendix A). His model, and much of developmental theory, assumes there is a single movement in the shift of the locus of authority from an uncritical trust in assumed Authority "out there" to a critically aware sense of authority within. A re-examination of this dynamic has illumined the puzzles of young adult dependence.

It seems to be more the case that the locus of authority shifts from without to within, not in a single movement from one place to another, but through a two-step process. When the locus of authority shifts from "assumed authority" outside the self to inner authority, it does so by means of an authority that is external, still "out there," but that *I* now choose, because this authority makes sense to me in terms of *my* observation and lived experience. Having some awareness that there are other authorities, other points of view, I nevertheless self-consciously choose *this* authority, who has the power to beckon and draw forth my own sense of truth and emerging critical awareness.

Indeed, young adulthood typically emerges in a relationship in which the emerging self is invited into greater strength. This is the fitting time for the mentor, guru, guide, coach, sponsor. Yet it is important to note that those who serve the mentoring function can be distinguished from the heroes and heroines of adolescent devotion. The mentor holds a very significant degree of power, but the "fusion" quality characteristic of the adolescent and hero/heroine relationship is absent.

When interviewing college seniors, we found that when we posed the question, "Is there someone whom you would like to be like?" the students always resisted it, insofar as they typically rephrased it in their responses: "No, there is no one who is a model for me, whom I would want to be exactly like, but there are people who exemplify certain qualities that I would like to have." Then they were always able to name one or several people who served as significant images of aspects of their emerging self.

This is to say that mentors anchor the vision of the potential self. They beckon the self into being and, in so doing, ground a place of commitment within relativism. As such, mentors exercise both cognitive and affective appeal, offering both insight and emotional support. But the young adult exercises at least a rudimentary sense of critical choice—at least at the level of requiring correspondence with his or her own experience. Indeed, the young adult will even make do without a mentor rather than betray the integrity of the emerging self.

A young woman we will call Shelly, torn between traditional and potential images of womanhood, reflects upon the significance of a woman who served her as a mentoring image. Recounting how a course in the psychology of women, taught from a feminist perspective, helped her to do some important integrating of conflicting tensions, she says:

Probably this course was extremely significant. . . . See, one thing I have not found at the college until this year with [name of woman professor]. . . . I have never before found a person with as strong a career interest as I have who is also very interested in men. And that has been very lacking. I've done without it, but it's been lacking and all my close friendships at home are with women for whom career is secondary and they're mostly interested in getting married. . . . My women friends here have been career oriented but not all that interested in men. . . . So what I finally did during the course was that I resolved that feeling . . . really feeling comfortable with being a woman and being very career oriented and being very independent. And that eased . . . conflict there.[18]

This reflection upon the need for a mentoring image fitting to the integrity of the emerging self reveals the dependence and vulnerability of young adulthood. Moreover, this observation enables us to see that just as it was appropriate to distinguish two eras in cognitive development, it is also appropriate to describe two eras within the affective dimension of development, within the form of inner-dependence.

In the young adult there is an appropriate dependence that differs from the dependence of either the adolescent or the older adult. Though the adolescent is subject to the power of the conventional milieu, the young adult is primarily subject to those voices that invite out the still emerging, but increasingly inner-dependent, self. This dependence is manifest in the relationship between the mentor and the young adult.[19] In the mentoring relationship, the young adult is not subject to the mentor in a condition of fusion (characteristic of the adolescent); nor is the relationship ordered by the negative tension of counterdependence. The young adult is better described as subject to the emerging self that is yet dependent upon authority "out there" to beckon and confirm its integrity. In young adulthood, the self depends upon mentors not so much for its integrity as for its expression, confirmation, and fulfillment.

It is appropriate to describe the emerging inner-dependence of the young adult as initially a *fragile inner-dependence*. *Fragile* here is not intended to connote weak, feeble, or puny. Rather, it is more like the fragility of a young plant as it emerges from the soil—healthy, vital, and full of promise, yet vulnerable. The feelings are those of special promise, hope, glimmering possibility, challenge, and sometimes exhilaration. The feelings to which the young adult is therefore correspondingly vulnerable are special forms of disappointment, failure, exclusion, abandonment, emptiness, and hopelessness.

The adult, in contrast, is less dependent upon others for the ordering of his or her own sense of value and promise and has become strong enough to let the mentor be other—even to have feet of clay; the mentor becomes peer. Authority that was located outside the self, though ratified within, becomes fully equilibrated within (though the self does not cease to require confirmation without). The adult manifests a *confident inner-dependence*.

	Adolescent	Young Adult	Adult	Mature Adult
Form of Dependence	Dependence/ Counter-dependence	→ Fragile inner-dependence	→ Confident inner-dependence	→ Inter-dependence

FORM OF COMMUNITY

For the young adult, the mentoring era finds its most powerful form in a mentoring community. The emergence of the more critical and more autonomous self in no way means a shedding of the need for a network of belonging—quite the opposite is the case. Young adulthood is nurtured into being most powerfully by the availability of a community that poses an alternative to an earlier assumed knowing, vividly embodies the potential of the emerging self, and offers the promise of a new network of belonging. A critical awareness of one's conventional ethos alone is not enough to precipitate a transformation in faith—a transformation in the meaning that grounds one's very existence. Typically, a critical awareness and a single mentoring figure, while influential, are by themselves insufficient to reorder faith itself. Rather, it is the combination of the emerging truth of the young adult with the example and encouragement of the mentor, grounded in the experience of an ideologically compatible social group, that generates the transforming power of the young adult era. An ideologically compatible, mentoring group serves to confirm the faith that one will be held in a new knowing—that there will be a new "home."

The character of the social context to which the young adult has access may be the most crucial element in the transformation and/or maintaining of what a young adult "knows."[20] But again, the young adult will have to feel that the truth that orders the social context is compatible with his or her inner truth—or at least with some very important part of that truth. The new self depends upon and responds to those individuals and groups who express patterns of meaning resonant with the experience and new awareness of the fragile, emerging self. There is a profound receptiveness to any network of belonging that promises a place of nurture for the potential self, even if (and sometimes especially if) its forms are demanding.

A place that offers confirmation of one's potential competence and specialness, while also confirming a solid belonging that exempts the fragile self from having yet to stand alone in any real sense, meets the yearnings for agency and communion in their young adult forms.

Thus, in the journey from conventional forms of community to a self-selected class or group, there is also a form of community particular to the young adult. This form of community may be described as ideologically compatible communities. The important word here is *ideological*. As the young adult composes meaning with a new self-awareness, not only does the form of world awareness shift from a tacit to an explicit form; initially, this new meaning is held onto and affirmed with great tenacity. This is because the new meaning must ground an equally new and yet fragile self. The very tentativeness and ambivalence of young adult meaning-making renders it "inevitably ideological."[21] By ideology I mean structured and largely rational attempts to understand self and world and to prescribe directions and corrections. By this definition, it may, of course, be argued that all structures of meaning are ideological. *Ideology*, however, tends specifically to connote a cognitive, tight, and even rigid orientation. In the case of the young adult, this is inevitable, because here the self and system are still one. The person emerging from embeddedness in conventional meanings composed by affectively grounded relationships tends to hold fiercely to the new system of meaning that now transcends the earlier conventional system and promises more being. The young adult must sometimes hold new meanings most fiercely when mustering the courage to make the passage off a once-stalwart (but now seemingly leaking and inadequate) "ship" that has hitherto held the self and onto a promising, but unknown, new shore.

The young adult (and his or her culture) most thrives when there is access to a network of belonging anchored in the strength of worthy and grounding meanings that provide a sense of distance both from the conventions of the young adult's past and from the larger society with which the young adult must still negotiate terms of entry. Keniston describes the affiliations of this period as having an "over-against" quality.[22] This quality is, however, to be distinguished from the simple counterdependence described earlier. The young adult is "over-against" the world-as-it-is, but in a mode that is more discerning and more dialectical than "pushing away from the dock."

The dialectic between self and society-world-other initially takes the form of a dichotomy. As Fowler has recognized, a person beginning to take responsibility for his or her own meaning-making encounters certain unavoidable tensions between competing values and possible life choices such as personal fulfillment vs. communal commitments, work vs. play, tradition vs. innovation, social action vs. academic study—or any number of other possible polarities conditioned by the particular historical and cultural context. Fowler has sometimes suggested that individuating faith finds it necessary to collapse such tensions in one direction or the other; elsewhere, he has suggested that individuating faith can tolerate these tensions (as tensions, in contrast to the next stage, which can more comfortably hold the truth of paradox).[23]

I suggest that this contradiction in Fowler's early work is another instance of the discrepant data that, under re-examination, distinguishes the young adult from the adult. The young adult seeks an ideology, a certainty, and a purity of vision, but the character of this vision differs from the Authority-bound and dualistic mode of the previous era. It is precisely the awareness that all perspectives are relative that may energize a fierce, and sometimes tenacious, bid for a place to stand within the anxiety of that reality. Therefore, in a premature bid for confidence, the young adult is vulnerable to collapsing the tensions of felt dichotomies.

Shelly, who earlier described an integration of conflicting images of womanhood, had suffered a very strong sense of irreconcilable tensions, which she described as

parents	vs.	self
religion	vs.	agnosticism
sweet	vs.	sassy
sexism	vs.	feminism
"God"	vs.	empiricism
believer	vs.	psychologist
marriage	vs.	graduate school
helping others	vs.	materialism
men	vs.	career
values-control	vs.	experience-emotion

In the midst of these tensions she did, on different occasions, collapse the tension in various directions. When the voice of a boyfriend prevailed, she abandoned her feminist perspective; when anxiety over her mother's health became too great, she tried to return to an earlier faith; when the study of behavioral psychology was compelling, she dismissed "God" for empiricism.

Yet in Shelly's description of this sort of push and pull, there also seems to be a good deal of transitional counterdependence, or "pushing away from the dock." What is significant for the formulation of our hypothesis is that when Shelly describes her resolution of these tensions, she seems not to stand somewhere where everything is resolved into a harmonious whole but where she is relieved to have the freedom to describe herself as "deviant". Deviant is a strong word, but it seems to reflect both the freedom and the over-against-the-world-as-it-is quality that marks the emergence and self-aware maintenance of the young adult self. The new self is able to accept, articulate, and affirm a sense of engaged choice and struggle, and she seeks alliances with those who share her stance:

I worked with [the dean] in an internship and we talked about religion . . . and . . . just lately people have been really reaching out to me. [A psych professor] and I are in similar places. We really have trouble with empiricism and we're wrestling, so we've spent time talking . . . and so it's suddenly . . . again the hot issue and I'm open to being a believer but . . . I'm comfortable and aware now that whatever I come up with will not be the traditional, and that's O.K. It can still be bona fide even though I know everyone doesn't agree with it . . . and I don't have to fit into a niche. So I'm working it through and it feels comfortable and it feels like it'll come.

And also I always thought I would get married when I was twenty-three or, the latest, twenty-four. Well, right now I probably project to twenty-six or twenty-seven. It is helpful and it's also very freeing 'cuz I don't feel . . . I am a deviant. I'm way off the scale as a deviant and I feel very good about that, in fact I'm . . . I'm probably proud of it more than anything else and I know I'll get flak from my parents. They've taken awhile to adjust to my being a Ph.D. which has not happened yet, but I'm on the road and they know it and marriage is something that . . . they wanted me to get married, maybe get a master's degree but get married and then get pregnant right after that and start a family. . . .

I want to go to an environment where I'll really be tested. It seems so often here [religiously affiliated school] that I haven't needed a God, and I think maybe in [name of larger city] I'll need one.[24]

We hear Shelly accept "deviance," testing, struggle, and tentativeness as a "place to stand" over-against and apart from previously held patterns of meaning and affiliation.

The yet more tested adult, in contrast, can maintain the tension of this earlier dichotomy between self and the larger social world. Only as one becomes confident, having composed a meaning and a voice of one's own that will not be overwhelmed by every competing point of view—only then can one relinquish the ideological and over-against mode and can engage as well as critique the world-as-it-is. The form of community of this more confident adult self is not the ideologically compatible community upon which the young adult is dependent in a primary way, but the self-selected class or group described earlier that confirms from without what is confidently known within.

The cognitive style of inner-dependent and tested adult faith remains dialectical, but in light of its greater confidence, tensions may be maintained rather than collapsed. The explicit character of inner-dependent faith shifts from being ideological to being world engaging, confident of its ability to engage on its own terms. The quality of engagement, however, is tempered by a corresponding willingness to make pragmatic accommodations, which no longer appear to threaten the essential integrity of the self—a self that now is felt to be capable of survival in any case.

This is to say that, if young adult faith is confirmed and given place, it can emerge from its fragile form to a self-confident adult strength to make meaning in the world-as-it-is, while maintaining sufficient integrity with the young adult's vision. Adult faith can sustain a respectful awareness of communities other than its own; and it can tolerate, if not embrace, the felt tensions between inevitable choices. Adult faith can engage the world because it has a confident sense of agency, the power to act. The fragile young adult must stand over-against the world to observe it, to critique it, to test it, and to save it. The tested adult has the confidence to stand within the world to engage it, to contribute to it, and (if one's faith requires it) to transform it.[25]

The mature adult, as described in chapter 4, has deepened into a form of meaning-making in which the tension of dichotomies resolves into the truth of paradox. A wise-hearted self emerges from the journey that the ideological self must make, from the formal tenacious bid for certainty through a testing of it in lived experience. This testing may strengthen the capacity to trust the integration of heart and mind—the whole community of the self—reflected in a trust of community in the social world.

What I have done here is to re-examine the three strands of development considered earlier and draw them together in such a way as to distinguish an identifiable "new" era in development. This era lies between that of adolescent or conventional meaning-making and full adult meaning-making. Thus, the framework proposed earlier may be nuanced and re-composed as follows:

	Adolescent (Conventional)	Young Adult	Adult	Mature Adult
Form of Cognition	Authority-determined (Tacit) Unqualified relativism	→ Probing commitment (Ideological)	→ Tested commitment (Explicit)	→ Convictional commitment (Paradoxical)
Form of Dependence	Dependent/Counter-dependent	→ Fragile inner-dependent	→ Confident inner-dependent	→ Inter-dependent
Form of Community	"Those like us" Diffuse Conventional	→ Ideologically compatible groupings (mentoring)	→ Self-selected class or group	→ Open to those genu-inely "other"

(For further elaboration, see Appendix B.)

When we take the three strands of development identified here—forms of cognition, dependence, and community—and weave them together again, we now have a tapestry that portrays the place and role of young adulthood in the journey toward mature adult faith.[26] Insofar as this tapestry can only serve as one heuristic model, it is, of course, finite. It is but one way of portraying a story that could be woven with other colors, other images, and in other proportions—each bringing to our awareness yet other facets of human meaning-making. One of the most serious limitations of this model is the possible implication (and not infrequent charge) that the activity of faith is being represented as linear and fixed, rather than as the dynamic, multidimensional, creative process that it is in reality. Concentric circles, spirals, and moving pictures would better capture these dimensions of truth that elude the printed word.

Another distortion of the tapestry woven here is that the strands of development appear side by side—not interwoven as an intricate but unified whole. Moreover, we might also think of these strands of development more accurately as representing the fibers that join to make up the strand of a single life, suggesting that the real tapestry of faith is woven from the collective strands of many lives, composing the rich and variegated story of human interdependence in faith itself. Nevertheless, the strength of this tapestry is its capacity to awaken our attention to both the promise and the vulnerability of young adult faith.

PROMISE AND VULNERABILITY

With this model we can begin to see that the potential of young adult faith is powered, first of all, by its freedom. On the one hand, the young adult has struggled, as we have seen, to push away from the safe but constraining harbor of inherited family, conventional knowing, in order to achieve some sense of a capable and distinctive self. On the other hand, the young adult is not yet engaged in the full range of adult commitments. This circumstance creates, not only a certain freedom, but also the second condition of young adult faith—a unique capacity to critically conceptualize the "ideal," unconstrained by the investments of the older adult. By "ideal" the young adult means that which is pure, consistent, authentic, and congruent. The young adult's search for the ideal is the search for what will most adequately or worthily ground, shape, and orient the commitment and investment of the emerging self. Once again, this is not to suggest a self necessarily absent from relation. As we shall see, quite the contrary is the case, and notably so when the young adult becomes a parent and yearns to create that which will be worthy of the child born from the young adult self.

Much is lost to the quality of individual and collective life when the potential contribution of this era in human development is dismissed as "youthful idealism." Young adulthood is the birthplace of adult vision. Never before and never again in the life cycle is there the same constellation of forces available to enable the formulation of life-transforming vision. The vision that grounds the young adult self will, for better or worse, enhance or diminish the possibilities of the whole of adult life. The era of young adult faith—in which truth, meaning, and ultimacy are recomposed—is a vital opportunity given to every generation for the renewal of human life. The tension between the critical capacity of the young adult and the world-as-it-is can potentially empower a creative, transforming critique. Erikson recognized this dynamic in his observation that "youth selectively offers its loyalties and energies to the conservation of that which feels true to them and to the correction or destruction of that which has lost its regenerative significance."[27]

A central strength of the young adult is the capacity to respond to visions of the world as it might become. This is the time in every generation for renewal of the human vision. In young adulthood, the primal force of promise is again recomposed. In the language of Jewish and Christian religious traditions, in this developmental moment there is a particular readiness to envision and experience the Kingdom or Commonwealth of God. The young adult soul can be beckoned beyond the conventional, the mundane, and the assumed, to investment in the promise of all life. It is unfortunate when the energy of the young adult life is simply resisted and feared as counter to culture rather than prized for its potential as prophetic power.

Daniel Levinson describes the task of early adulthood as the formation of "a dream."[28] He has done his study with men, but I am persuaded that the same is true for women, though our dreams may take different forms, and we may have less cultural permission to recognize and to prize them. The critical vision and prophetic power of young adult faith is manifest in the young adult dream. The power of this dream is twofold: it initially has power to inspire and ground the young adult, but the young adult dream may also resurface periodically in later adulthood, each time with a power of potentially greater maturity and depth. This dream may first present itself with eager passion and confronting energy in the voice of a twenty-year-old. Its energy may forge a passionate investment of the self in the "ideal"—as one sees it—perhaps necessitating accommodation and renewal on the part of the established culture (as many parents and administrators are well aware). But it also appears that the power of young adult faith does not end with young adulthood. Developmental insights in dialogue with depth psychologies suggest that the young adult dream may re-emerge in later adulthood to renew (or block) the power of the adult life. Particularly in mid-life and perhaps again at sixty (or whenever the essential forms of a person's life come under review), the vision that has oriented the set of the adult soul is reawakened for testing and recomposing, and depending upon its adequacy to the conditions of ongoing experience, it may nourish a renewal of energy, vision, and commitment, thus retaining and enlarging its regenerative strength.

In contrast, the initial strength of the young adult dream may be at once "ideal" and ambivalent, and, therefore, a fragile strength—the locus of the young adult's vulnerability. When young adults hold an alternative vision characterized by purity of the ideal and tenacious fierceness made possible by their freedom and need for security, they may manifest the "omnipotentiality" Keniston observes in the postadolescent.[29] Here everything can be seen "clearly and simply," and "everything ought to be possible." Thus the young adult may be vulnerable to his or her own "talent for zealotry and fanaticism, for reckless action in the name of highest principles, for self-absorption, and for special arrogance" (p. 18).

Keniston also alerts us to other vulnerabilities inherent in the ambivalence that is part of the task of finding a fitting relationship between the new young adult self and society. In the attempt to maintain personal integrity and simultaneously achieve effectiveness in society, the young adult is vulnerable, as described earlier, to collapsing dichotomies in one direction or the other. This may take the more typically recognized form of standing against society, but it may also take the form of standing against the self by muting one's dream and, for example, just "getting a job that will make money." Or one may try to continually re-form the self to fit society in "major efforts at self-transformation employing the methodologies of personal transformation that are culturally available in any historical era: monasticism, meditation, psychoanalysis, prayer, hallucinogenic drugs, hard work, religious conversion, intros- pection" (p. 8). This is to say that such experimentation may signal that a vulnerable but promising self is being fought for and is looking for a fitting home in society.

The vulnerability of this moment can eventuate also in a collapse of the dichotomy in the direction of the self, pro- foundly rejecting society or the "other." Drifting or estrange- ment (or its more extreme form, alienation) is another shadow dimension of the omnipotence and ambivalence (and the integ- rity) of the young adult life.

Young adults are vulnerable in other respects: The young adult's critical awareness suddenly makes it possible to re- cognize the tenuousness of all of life. To become aware that an ideology of meaninglessness may possibly have its own integrity renders one vulnerable to intellectual des- pair. This vulnerability is only sharpened when young adults can find no effective connection with society. They are, therefore, particularly vulnerable if there is no network of belonging that can incarnate a significant sense of con- nection against the threat of meaninglessness. Young adults require a meaningful ideology (a dream) and a grounding community.

The promise and vulnerability of the young adult, therefore, is shaped by two primary conditions. The first is charismatic leadership. The young adult is appropriately dependent upon charismatic leadership to awaken and beckon the promise of the emerging self. This is not to say that they are so many sheep, ready to follow any goat with its bell. I stress again that young adults will not indiscriminately pledge allegiance to just any charismatic leader or group. Indeed, they will go without a guru or mentor or guiding group rather than follow someone who does not "make sense." People and institutions who hope to serve as an anchoring authority for young adults must offer a vision of self, world, and "God" that resonates with the experience and critical capacity of young adults themselves.

However, once young adults do make that powerful connection with the one or ones who have called out the energy of the young adult life, they are vulnerable to exploitation, or at least to the limits of the mentors' wisdom and the community's vision. When they respond to a guide, they become vulnerable to meeting the guide's expectations; they are not yet able to critically discern the limits of the perspective and person offering compelling direction and affirmation to the young adult self—especially if this guide is located in an alternative social context, isolated from, rather than critically related to, the larger society.

These dynamics were tragically illustrated at the time of the Jonestown suicides. Jim Jones attracted a large following by holding up the ideal of a human community in which the elderly and the orphaned would have place and dignity, a community of love. This vision captured the imagination of those who were "young adult" in faith (which, please note, may represent many different ages). Among these people was a twenty-one-year-old woman whose father, a psychologist, was deeply concerned about her following Jones to Guyana. He went to several government offices for assistance but was told that, as his daughter was twenty-one and therefore an "adult," nothing could be done.

In many respects, she was, in all likelihood, an adult; but in terms of faith, it is probable that she was a "young adult," and perhaps never more vulnerable to charismatic leadership and ideology. We see, then, with all too painful clarity, that a community capable of meeting the frontier of the young adult's longing for meaning, becoming, and belonging can be sponsoring or it can be exploiting. This recognition requires us to consider not only the structure of young adult faith but also its content, the second crucial dimension shaping the potential and vulnerability of the young adult.

STRUCTURE AND CONTENT

I have suggested that insights from constructive-developmental theory present us with a flowing sequence of developmental structures that may tell us something about the formal aspects of the way of faith. But a structure is analogous to an empty container. Although the shape of the container will, of course, shape whatever is put into it, the container—or structure—itself does not determine the full nature of its significance. The content (and, therefore, the purpose) of the container is also of utmost importance.

Finally, therefore, young adult faith is not shaped only by its structural features—the promise of its freedom and critical idealism and its vulnerability to arrogance, estrangement, despair, and the exploitation of mentors and their communities. Young adult faith—both its promise and its limits—is dependent also upon the content (images, symbols, and ideology) held by its structures.

The power of content and its relationship to structure in young adulthood comes into sharp focus in Carol Gilligan's study of students who took a course on moral and political choice taught by Lawrence Kohlberg at Harvard. This course, the hope of which was "to save sophomores from relativism," revealed that "relativism" was often more tenacious than could be accounted for by defining it as a transitional place between Kohlberg's definitions of conventional and principled (postconventional) moral reasoning.[30]

Gilligan reports that some of the relativists and women, in their insistent though somewhat different attention to the context of moral dilemmas, resisted assimilation to the categories of the Kohlberg coding scheme (p. 148). She reports that these students seemed to be dealing seriously with real experience, such as starvation in Biafra, competing obligations, and the reality of human pain and suffering. Such wrestling with the complexity of reality seemed to have the power "to undo the most principled moral understanding" (p. 148). As a consequence, students came to see that "reason had outstripped morality, as Kant and Dostoevski had seen, and, in the absence of knowledge, moral judgment became a matter not of logic but of faith" (p. 148).

As an example, she quotes one student's response to Kohlberg's classic Heinz Dilemma. To study forms of moral reasoning, Kohlberg has developed a form of interviewing in which people are asked to respond to a hypothetical moral dilemma. The best known of these is the Heinz Dilemma, in which Heinz, who lives in an unnamed European country, knows of a druggist who has a drug that might save the life of Heinz's wife, who is dying. He has tried by every means possible to purchase the drug, but he does not have enough money to pay the price the druggist is asking. The first question posed to the interviewee is, Should Heinz steal the drug?

The student had experienced a period of extreme relativism, beginning at the end of his sophomore year when he "came to" the conclusion that "morality was by and large, a lot of bunk, that there were no right or wrong answers whatsoever." This had marked for him the end of "huge theoretical moral constructs and systems."[31] (We might say that this had marked the shipwreck of the hope that assumed intellectual Authority could lead to certainty.)

She then writes, "Thus, while formerly this student had considered the preservation of human life to be the paramount value in all situations—a view, he said, that guided his participation in anti-war activities—he now believed that 'what we think is very much a part of how we live' and that in detaching thought from life he had been 'building a castle in the air.' Still, the moral problem remains, not in terms of a 'Platonic system which says a certain thing may be wrong in itself,' but because 'human beings come in contact with each other's lives.' Moral values are human constructions, conventions of thought that inevitably are tied to the conditions in which people live and in which they must act" (p. 151).

She continues with the thought of the student (p. 151):

A truly moral experience, if there is such a thing, [would be] relating to any person one comes across, not as a means, but as an end in himself and essentially as a human being and nothing more and nothing less, not as my client, not as my waiter. When one is "beyond good and evil," you talk about human beings vis-à-vis other human beings rather than talking about right or wrong. . . . I guess to me the *ideal* societal situation is where everybody related to everybody like that and did not worry about right or wrong, because then moral dilemmas might not exist or might not arise. Maybe if Heinz comes in to the druggist and the druggist looks at this guy and says this is not some guy who may or may not be able to pay me $2,000, this is a man and his wife is dying, maybe that is the *ideal* way for the druggist to perceive this problem and then he gives him the drug.

This voice begins to sound different: what we hear from this student is a composing of meaning on the other side of relativism, a composing that is at once "ideal" and, at the same time, profoundly "contextual"—related to the complexity of real experience. It is aware of the relative character of all knowledge, but not in the earlier unqualified form, in which there were "no right or wrong answers whatsoever." It expresses a contextual relativism in which commitment may also dwell.[32] Accordingly, I suggest that the voice heard by Gilligan in this study was that of young adult meaning-making, young adult faith.

This report supports our contention that there can come a time in young adult development when one ceases to make meaning in terms of inherited or assumed conventions (albeit highly "principled" ones) and begins to compose meaning in terms of one's lived and observed experience. This study witnesses to the young adult's capacity to recognize in a newly self-conscious way that moral judgment and behavior are matters of faith—that is, matters of how one composes self, world, and the character of ultimate reality. In the voice of the young adults reported here, we hear a capacity for self-aware critical discernment and inner-dependence. We hear a clear if tentative capacity to see the ideal and a need to find congruence between experience and ultimate meaning. All of these are hallmarks of young adult faith. Moreover, this is a voice in which we can hear a tilling of the conceptual ground in which the strength to critique conventional morality, to recognize the dissonance between "belief" and behavior, and to renew human vision and hope may be planted. At the same time, however, we also perceive a fertile emotional ground that, depending on circumstances, may prove susceptible to the blight of disillusionment and despair. The correspondence between the developmental structure that Gilligan found in her study of moral reasoning and the structure we discern as characteristic of young adult faith confirms one half of our concern, the nature of young adult faith structure. But I am calling our attention to the fact that we must be equally concerned with the quality of the content held by these structures. Therefore, Gilligan's observation regarding the various contents that the same structure may hold is also of critical importance.

In the students who came under study, the researchers observed a variety of contents dwelling within the same formal structures of young adult meaning-making, observing ideologies that ranged from that of the New Left to that of the New Right. For example, among these students, the researchers encountered both a Nietzschean racist and a modern-day Raskolnikov.[33] At the same time, it appears that the researchers also observed the "ideal" quality we have attributed to young adult faith. Gilligan eloquently and poignantly notes: "When the injustices of conventional morality were apparent and there seemed no alternative way to judge, . . . then the flexibility of adolescent thought made anything seem possible. Given a morality that appeared both absurd and hypocritical, a matter more of rationalization than of reason, hedonism returned as at least an 'authentic' basis for choice" (pp. 145–46). This observation should alert us to the sobering awareness that when the young person has seen relativism and seeks a new integrity in which to stand, even hedonism or a comparable variant may appear as a viable "faith." In other words, whatever content (or ideology) appears to be at least consistent and authentic may appear to fit the yearnings for the "ideal," so long as it is liberated from the "hypocrisy" of the conventional (and inconsistent).

On the other hand, Gilligan also observed that those students most able to develop a capacity to grapple effectively and responsibly with moral issues seemed to be those "whose concept of morality as respect for persons entailed an 'obligation to relieve human misery and suffering if possible.' "[34] The implications of this observation are far-reaching. Gilligan's observation suggests that the content of young adult life and thought will affect not only the young adult's immediate thought and behavior but also the possibility of transition toward more adequate patterns of meaning. This is to say that if young adults are offered images that require an ongoing struggle with "otherness" (in contrast, for example, to an easy hedonism, which in its focus on the self can mask the presence of "the other"), they are more likely to continue toward increasingly adequate (that is, mature) forms of faith.

Moreover, this means that young adult faith and its promise and vulnerability is shaped, not only by the structures of faith as described by constructive-developmental theories, but also by the contents those structures hold. More developed or mature structures may, nevertheless, hold images with evil consequences as well as good. Therefore, if there is a time in human growth when the structures of faith are particularly open and vulnerable to the "ideal," to ideology, and to charismatic leadership and community, and if such a period shapes the potential strength and quality of all of adult experience, then the "content" of young adult faith—the images, symbols, and ideologies held by the young adult faith structure—ceases to be a matter toward which we can be indifferent. Once we recognize that the structure of young adult faith mandates a search for an "authentic" basis of moral action and that this search can be fulfilled by "contents" as diverse as hedonism, cynical moral nihilism, or an ethic of service to others, then we see that an understanding of development defined in merely structural terms can only be a part of what we seek.

Corporate America, professional guilds, traditional Western religion, Eastern religions, new religious movements, military programs, political causes, and organized crime all offer their "content"—their images of value and vision—in a bid to capture the confidence and loyalty of the emerging young adult. Our quest to understand the development of a faith worthy of the potential of the young adult necessarily, therefore, requires an examination of the relationship between the evolving structures of faith and the process of imagination—the part that content/image plays in the formation of faith, and the matter to which we next attend.

6. Imagination: The Power of Adult Faith

Some years ago, I began in the course of my studies to notice that various authors boldly declared what they perceived to be *the* unique characteristic of human beings. I began to record these declarations at random and, among them, accumulated the following:[1]

The human is first of all a promise-making, promise-keeping, promise-breaking creature.

—Martin Buber

There is a primary need in people which other creatures probably do not have. . . . This basic need is the *need of symbolization*.

—Suzanne Langer

The gorilla, the chimpanzee, the orang-outang, and their kind, must look upon humans as feeble and infirm animals, whose strange custom it is to store up their dead.

—Miguel de Unamuno

No fact in human nature is more characteristic than its willingness to live on a chance.

—William James

On first reading, each of these statements appears distinctly different from the others; a closer reading suggests, however, that this is not the case. Rather, each one reflects what Philip Wheelwright describes as the experience of "threshold existence." Human beings live "always on the verge, always on the borderland of something more." Human beings bear a consciousness of something beyond the immediate. Human life finds itself forever on the thresholds of time, of space, and of the unseen—"reaching up to the gates of Heaven while one foot is slipping off the edge of the Abyss."[2] In spite of the massive evidence of the mundane and the ugly in our experience, we human beings tenaciously harbor the conviction that we were "made for more." Something more was promised. There is more for us to live into, to embrace, or to be embraced by. We have a sense that we participate in something wider and deeper than we have yet realized—a more inclusive patterning of relation, a more profound ordering of justice, a richer loving of life in its manifold forms. We intuit a unity of the whole. Time, the world-as-it-is, the world of space and sense—all may be lived into and transcended. We human beings harbor a conviction of a "Beyond filled with Holiness."[3] Having the capacity to intuit the whole, we have the capacity for faith.

Young adulthood is, as we are beginning to see, the critical period for forming a conviction of threshold existence and a passion for the "ideal." But the strength of the formation of vision and commitment in young adulthood is contingent upon two factors. The first is the evolution of its undergirding structure: for example, the development of critical thought. The second, equally indispensable, is an ability to adequately recognize and name the ideal, the worthy, the good.

This second, crucial factor, the apprehension of the unseen potential of life, occurs only by means of metaphor. We can name the unseen and intuit the character of ultimate reality only by indirection. We can only say, "It is like . . . " The seen provides a vehicle for the unseen.

We know this on many levels of experience. For example, if we want to name tears (as in weeping) we need only point to them and agree upon a single sound that serves as a sign. If, however, we want to express sadness, we must point to a tear, meaning "sadness is like tears," or we may speak of a "heavy heart." Likewise, whatever we know of transcendent truth, we know by means of an image—an object or act of the sensible world—that gives form to our intuition of the character of ultimate reality. And so we speak of ultimate reality as like No Exit, or a father, or a mother, or Nothingness, or the Way, or a unified field, or the Holy One.

If, therefore, we recognize that the quality of faith utterly depends upon the adequacy of the images it employs and how those images are held, then we will see that the composing of faith is, in essence, an act of imagination conditioned, in part, by structural development.

Young adults share a similar way of composing meaning—a particular structure for seeking and holding images of faith—but this structure may hold various contents. Those who become young adult in faith have the capacity to think critically, to passionately search for the ideal, to be appropriately dependent upon a self-chosen authority outside the self, to fiercely affirm what is ambivalently held, and to pledge fidelity to a community that will hold and confirm the promise of the emerging self and its vision of the world and ultimate reality. This structure, however, may hold the faith of a peace activist whose life is ordered by a commitment to the preservation of the planet, a marine whose life is ordered by allegiance to a nation, a newlywed homemaker whose life is ordered by the values of marriage and family, a medical student whose life is ordered by the desire to heal and by the priorities of the medical institution, a drug pusher whose life is ordered by financial survival, a junior executive in an advertising firm whose life is ordered by material success, or a computer entrepreneur whose life is ordered by the delight of intellectual and business puzzles and the desire to belong to the crowd in the fast lane of the career track. Each of these may represent the same structure of meaning, but each meaning structure holds a different content. Therefore, their forms of faith are similar in significant ways, yet distinctly different.

Constructive-developmental theory has tended to separate

the issues of structure and content and to focus almost exclusively on the development of structures. Yet we can neither adequately understand the dynamics of young adult faith nor assess the relative worthiness of various faith choices if we do not attend to the matter of content as well. We must recognize that the function of structures is to hold life in meaningful patterns and that, as this chapter will attempt to make clear, life's patterns are given form, not only by the structures already described, but also by the images the structures hold.

The character of the structure and the quality of the content it holds are mutually interdependent in the activity of meaning-making. Piaget described the dynamic interdependence of structure and content as the process of assimilation and accommodation. Content—images, symbols, concepts, stories— gives form to our intuitions of life; but the power of the content is conditioned by the capacity of the structures that hold it (much the way a computer program conditions what the images of letters or numerals can or cannot do). Images (the content), in turn, have the power to modify structures, because, as Piaget described it, it is only when one encounters images that cannot be assimilated into the present structures that the structures must be transformed so as to more adequately accommodate the image or pattern of images. The character and quality of one's faith, therefore, are dependent upon both structure and content.

Recognition of the mutual interdependence of structure and content draws us inexorably beyond the fact of the formal structures of meaning-making (a fascination with stages per se) and more deeply into the process of meaning-making itself and the question of its correspondence to truth. It compels us to attend to both of the questions of epistemology: How do we know? and What can we know?

Therefore, once we recognize that everything of importance to us is inevitably and unavoidably shaped and determined by the meaning-making activity of faith, we are overwhelmed both by our need to know the character of ultimate reality and by our awareness of the finite nature of all knowledge. In other words, we must find meaning in order to act; we must orient our action to a center or centers of power, confidence, loyalty, and affection—to a fabric of trustworthy pattern. We must compose a "God." And yet we recognize simultaneously that even the most worthy composition of faith is, finally, partial and inadequate—that is, an idol—insofar as metaphor is a vehicle that can convey no more than a limited aspect of the real, and the structures, which determine how profoundly metaphors are held, also cannot match the complexity of reality.

Hence, we must realistically appraise the strength and the limits of the human activity of meaning-making; as we shall see, this is to say that we must understand and test the power of imagination.

PIAGET AND THE NEGLECT OF IMAGINATION

Piaget was primarily interested in the formal properties of knowing. But, as we are beginning to see, if we are concerned with faith and therefore with image as well as with structure, an exclusively structural appropriation of Piaget's thought is inadequate. The concerns of faith development require attention to an element of Piaget's insight that Piagetians have "forgotten," and about which psychologists, educators, theologians, and others may be usefully reminded.

Earlier, in chapter 3, we noted that the Piagetian paradigm has manifested a number of "neglects"—namely affect, being, continuity, process, and the social dimension of experience. Kegan has addressed these by arguing that Piaget's insight into cognition partakes of a larger conception—meaning-making activity—and that this larger activity embraces all of these "neglects." However, there is another "neglect" that Kegan has not addressed. Piagetians and other developmentalists have attended to structure to the neglect of content.

Piagetians have forgotten that the power of developing structures, or "operations," of the mind is the power of their enhanced capacity to handle images—what Piaget termed representations.[4] This power of symbolization is the power of

imagination. Piagetians have participated in the Enlightenment myth that one can shear structure (or method) from
content, separate the subject who knows from the object that
is known. Consequently, developmental theorists have separated development from imagination, neglecting to recognize
the power of the latter. They have focused on seeking to understand the method or conditions of seeking truth. In so
doing, they have neglected to give comparable attention to the
adequacy of the "truth" itself. The power of process and method
has been divorced from the power of content and name. Yet
Piaget himself recognized that the significance of each new
developing structure is precisely its greater capacity to hold
and handle representations. Thus when we appropriate this
paradigm to make linkages between the structure and the
content of faith, we are again in continuity with Piaget's essential genius. His thought is, however, rooted in the thought
of the Enlightenment and, as already suggested, reflects both
the strengths and limits of that intellectual tradition. It is
useful, therefore, to examine earlier understandings of imagination if we are to renew our understanding of the relationship
of structure and content in the composing of faith.

KANT, COLERIDGE, AND IMAGINATION

We have already remarked that, at least since Kant, we have
been aware that all of our knowing is a composing activity.
The human mind does not receive the world as it is in itself;
rather, we act upon it to compose it (or better, we interact
with it in a mutual composing). In the era of the Enlightenment (1675-1830), it was almost as though Western philosoph-
ical-theological thought came to the same point in the
epistemological pilgrimage as does the emerging young adult
described earlier. Philosophical reflection articulated a renewed awareness of the powers and limits of its own knowing.
Philosophers began anew to critique, to purify, and to restore
their understanding of the power and processes of the knowing mind.

In Germany, Immanuel Kant (1724-1804) made distinctions between theoretical, speculative, and practical reason, thereby distinguishing the knowing of the sensible from the supersensible.[5] Only that which could be apprehended through the immediate senses could be "known." The apprehension of moral and religious claims was perceived as inaccessible to "knowing," but he perceived the postulation of religious categories as necessary to practical or moral life. Philosophical and theological reflection became aware of and responsible for its own composing activity—particularly in the realm of the supersensible or the spiritual.

As a part of his critique of the powers of the mind, and central to our concerns here, Kant identified imagination as the active, creative, constructive power of the knowing mind. He recognized imagination as the power that acts upon the *sense* in a way that organizes perception, unifies, and creates the categories of interpretation, or "understanding"—at the same time that it is free from the laws of "understanding." Imagination for Kant, then, is the free composing activity of the mind, essential to all perception and to the power of the mind to hypothesize.[6] But as critical a role as Kant gave to imagination in the knowing of the sensible world, he did not allow imagination a central role in practical reason, the deducing of the supersensible world necessary to moral choice and action.

In England, Samuel Taylor Coleridge (1772-1834), influenced by the Enlightenment and specifically by Kant, also identified imagination as the composing activity of the mind. Coleridge was intrigued with Kant's word for imagination, *Einbildungskraft: Kraft* denoting power; *Bildung*, shaping; and *ein*, one. Imagination—the power of shaping into one.[7] However, Coleridge not only noted this meaning but, as we shall see, brought it to a level of significance that went beyond Kant. In so doing, he made visible the indivisible bond between imagination and faith—understanding both as shaping and unifying activities integral to being human and to discerning the character of "eternal truth" (or ultimate reality, as we have termed it).[8]

Therefore, in order to understand the relationship of imagination and faith, we first direct our attention to the thought
of Coleridge. (As William F. Lynch has noted in his own
reflections on imagination, "new theorists are modest because
they acknowledge that poets like Coleridge and Wordsworth
anticipated them by far.")[9]

Before proceeding further it is essential to distinguish imagination from mere fancy, fantasy, or the fanciful. *Fanciful* in its
common usage connotes "the unreal." And, indeed, Coleridge
identified fancy as having a function quite other than the act
of composing reality. In his perception, fancy simply takes the
images already in the memory and arranges and rearranges
them in an associative or aggregative manner.[10] Fancy, for
example, can associate talking and mice and can compose a
Mickey Mouse to reign over Fantasyland. This is not to say
that fancy is necessarily trivial. The free association of fancy
can play a role in the composing of more adequate truth, as
demonstrated in psychoanalytic method. Fancy alone, however,
cannot finally compose truth. By contrast, the task of the
imagination, and particularly of the religious imagination, is
to compose the real.[11]

Coleridge describes imagination itself as the highest power
of Reason, which includes all of the powers of the mind.
Coleridge's sense of Reason is like Kant's "practical reason" in
that Reason can apprehend transcendent, moral truth. But,
unlike Kant, Coleridge is persuaded that Reason "knows"
eternal truth and does so by means of the imagination. "Reason is the power by which we become possessed of principle
(eternal verities) and of ideas (N.B. not images) as the ideas
of a point, circle, Justice, Holiness, Free Will in Morals."[12]

Reason is the knowledge of the laws of the whole considered as one;
and as such it is contradistinguished from the understanding, which
concerns itself exclusively with the quantities, qualities, and relations
of particulars in time and space. . . . The reason . . . is the science of
the universal, having the ideas of oneness and allness as its two
elements or primary factors.[13]

Above all, writes Coleridge, Reason is the integral *spirit* of the regenerated person, reason substantiated and vital, "one only, yet manifold, overseeing all, and going through all understanding; the breath of the power of God."[14]

The power within Reason by which the contradictions of understanding are transcended and the oneness of reason is accomplished is the imagination—"the completing power."

Thus, for Coleridge, Reason, which "dwells in us only as far as we dwell in it," and which constitutes the human relationship to the divine, is the highest and most complete power of any human mind; it is, if you will, the "animating essence" of the mind. And its completing, unifying, transcending activity is wrought by means of the imagination. Reason grasps the infinite, unseen ideal, and does so by means of the power of imagination. Since Reason is the regenerate Spirit in the human, imagination is also the activity of Spirit—"the breath of the power of God." For Coleridge, imagination—the power of shaping into one—is the power by which faith is composed.

A central insight of Enlightenment thought was the insistence that if human beings were to awake to the fulfillment of their own humanity, they must become aware of and responsible for the power of imagination. Mature faith was perceived to depend upon an awakening to the nature, power, and limits of imagination. The human being is thus most true to his or her own nature when the powers of imagination are fully awake—alive to the presence of Spirit and to the power of the human person and community to compose (and to distort) self and world.[15]

We turn, therefore, to examine the process of imagination and its relationship to human development. After we have explored these dynamics we will consider the adequacy of the imagination to determine truth. Finally, we will consider the role of human community—specifically the academy—in shaping the imagination, and therefore the truth, of the young adult. To explore these dynamics is to examine further the "how" of human development and the underlying grammar of the formation of adult faith.

IMAGINATION: ESSENTIALLY VITAL

Coleridge's most focused statement describing imagination is a brief, "packed" definition in his *Biographia Literaria*:

The IMAGINATION then, I consider either as primary, or secondary. The primary IMAGINATION I hold to be the living Power and prime Agent of all human Perception, and as a repetition in the finite mind of the eternal act of creation in the infinite I AM. The secondary Imagination I consider as an echo of the former, coexisting with the conscious will, yet still as identical with the primary in the *kind* of its agency, and differing only in *degree*, and in the *mode* of its operation. It dissolves, diffuses, dissipates, in order to re-create; or where this process is rendered impossible, yet still at all events it struggles to idealize and to unify. It is essentially *vital*, even as all objects (*as* objects) are essentially fixed and dead.[16]

For our purposes, there are five concepts in this definition that are important. First, imagination participates in all human perception as its "living Power and prime Agent." This is to say that all people imagine their world into being. It is not to say that the world somehow does not really exist and that the imagination conjures it up. Rather, we compose what we find.[17] The imagination orients one to choose and notice certain details over countless others. The imagination then informs the way in which one makes sense of the details, forming pattern out of disparate elements. In other words, it acts first as a kind of filter and then as a kind of lens. Consequently, the mind is never a mere onlooker—it composes its world. Everything that we sense or perceive is "created" by the power of the imagination. "To know is in its very essence a verb active."[18] Second, some of the activity of imagination is conscious (and this dimension we will discuss at some length). Third, the imagination is a power that "dissolves . . . to re-create" and "struggles to unify." Fourth, it is essentially vital; the imagination, as we shall see, is the motion of life itself, enlivening existence. And, therefore, fifth, as Coleridge saw, it participates "in the eternal act of creation." (It is one with the Spirit that in the biblical story of creation "hovered over the face of the waters" at the dawn of Creation—imagination is the activity of Spirit.)

Coleridge was a powerful thinker, but not a systematic one. Nowhere did he lay out a comprehensive statement of his reflection on imagination. Instead, he tucked his thoughts here and there into notebooks, elaborated upon them in poetry, and wove them into other writings as fleeting flashes of insight. In our own consideration of the imagination, therefore, we are assisted by others whose reflections on imagination serve to order the thought of Coleridge.

I find particularly helpful the work of James Loder, an educator, clinical psychologist, and theologian. Loder describes a grammar of transformation or a paradigm of the process of creativity that identifies the critical elements of the process of imagination as these bear on human development. He has described what I term five "moments" within the act of imagination: (1) conscious conflict (held in rapport), (2) pause (or interlude for scanning), (3) image (or insight), (4) repatterning and release of energy, and (5) interpretation.[19]

1. *Conscious Conflict*: Whether or not we hold a theory of change and growth, we know from our own experience that new life, insight, and transformation often arise out of circumstances that are initially at least somewhat uncomfortable. The moment of "conscious conflict" occurs when one becomes aware that "something is not fitting." Conflict may be present in an unconscious or preconscious sense, but it does not become available for the recomposing of meaning and for the transformation of faith until it is brought to the conscious level. This may emerge as an increasing curiosity, a devastating shattering of assumptions, a vague restlessness, an intense weariness with things as they are, a body of broken expectations, an interpersonal conflict, or a discovery of intellectual dissonance. In this moment, equilibrium is thrown off balance. Individuals (and sometimes whole communities) from time to

time experience some degree of such disequilibrium. Within the moment of disequilibrium lies a threefold task: the conflict must be felt, allowed, made conscious; the conflict must be clarified; the conflict must be suffered with the expectation of a solution.

The conflict is initially experienced as a "baffling struggle with irreconcilable factors."[20] Whatever the factors, they generally represent a tension between established meaning that is deeply rooted in both mind and heart—and new experience, which now stands in strong opposition over-against established meaning. In this tension are embedded echoes of the yearnings described earlier, the simultaneous longings for preservation and transformation, for continuity and for new life, for communion and for distinctness: "the tendency at once to individuate and to connect, to detach, but so as to either retain or reproduce attachment."[21] (Therefore, this is typically the moment of trying to figure out and to name "what's wrong," while at the same time feeling some resistance to "finding out.")

It is Coleridge's great conviction that this moment of opposition must serve to distinguish, but not to divide.[22] To distinguish is to clarify; to divide is to destroy the underlying and ultimate unity, which would preclude the activity of recomposing the whole that is the activity of imagination when vitalized by Spirit. Thus, for Coleridge, thought distinguishes but is essentially connective.

Philip Wheelwright sharpens the description of this moment with his discussion of the "*confrontive imagination*."[23] The confrontive imagination particularizes; it makes things specific. The moment of conflict has not exercised its potential power as long as there is only a contradiction of vague generalities. One must enter into the particularity of the puzzlement, tugging unruly thoughts and feelings into view. In so doing, one faces an enlarged complexity and sometimes a deepened terror. This not only demands rigorous and disciplined care for thought, but may sometimes also require a measure of courage.

This is to say that, in the activity of faith, "the bombardment of forces" experienced in the disparate character of existence must be transformed from a welter of overwhelming blur into a perception of the particular nature of each element of power in the force field of life. This particularizing function, integral to the search for truth, accounts, in part, for the vitalizing, intensifying nature of imagination; for in the moment of conscious conflict "everything comes alive when contradictions accumulate."[24]

This particularizing requires also the imaginative distancing of the "*stylistic imagination*." Wheelwright uses this term to identify the imaginative achievement of "right distance." Right distance is "not mere distance in space and time," but a "putting of the phenomenon, so to speak, out of gear with our practical, actual self" and thereby looking at it with a freshness of attention. This distance is "the primary factor of style, both in life and in art."[25]

The perils of this moment of conscious conflict are two: overdistancing and overwhelming anxiety. Overdistancing, or a reified objectifying, breaks the connection with one's own field of receptivity, with affective grounding, and with Spirit. Overdistancing breaks the felt tension of conscious conflict by dividing the conflicted self from the rest of self at the cost of a broken spirit and the emptying out of all that is vital. Overdistancing has occurred when intellectual engagement with significant issues becomes mere academic swordplay, alienating the student from learning; overdistancing is manifested when domestic conflict shifts to domestic violence; and this same dynamic marks the erosion of political passion into a mere exercise of power.

The moment of conscious conflict that serves to recompose meaning and fulfill the promise of life is not one of brokenness in this sense; it is, rather, a distinguishing that fosters an enlivening restlessness (or even torment) suggesting new possibility—be it intriguing, irritating, painful, or awesome. The moment of conscious conflict is the location of much of the suffering dimension of faith, and the temptation to avoid this moment is understandable.

If either overdistancing within the conflict or an avoidance of the conflict altogether are to be averted, the conflict must be held in a "context of rapport"[26] lest the maintaining of the tension create an overwhelming anxiety. We must particularly note that when faith itself is being reordered, when meaning at the level of ultimacy is disordered and under review, a community of rapport is especially crucial. This notion is similar to Winnicott's concept of a "holding environment."[27] If disequilibrium is to be tolerated, there must be a sustaining "holding environment." Moreover, it must continue to hold over time, for once the conflict is conscious there is an inner momentum that drives toward resolution, seeking and waiting for its fulfillment. Momentum of this kind can only be ignored, thwarted, or submerged at the great cost of the betrayal and diminishment of the potential self and the consequent impoverishment of the human community. Yet here, once again we see that transformation is dependent upon the strength of the community itself, in this case, the capacity of the community to tolerate, sustain, and even nurture conscious conflict.

2. *Pause*: Once the nature of the conflict has been clarified, it is no longer fruitful to continue to focus intensely upon it. This is the time for the second moment in the composing process, the moment of *pause*, or incubation, an "interlude for scanning." One puts the conflict out of consciousness, but not out of mind. This moment is one, not of escape, but of relaxed concentration. In the moment of pause the conscious mind remains passive, or better, "permissive." Here, the mind is asleep, but "the soul keeps watch with no tension, calmed and active."[28] The activity beneath the surface may be likened to "an interlude for scanning"[29] for integrative patterns—some of which may already be present, others of which may have yet to appear in experience. Coleridge described consciousness as "connected with master-currents below the surface."[30] In the moment of pause, the master-currents are at work.

Humankind has formalized modes of giving itself over to the deep master-currents of the soul, and a recognition of the essential and powerful nature of pause is embodied in all contemplative traditions. One finds it in Quaker silence and in yoga meditative practice, as well as in such contemporary formulations as Transcendental Meditation. But "pause" also occurs in more mundane forms, which is to say that something really does happen to us while the bathtub is filling. An intuitive sense of this moment is reflected in such phrases as "Let me put it on the back burner for a while," or "I'll sleep on it."

The experience of "pause" is illustrated in a passage in which Virginia Woolf begins to account for how it was that when she was asked to speak about women and fiction, she came to speak about "a room of one's own":

Here then was I . . . sitting on the banks of a river a week or two ago in fine October weather, lost in thought. . . . Women and fiction, the need of coming to some conclusion on a subject that raises all sorts of prejudices and passions, bowed my head to the ground. . . . The river reflected whatever it chose of sky and bridge and burning tree, and when the undergraduate had oared his boat through the reflections they closed again, completely, as if he had never been. There one might have sat the clock round lost in thought. Thought—to call it by a prouder name than it deserved—had let its line down into the stream. It swayed, minute after minute, hither and thither among the reflections and the weeds, letting the water lift it and sink it, until—you know the little tug—the sudden conglomeration of an idea at the end of one's line: and then the cautious hauling of it in, and the careful laying of it out? Alas, laid on the grass how small, how insignificant this thought of mine looked; the sort of fish that a good fisherman puts back into the water so that it may grow fatter and be one day worth cooking and eating. I will not trouble you with that thought now, though if you look carefully you may find it for yourself in the course of what I am going to say.

But however small it was, it had, nevertheless, the mysterious property of its kind—put back into the mind, it became at once very exciting, and important; and as it darted and sank, and flashed hither and thither, set up such a wash and tumult of ideas that it was impossible to sit still.[31]

This "pause" after the recognition of the conflict may require only a few seconds, or many years. Its gift is a unifying image or insight—a gift that, no matter how intense the struggle that precedes it, always "takes awareness by surprise."[32]

3. *Image (or Insight)*: The period of pause has completed its work when it gives rise to an image or insight capable of simplifying and unifying all that had seemed so unreconcilably disparate and complex. The image incorporates the conflict into a single unified whole, thereby repatterning it. This is the moment of insight, the moment of "ah-ha!" Hitherto unrelated frames of reference converge to create a wholly new outlook.

The image that works creatively simplifies and unifies the disarray of the conflict, "shaping it into one." The image is in itself merely an object or act of the sensible world; it becomes an "outward form that carries an inward sense."[33] When wishing to express a thought, emotion, or intuition that cannot be pointed at because it lies beyond the senses, we must use objects and acts of the sensible world as mediators. To convey our meaning, we point to an object or act of the sensible world, not as a one-to-one correspondence, but as metaphor. The image then loses its own "gross material quality," so to speak, and lends its form as a vehicle to convey inner life or spirit. For example, "the word *sincerity* is supposed to be the same as *sine*, without, and *cera*, wax; the practice of the Roman potters being to rub wax into the flaws of their unsound vessels when they sent them to market. A sincere (without-wax) vessel was the same as a sound vessel, one that had no distinguished flaw" (p. 25). To take another example, the word *spirit* originally meant "breath" or "air in motion," suggesting a power that moves unseen.[34]

Thus, as Bushnell saw, "the soul that is struggling to utter itself, flies to whatever signs and instruments it can find in the visible world, calling them in to act as interpreters, naming them at the same time, to stand, ever after, as interpreters in sound, when they are themselves out of sight."[35] Objects and acts of the sensible world serve as forms for thought. "Thinking . . . is the handling of thoughts by their forms."[36]

This awareness of image used as metaphor leads us to the important insight that every image that functions as a bearer of inner life is at once both "true" and "untrue." Since the image only gives *form* to the truth it attempts to convey, it can only represent that truth; it cannot fully reproduce or embody it. Consequently, the image is simultaneously both like and unlike the intuition or feeling it mediates. This occurs of necessity, if only in that the image gives form to what is without form. Thus, there is inevitably some distortion in every image, and, therefore, in every apprehension of truth. All images, as well as the words, concepts, and rituals that derive from them, are merely forms we employ for the handling of reality. Insofar as they convey some essential aspect of truth, they are faithful to that truth. Their deception—their untruth—lies, in part, in their tendency, as earthen vessel in which truth is borne, to offer "their mere pottery as being truth itself" (p. 48). When the earthen vessel is regarded as truth itself (rather than a participant in truth), we lapse into idolatry.

Such idolatry is further conditioned by the fact that when any image is appropriated to grasp, name, and give form to unseen reality, the image is always peculiar to the individual or group who selects it. The image carries particular associations—social, political, and psychological. The same image, therefore, may bear quite another meaning (or no meaning) for another person, or for a different group.

This awareness of the strengths and limits of images, and of the words that derive from them, enables Bushnell (perhaps overstating the point) to assert that there are few creeds one could not affirm if one were to return to the standpoint of those who made the creed and were to receive it in its "most interior and real meaning." Conversely, he also notes that, given the fluctuations of language and its ongoing "peculiar" appropriation of images, over time "we cannot see the same truths in the same forms. It may even become necessary to change the forms to hold us in the same truths."[37]

Whether as mathematicians, physicists, sociologists, philosophers, theologians, or historians, human beings give form to their meaning with images. When the image becomes so complex as to serve as a key to a whole pattern of relationships, the image becomes a symbol. Meaning is constituted by a pattern of connections, unified and expressed by symbols. Because the task of faith is to shape into one the whole force field of life, when an image functions to give form to meaning at the level of faith, it necessarily engages a degree of complexity only held by symbol. Its form may be that of concept (i.e., God), event (i.e., Passover), person (i.e., Muhammad), or thing (i.e., bread and wine); its function is to grasp and to shape into one a conviction of fitting reality.[38]

As noted earlier, Langer asserts that the distinctive activity of the human being is this act of symbolization. She writes:

I believe there is a primary need in human beings which other creatures probably do not have, and which accentuates all . . . apparently unzoological aims, . . . wistful fancies, . . . consciousness of value, . . . utterly impractical enthusiasms, and . . . awareness of a "Beyond" filled with holiness . . .

This basic need, which certainly is obvious in any person is the need of *symbolization*.[39]

For example, every nonutilitarian act of humankind—including the "chattering" speech-play of small children that occurs apart from the need for communication, as well as ritual, art, laughter, weeping, love talk, superstition, dreaming, and scientific genius—is the transformation of experiential data into symbolic forms. Such symbolic transformation has no purpose in the sensible world apart from the human need for "meaning," which transcends, permeates, and shapes into one the whole of being (Langer, chap. 2).

Thus, we may now be prepared to recognize that religion,

at its best, is a distillation of images (symbols) powerful enough to shape into one the chaos of existence—powerful enough to name a community's conviction of the character of ultimate reality. "Religion . . . is a metaphysical poem tied to faith."[40] The great religions of the world have survived only because countless people have been able to confirm that, "Yes, life is like that."

The moment of image/insight in the process of imagination is, in religious experience, the moment of revelation. Revelation is that part of the inner experience of a people that "illuminates the rest of it."[41] Revelation is the event that provides an integrative, unifying image of meaning. H. Richard Niebuhr writes:

By revelation in our history . . . we mean that special occasion which provides us with an image by means of which all the occasions of personal and common life become intelligible. What concerns us at this point is not the fact that the revelatory moment shines by its own light and is intelligible in itself but rather that it illuminates other events and enables us to understand them. Whatever else revelation means it does mean an event in our history which brings rationality and wholeness into the confused joys and sorrows of personal existence and allows us to discern order in the brawl of communal histories (p. 109).

Niebuhr likens such revelatory images to a luminous sentence in a difficult book, "from which we can go forward and backward and so attain some understanding of the whole" (p. 93). This is to suggest that the new image or insight enables us to do and to see the whole of life in ways that previously eluded us. Occasions of just such revelatory insight are the motivating purpose of all truly liberal education, and it is this moment in which the purposes of education and the journey of faith are most inextricably linked. As Niebuhr expressed it, "When we speak of revelation we mean that moment when we are given a new faith" (p. 154). This is what Whitehead understood when he wrote that finally the essence of education is religious.[42]

That one is now able to engage the whole of reality in a new way points us toward the next moment in the process of imagination: the repatterning and the release of energy made possible by the new image.

4. *Repatterning and Release of Energy: Repatterning* is the term I use to name the moment that Loder refers to as release of energy or release of tension and reconstruction of phenomena. "This is a felt decathexis of the conflict that makes new energy available for reorganization of the personality and its 'world' relative to the insight gained. New energy is available because the mind has found an easier way to assemble all the aspects of the conflict."[43] At the level of faith, the recomposing of the whole, this moment must include what in educational contexts is described as teaching for transference. This is to say that, in light of the new insight, the whole of one's knowing and being is reordered. There is a re-visioning of the connections between things—from the point of insight there is a "going back and forth" so as to order a new pattern, a new seeing of the whole; whether the transformations be dramatic or subtle, the reordering of the particular is, in actuality, a repatterning of the whole.

Such repatterning may be recognized in everyday experience. It happens, for example, when one notices that something one has known for a long time in one arena of life also pertains to another aspect of one's world. This is the continual making of connections, the recognition and deepening of associations. One of the consequences of the release of tension and energy is a feeling of enlargement, a new quality of openness to self and world. Releasing one from the tension of the conflict, it also frees one for a measure of fresh awareness and engagement. "We might say consciousness is expanded by, and to the measure of, the resolution."[44] The surest sign of healing insight is this release of tension and new openness. Repatterning makes possible a "freshness of sensation" that is a "seeing with new eyes as on the morning of the first day of creation."[45]

Obviously, therefore, this moment also contributes to the vitalizing power of imagination. New vision combines with new energy; together they compose and exhilarate the soul so as to affectively ground a sense of confidence, assurance, and new power. There is a sense of more adequate access to reality. Imagination is, therefore, the power of realization: to image is to realize. And as imagination is the activity of faith, the task of faith is to imagine the real.[46] Faith is, indeed, something quite other than wishful thinking or mere assent to irrelevant dogma. But if the image which gives form to faith is to serve its vocation to truth, the image, no matter how compelling it may appear, must be tested before the act of imagination is complete. The testing of this new reality and the power of its energy is the next moment, and the completion, of the act of imagination.

5. *Interpretation*: The transformation of knowing and trusting is not complete until it has found public form. This moment brings "insight" to a public test of its validity.[47] This effort to interpret the revelatory insight to an interested public functions in two ways: First, we do not seem to grasp the new insight fully, and we are not at ease with it, until it has been confirmed by others. In other words, we are dependent upon a community of confirmation for the completion and anchoring of our knowing. We feel this to be necessary because we feel a need for assurance of correspondence, coherence, and connection between the original conflict, the new image, and a concerned or interested public. Hence, we test our knowledge with the knowledge of others. This test is crucial to the formation of our sense of inner conviction, but it is crucial in a second respect as well.

Having examined this process of imagination as the process by which we formulate our knowledge and our trust, we cannot help but recognize both how strong and powerful a process it is and how seemingly precarious. That so much depends on the search for fitting and right images and that images are so conditioned by context should give us pause. Northrop Frye has said that the use of metaphor can seem "like crossing a deep gorge on a rope bridge: we may put all our trust in its ability to get us across, but there will be moments when we wish we hadn't."[48]

We most wish we did not have to when haunted by the question, How is the knower to be saved from the distortions of subjectivity in his or her quest for a truthful faith? Sometimes even the most compelling images are, nevertheless, seriously distorting, unfitting images that lead away from truth. Images may be held with deep feeling, but "depth" is no guarantor of truth. If we compose our knowing by means of the imagination, how do we account for, and how are we saved from, what H. Richard Niebuhr calls the "evil imaginations of the heart"?[50] Is it not the case that though we have been following Coleridge's perception of imagination as the act of Reason—the divine in the human—imagination, nevertheless, persists in common usage as a "slippery term designating a power that penetrates the inner meaning of reality but also a power that creates substitutes for reality"?[51]

Indeed, Coleridge also recognized the possibility of an evil imagination. He understood the evil imagination to be the isolated imagination, divided from the unity of the "One Life" and therefore cut off from its Source.[52] This is to suggest that when the imagination of an individual, a community, or a nation becomes isolated, whether as a result of arrogance or oppression, such isolated imagination becomes vulnerable to the distorting features of its own metaphors.

All images must be brought to the test of "repeated, critical and common experience."[53] The interpretive moment is essential, not only as the completion of an inner process, but as a participation in the forum of common experience that alone can confirm or refute the capacity of the image to grasp the real. For which "gods [images of defining and unifying power] are dependable, which of them can be counted on day after day and which are idols—products of erroneous imagination—cannot be known save through the experiences of . . . history."[54] This is to say that the human community must serve not only as a community of confirmation but also as a community of contradiction. Emancipation from "narrow faith" and from distorting subjectivity may occur only in a community that distinguishes between evil images—those that separate and diminish selves and communities—and life-giving, truthful, vital images.

However, we must not give a too-facile endorsement of the power of finite communities to serve the search for truth. It must be acknowledged that even a rudimentary acquaintance with the history of faith communities abounds with examples of the abuse of the process in which "spirits" and "images" are discerned. Too often, inadequate images are greeted with acclaim, whereas the true prophet is rarely popular. Therefore, the community of confirmation must be defined finally in terms of the historical experience (past and future) of the whole human community.

Having recognized that all images are finite and now acknowledging that the process of imagination itself is fragile and vulnerable to distortion, one may ask if one can have confidence at all in any meaning, truth, or faith so composed. An awareness of the imagination process could lead us into the cul-de-sac of unqualified relativism. Yet as Niebuhr states so clearly, "the heart must reason," and "the participating self cannot escape the necessity of looking for pattern and meaning in its life and relations. It cannot make a choice between reason and imagination but only between reasoning on the basis of adequate images and thinking with the aid of evil imaginations" (p. 108). Thus "anyone who affirms the irrationality of the moral and religious life simply abandons the effort to discipline this life, to find right images by means of which to understand oneself, one's sorrows and joys."[55]

Mary Moschella, while a graduate student in religion, gave a baccalaureate address, the following excerpts from which illustrate something of the dynamics of imagination as the power of shaping into one—the power of adult faith:

Many of us might admit that we . . . were drawn to this place by the modest desire to learn to see everything clearly. Though it sounds presumptuous, we who have spent two or more years here, dissecting holy Scriptures, comparing world religions, constructing and deconstructing the concept of God, cannot pretend any lack of ambition. We did not come here to satisfy cool academic curiosities, but rather to learn how to see everything—the whole picture of life—clearly. We came to explore the very mysteries of God, to expand our view of the world, and to discern what it is that the universe demands of us.

After being here for a while, we have discovered that the process of learning to see religiously is a difficult, if not overwhelming, endeavor. For in delving into questions of ultimate meaning, we have learned how blurred is our vision, how tenative and partial our . . . insight. In this, we are like the blind man from Bethsaida, who even with a miracle, could only slowly and gradually learn how to see. . . .

Our studies and our common life have bombarded us with more . . . than we know how to manage. For our study . . . has caused us to examine our own faith and values: To decide what it is that we treasure . . . and what is essential to human be-ing.

Thus we have been involved in the process of naming our Gods. This process has demanded not only that we clarify issues of personal faith and belief, but also that we regard anew some of the global issues of human struggle. It is not that horrors such as world hunger have just recently come into being. But somehow before we hadn't quite seen (or faced) the magnitude of suffering involved, or the ethical challenges that such suffering presents.

So in the process of naming the Gods, we have been naming some demons too. We have seen and named the terrifying demons of militarism, racism, and sexism in our world. These appear to us as horrifying patches of darkness, frightening shadows that make us want to shut our eyes tightly and return to the comforts of our former blindness. . . .

Last summer I was in Israel, working on an archaeological dig. At the site of the ancient city of Dor, each day as I swung my pick into the age-old soil, I was inwardly chipping away at just these sorts of issues. I expended a good deal of energy cursing the facts of human suffering in the world, and trying to imagine some kind of hope of restoration.

Excavating at the level of the Iron Age can be rather tedious; only rarely did we turn up any precious small finds. Most of the time was spent staring at dirt walls and broken pottery shards. In my square, not even one whole vessel was uncovered all season—just so many broken pieces, scraps of ancient civilization. All of the brokenness appeared to me as an accurate metaphor for understanding the world. Broken and crushed, every piece of it; broken with small personal pains, as well as with overwhelmingly large human struggles. Yet as the summer went on, and I kept staring at the pottery, I slowly started to notice something more than just the brokenness. Some of the pieces of clay, however broken, were really quite beautiful.

Later in the summer, I found out about the business of pottery mending. This tedious work goes on year-round in a cathedral-like building not far from the tel. Here ancient vessels have been slowly and carefully reconstructed. I remember being completely amazed at seeing those huge restored jugs for the first time. How could anyone have possibly managed to piece together so many small nondescript chips of clay?

Seeing those restored vessels encouraged me to imagine perhaps that at least some of the world's brokenness could be overcome. I began to picture myself in a kind of vocation of mending, of repairing some of the world's brokenness.

To mend the world. To proclaim a radical vision of social transformation that would prevent future brokenness from occurring. These are the tasks that I perceived the world to be demanding of me.[56]

Robert Lifton has written that "human existence itself can be understood as a quest for vitalizing images."[57] Not only to the study of religion, but to every discipline, academic department, and professional school, the young adult comes seeking vitalizing, fitting, and "right images" by which to name self, world, and "God." The young adult has a unique capacity to receive images that can form the vision and fire the passion of a generation to heal and transform a world. It is the vocation of higher education to inform and nurture the young adult imagination—the power of adult faith. It is higher education, therefore, to which we now direct our attention.

7. Higher Education: A Community of Imagination

Daniel Levinson describes the young adult as a "novice adult."[1] Traditionally the novice was a new one, a beginner, in a religious order. Having completed an initial period of testing and no longer a postulant, the novice was clothed in the manner of the order, but was still recognized as dependent upon the guidance and support of more mature leadership in the continuing journey of spiritual and vocational formation.

The "novice adult" today is sent far less frequently to a monastery, convent, or seminary, and much more frequently to higher education. Although there are other contexts for young adult formation (the military, work apprenticeships, marriage, programs like the Peace Corps, prisons, and sometimes travel), it may be said that higher education is the institution of preference for the formation of young adults in our culture. (Indeed, military recruitment depends, in part, upon the promise of educational opportunity.)

Young adults in higher education (both undergraduate and graduate) quickly don the trappings of adulthood—an aura of independence, a measure of responsibility for self, and cultural permission for participation in all adult behaviors (short of full participation in the world of work). But the young adult is still in formation, still engaged in the activity of composing a self, world, and "God" adequate to ground the responsibilities and commitments of full adulthood. The young adult is searching for a worthy faith.

Since, as we have seen, young adults are yet psychologically dependent upon competent leadership for their formation, higher education—self-consciously or unselfconsciously—serves the young adult as his or her primary community of imagination, within which every professor is potentially a spiritual guide and every syllabus a confession of faith.

Such a point of view may seem to run counter to the commitments of the academy and therefore appears to speak of a domain beyond the academy's responsibility. For, since the nineteenth century, higher education has been increasingly dominated by a particular interpretation of "academic objectivity" that has seemed to preclude a self-conscious searching for and teaching of value and meaning. As a result, a commitment to the true has been divorced from the question of the good. Responsible teaching has seemed to require a dispassionate presentation of "value-neutral fact" or the mere presentation of multiple points of view. Teachers, individually and collectively, are more inclined to say, "The data show . . . " than, "I have found . . . " or "We contend . . . " or "I believe."[2]

Correspondingly, the academy tends to perceive students either as conventional, dependent neophytes in need of being awakened to the complex and relative character of all knowledge or as independent thinkers prepared to adjudicate objectively among competing alternatives. These assumptions extend to residence hall life, where *in loco parentis* once prevailed but where it is now assumed that students are fully "adult."

These conventions within the academy have their roots in the assumptions of Western epistemology—that is, assumptions about what we can know and how we come to know it. The nineteenth century influence of the Kantian perspective discussed in the last chapter pervades the modern academy. Members of the academy either perceive little utility in engaging any subject that cannot be submitted to empirical investigation, or, following Kant more explicitly, we distinguish the knowing of the empirical world (pure reason) from the world of meaning or ultimate truth (practical reason). This distinction has increasingly circumscribed the limits of the academy's domain and determined the focus of our attention. The phenomenal can be known, but noumenal reality cannot; and if it cannot, the reasoning goes, then questions of meaning, morality, ultimacy, and faith stand outside the realm of knowledge and are beyond (or irrelevant to) the concerns of the academy.

To state the case most sharply, the domain of "knowledge" has been reduced to the domain of "objective reality" (understood as empirical fact and theoretical analysis abstracted from fact, standing in contrast to "ultimate reality"). Further, the knowledge of the "object" that is known has been divorced from its relationship to the "subject" who knows, thus diminishing the significance of emotion, intuition, the personal, and the complexity emerging from the practice of lived experience (domains difficult to apprehend "empirically"). Reason has been domesticated; that is, reduced to those processes that can be analyzed and replicated—in short, produced and controlled.

As a consequence, we in the academy have reordered our understanding of our relationship to truth. Wilfred Cantwell Smith describes this shift as follows:

I would submit that one of the central and most consequential developments in intellectual life in modern times in the West, especially the academic West, has been the lowering of the idea of truth and knowledge from something higher than human beings to something lower than we. Traditionally, and essentially, universities were what they were—and uncontrivedly had the allegiance and respect that they deserved to have—because they were in pursuit of a truth that is above us all. Because it was above us, transcended us, it freely won our loyalty and—not so freely—our behaviour: we strove to live (not merely to think) rationally, in the sense of conforming our wills (sic) to an intellectual order higher than our individual persons; something that could be attained at times only at great cost, and never without firm discipline—but worth it. . . .

These ideals were approximated to in actuality, of course, only partially . . . ; and at times hypocrisy was substituted for even a distant loyalty. Nonetheless the vision informed and sustained academia for centuries; . . . many persons . . . were touched by it and in some small or large degree transformed. Ideally, education consisted in that transformation.

The shift in recent times has been from this notion of truth that we serve, to a different notion of it as something that serves us. . . . We manufacture knowledge as we manufacture cars, and with similar objectives: to increase our power, pleasure, or profit—or if we are altruistic, to offer it to others that they may increase theirs. The university has been becoming "the knowledge industry," its products ours to command (to buy and sell).[3]

Initially, this shift, brought about by the recognition of the limits of the knowing mind and requiring a more modest stance in relation to claims of ultimate truth, was a great relief. The academy relinquished some forms of hypocrisy and elite moralism and arrogant impositions of unselfcritical assertions of Truth. Modern scholarship has made important progress as a result of its now more self-conscious methodologies. Yet wherever a strict dichotomy between the objective and the subjective has obtained, we have also exchanged wisdom for knowledge and moral commitment for method.[4] Therefore, the tenets of modern scholarship have led also to the muting of the professor, the impoverishment of the vocation of higher education, and the abandonment of the young adult searching for a fitting orientation to ultimate reality—a faith. The young adult has no guide; the professor has become a mere technician of knowledge; higher education can articulate no orienting vision, and discrete and isolated academic disciplines, therefore, disclose only limited aspects of truth.

How might the academy maintain its commitment to truth, proceed with integrity in light of the relative character of all knowledge, and serve the formation of young adult faith? Is the epistemology assumed in the modern academy true? Is there an alternative epistemology, a more adequate way of perceiving the relationship of human understanding to the apprehension of the whole of reality?

George Rupp argues that neither a stance that claims to be immune to relativism (the stance, for example, of some religious communities) nor a stance that accepts unqualified relativism as unavoidable (the stance of the seeming practice of the academy) is adequate. Rupp contends that there is a sense in which both these positions presuppose a Kantian episte-mology, and, on the basis of a Hegelian critique, he asserts that a strict dichotomy between phenomenal knowledge and noumenal reality is untenable.[5] Rupp interprets Hegel's cri-tique of Kant as one that enables us to recognize that "It is, to be sure, useful and even necessary to distinguish between the object as it is in the consciousness [the imagination] of the knower and the thing in itself. But while the intention of this distinction is to call attention to the limitations of a given claim to knowledge, its effect is [also] to drive the knower toward more adequate comprehension" (p. 9).

Rupp's understanding of the search for truth is not, then, one in which the knower stands on one side of an impenetrable barrier and reality on the other. Instead, there is an ongoing process of interaction between the knower and the real (the knower him- or herself also being part of the real). It is a process that, in principle, acknowledges no limits to what can be known—even if, in practice, it can never attain a totally adequate comprehension of what Hegel termed "absolute knowledge" or "the truth" (p. 9).

This third (Hegel-Rupp) position, then, is a perspective from which to reject both uncritical conventional dogmatism and unqualified relativism. This epistemology recognizes that every perspective is rooted in and, therefore, relative to particular personal, social, and cultural conditions. Yet because each incomplete perspective is, nevertheless, an attempt to compre-hend the one reality there is, it is possible to make judgments about their measure of validity as multiple perspectives mutually inform and correct each other (p. 9). The interaction this understanding of knowing articulates is consistent with Piaget's epistemology in its dependence upon the ongoing in-teraction between subject and object, and as a critique of Kant, it presses in the same direction as Coleridge. This model too renders the boundary between the knower and "the one reality there is" more permeable, setting in its place an ongoing, dynamic process between the knower and the real, between the knower and the whole of being—the process Coleridge identified as Reason, with imagination as its highest power.

This way of understanding our search for truth recomposes the relationship of the academy to issues of transcendent meaning. The reified boundary between empirical truth and questions of meaning and faith that has characterized (if not tyrannized) the academy, is, in principle, dismantled, and the whole of reality becomes the concern of the academy in its commitment to truth. Academicians are thereby invited to bring the competence of modern scholarship to the search for critically composed and worthy forms of faith within a relativized world.

Certainly this perspective does not negate—indeed, it affirms—the responsibility of the academy to facilitate the learner's encounter with the relative character of all knowledge. But this perspective frees the academy to serve the young adult by moving beyond the teaching of mere unqualified relativism (and its incipient dogmatic forms) into the composing of worthy commitments to self and society within a relativized world. For if finally all knowing is one, if truth is not adequately grasped by discrete, compartmentalized domains of knowledge (as not only theology but modern physics suggests is indeed the case), and if all knowing is inevitably also a valuing, then any absolute value neutrality is, in any case, in any field, spurious. The academy's commitment to truth requires an engagement with the whole of truth, the full scope of reality. In sum, a critical appraisal of the epistemological assumptions of the academy itself points toward a reordering of the relationship between the academy and the young adult's search for faith.

This reappraisal of epistemological assumptions does not arise from the needs of the young adult alone. Not only students but all thoughtful persons are increasingly overwhelmed both by the burgeoning of knowledge and by the inability of knowledge or data, narrowly defined, to address the most pressing concerns of this generation—how to survive the threat of ecological, economic, or nuclear holocaust. The need to discern competent and strategic ways of addressing issues of ultimate importance surfaces as a subtle, but intense, demand for principles of meaning. It is a demand for an apprehension of the fitting and true connection between things—a way of knowing that can order and ground a worthy path toward a survivable and desirable future. There is an emerging awareness that our quest is for wisdom—that rich blend of experience and knowledge that manifests itself as sagacious judgment and informed love.

As we have seen, the young adult imagination is particularly receptive to being inspirited by compelling wisdom, ready for initiation into a responsible faith. The young adult yearns for a vision that is both critical and worthy, and a future that offers a place of vocation within it. The dynamics of young adulthood conspire to make young adults forge some sort of dream for the orientation of self and world, "making do" with whatever images are accessible within their environment. It is thus that the institution of higher education inevitably has enormous influence on the lives of young adults. Higher education serves as the primary mediator of the images by which they will reimagine self, world, and God. Higher education is a primary context for the formation of the young adult dream— the faith that shapes (or misshapes) both the adult who is to be and the world for which the young adult will soon be responsible.

THE ACADEMY: A COMMUNITY OF IMAGINATION

As most educators are aware, the etymology of the verb *to educate* suggests that to educate is "to lead out" (or "draw," or "bring").[6] As we have seen, to educate young adults is to lead them out through the relativizing of all knowledge and into the responsibility of composing truth and commitment within a relativized, complex world. Yet as we have also discussed, there is a necessary interdependence between the leader and the one being led. Thus the education of young adults may be better conceived as an initiation into a conversation— a self-conscious participation in the dialectic toward truth.[7] In this conversation the educator initially assumes responsibility for making accessible the images that grasp the most adequate approximations of the one reality there is, but the educator will not remain unaffected by the young adult's engagement with that reality.

Derek Bok, president of Harvard University, in his book *Beyond the Ivory Tower*, carefully reflects upon the values of the traditional university, the present conditions of the multivers- ity, and the "activist view" so as to reconsider the purposes of the university in terms of its social responsibility. He then reasons that in a world in which millions starve and are ridden with disease, it is a vocation of the university to respond to that reality through the normal academic functions, such as teaching programs, research, or technical assistance, as well as through its policies and practices. The academy, he asserts, has a responsibility to invest its considerable resources to search for hardier crops and more effective vaccines and to teach moral reasoning and applied ethics in both its explicit and implicit curriculum. Furthermore, it is part of the teaching responsibility of the university to disabuse students of the hope that the specter of global poverty can be reduced to a struggle to persuade university trustees to boycott lettuce or companies that make infant formula. But he also thoughtfully observes,

Despite our distaste for the violence and conflict of the late sixties, we often forget how many of the demands from that time have since been accepted and incorporated into the daily life of the university. Most academic institutions now think carefully about voting their stock, make conscientious efforts to recruit minority students, and exhibit concern for the interests of tenants and neigh- bors in planning institutional expansion. Only rarely did these prac- tices begin at the initiative of the administration; in most cases, they emerged only after bitter student protest. In contrast, it is hard to think of many important ethical responsibilities in this period that were adopted spontaneously by the typical university administration.[8]

The possibility that higher education might serve as a context for initiation into a two-way conversation of this scope requires, first, the recognition that no single educator may provide all that is necessary to sponsor the journey toward a competent and responsible adulthood. This educational task necessarily requires a community of educators—faculty across all disciplines, administrators, residence hall staff, support staff, and students themselves—who only collectively may embody what is required. Further, the academy will adequately serve the ongoing transformation of human knowing only as it embodies in its everyday life the dynamics of imagination—the power by which we come to recompose reality intuited as a whole. To see how this is so, we will reconsider each of the moments of imagination described in chapter 6 in terms of the academy's potential to serve as a community of imagination.

CONSCIOUS CONFLICT

In higher education, the moment of "conscious conflict" is the celebration of a primary strength. When serving at its best, the college or university "pulls together a livable tension of restless opposites."[9] The academy has a particular responsibility and a unique capacity to serve as a center of conflict. The academy may bring together "with real power and seriousness those subjects which are at the present time thought to be major aspects of reality,"[10] no matter how threatening their mutual contradiction. To do so is to engage in what Perry sees to be the function of a college: "to present to the student's attention in concentrated form all the questions that the sophomore in humankind has raised . . . through the ages and . . . has then spent the rest of . . . history trying to resolve, rephrase, or learn to live with."[11] Educators introduce appropriate conflict, dissonance, and wonder so as to awaken the learner to a serious, disciplined, and vitalizing engagement with reality.

But this is also the moment of discipline. The educator must do more than raise issues and heighten curiosity. It is part of the educator's task to initiate the learner into a discipline of definition and critique so that the nature of the dissonant, the unresolved, and the mysterious is clarified. This is what we best mean when we speak of the "disciplines" of knowledge: the "disciplines" represent methods for determining the distinctions between phenomena so as to name and handle and know them in the service of discerning truth.

If truth is to be served, however, the academy needs to be reminded that the vulnerability of this moment is "overdistancing" or the forgetting of the Coleridgian insight that we separate to distinguish, but never so as to divide the one reality there is. In the modern university, not only has the tension of opposites been distinguished into disciplines; typically, they have been utterly divided from one another to the point that "interdisciplinary" work has become necessary—and difficult. It is all too rare for faculty from separate academic departments and autonomous graduate schools to meet and to engage the most central issues of human concern together. Such rigid divisions disorder truth.[12] For, as Coleridge warned, to divide the one reality there is, is to be cut off from Spirit, which unites the whole; when the imagination becomes isolated, its potential for distortion, evil, and deadness appears. Indeed, as James Loder has commented, "Our reification of disciplines has 'devitalized diversity.'"[13]

When such division becomes normative, as it has in the contemporary multiversity,[14] the academic imagination disengages from the one reality there is, in which all issues and subjects live in the restless and creative tension of profound interdependence. Neglectful of these interdependencies, the academic imagination becomes only the "modular" imagination,[15] characteristic of contemporary life. Ours is an era in which conflicting forces bombard us to an unprecedented degree. So extreme are the demands on our attention that one way of coping is simply not to engage the whole of one's world. Rather, the temptation is to engage some "manageable" part (in which one may become expert and "secure"). One can then, of course, accomplish the proverbial feat of knowing more and more about less and less. But the most serious consequence is that truth is distorted. Partial knowledge inevitably leads to disproportion—either by inflating or by diminishing the significance of the perspective achieved. The knower who sees through the lens of only one discipline fails to see "the connections between things," and his or her composition of reality is, as a consequence, not an adequate construct from which to determine responsible action in the world. For example, as Everett Mendelson has reflected, the dropping of atomic bombs on Hiroshima and Nagasaki was at once both magnificent physics and catastrophically untrue.[16]

When the social sciences, the physical sciences, the humanities, and each of their subdisciplines no longer share a common conversation, there is no adequate way to address the challenges confronting the world community. The academic imagination must recover the capacity to engage the whole of the field of conflict that confronts the young adult mind searching for meaningful truth.

If higher education is to initiate the young adult into a conversation with the full force field of life, typically the student's experience must be enlarged. Faith is the place of experience and the imagination.[17] The imagination must have plenty of experience to work upon if truth is to be apprehended.

The range of experience addressed by the academy may be extended, first, by recognizing the experience of the student as it already exists. The student may come to the academy with rather limited, homogenous experience; increasingly, however, particularly as many students are older than used to be the case, students bring a good deal of complex experience to the academy. In either case, the student's experience should not be ignored nor should false assumptions be made about it. And in both instances, but in differing ways, the academy can further extend that experience by giving access to those disciplines that mediate human experience—including (but not limited to) history, literature, the sciences, and the fine arts. The methods are many: lecture, research, travel, film and other art forms, field study, internships, the employment of various technologies, laboratory experiments, participation in communities of genuine diversity, and so on. It is the lively and sobering encounter with the fullness of life that confounds the soul, enlivens curiosity, and reveals the partial character of every discipline and theoretical perspective.

This encounter is most powerfully achieved when the learner is not a detached observer but a responsible participant. Harold Loukes, a Quaker educator, has rightly asserted that "the young do not need to be preached at; they need to be given a task."[18] It is in the task, in the need to take responsible action, that the discernment of truth is re-joined with moral act and that faith must be recomposed. Further, as students and their teachers experience the discernment of truth as indissolubly linked with act and its consequences, the dichotomies between method and morality, theory and practice, knowledge and context, self and society, private and public— dichotomies that plague both higher education and society as a whole—are transcended, and the best impulses of the searching mind are honored.

In one of my classes I had been presenting a psychological theory. I began, one day, to suggest some of the strengths and the limits of the moral considerations implied by the theory. One of the younger, white members of the class interrupted the lecture to comment that he was uncomfortable with our raising questions of good and evil. After the class had finished, an older, Afro-American student stayed behind to comment in a thoughtful manner that it was his perception that some members of the class had not yet had life experiences that had required them to wrestle with raw questions about the nature of evil. I found his comment astute, and it prodded me to reflect again about how students' experience could be extended, such that they might see as essential to their intellectual reflection the testing of the moral implications of any theory.

Finally, if the moment of conscious conflict is to be sustained so as to make possible a new composing of truth and faith, the conflict must be held in a "context of rapport," which is to say, held in community, in communion, in trust. Teachers must have staying power. The conflict is creative only if one is not left alone with it, overwhelmed by it, or otherwise has to defend against it. We can face the largest challenges before us only together.

Many years ago, while teaching at a small college, I was talking with a student at a large university. As I described the depth and scope of the questions being raised for the freshman class in the smaller school, the university student (a senior) was aghast that we would expect first-year students to face questions of such magnitude and such potential for despair. I was puzzled by her response, until I realized that the quality of community at the two schools was remarkably different. The students in the smaller setting were not listening to lectures in amphitheaters from faculty they would never meet, nor were they returning to high-rise dormitories where they would not necessarily know anyone besides their roommate. The smaller school purposefully created both conversation and community, making tolerable an engagement with serious conflict and doubt.[19]

Educators take the initiative in creating a lively, disciplined, and comprehensive moment of conscious conflict and also assume responsibility for holding and sustaining that conflict in an ongoing community of imagination.

PAUSE

The modern academy had its genesis in the contemplative monastic tradition, but we have in large measure lost the essence of our heritage through our inattention to the power of pause. Though pause is essential to insight, the structure of the academy offers little opportunity for contemplation.[20] Congested urban campuses, lockstep class schedules, mass-feeding dining halls, crowded dormitories with little private space, interminable committee meetings and office appointments, competition for grades, pressures for "excellence" in research and teaching evaluated by a requisite amount of publication—all conspire to erode the quality of contemplation essential to the achievement of wisdom. Though the academy engenders a good deal of conscious conflict, it often fails to allow the pause so necessary to the gestation of new images and insight.

Instead, although the term schedule may provide a "reading period," faculty are all too quick to insert additional class meetings, and, ironically, students experience such periods as "the pressured time in the term," as they scurry about writing papers and preparing for exams. Faculty are given sabbaticals, but especially before tenure (and even after) they feel the pressure to "be productive," to justify their time away from the classroom. In a consumer culture, knowledge becomes a matter of production, and time becomes a matter of consumption rather than an occasion for contemplation. We must "use (up) our time well."

During my years of teaching in higher education, I have three times arranged for a class to begin with five minutes of silence. When I once commented on this before a large audience of university faculty, a professor from a law school expressed his concern that students might feel they were not getting their money's worth. I can only report the humbling fact that students found it to be integral to the course—perhaps even its most valuable component. Similarly, when I was serving as a chaplain and introduced significant periods of quiet into campus liturgical events, I do not think it insignificant that this was the only aspect of "religious programming" to which there was no negative response.

Parker Palmer, an educator who also incorporates silence

into his classes, writes that he not only uses silence at the beginning of a class, but

> I also use periods of silence in the middle of a class, especially in an open discussion when the words start to tumble out upon each other and the problem we are trying to unravel is getting more tangled. I try to help my students learn to spot those moments and settle into a time of quiet reflection in which the knots might come untied. We need to abandon the notion that "nothing is happening" when it is silent, to see how much new clarity a silence often brings.[21]

In a culture of "instant" everything, and the superficiality that follows upon this, educators may "lead out" by enabling the human spirit to learn once again the value of waiting and to rediscover the relationship between contemplation and wisdom—the richness of insight that emerges in the space of "empty time."

IMAGE

In the recomposing of faith, the gift born out of the "pause" is a unifying and simplifying image that shapes into one the disparate elements of the conflicts that experience—past, present, and anticipated—has rendered conscious. In the formation of young adult faith, four types of images are of particular importance. Young adults need access[22] to images (1) that give fitting form to truth, (2) that resonate with their lived experience, (3) that capture the "ideal," and (4) that recognize and name the dynamic character of ongoing transformation.

First, the young adult needs access to images that give fitting form to truth. This may appear to be self-evident, since the academy is, of course, concerned with truth. But our concern here is to remember that the young adult still appropriately depends upon outside authority. Even young adults who appear self-sufficient are dependent upon others in making their way among the images available in the environment. Therefore, the educator bears a responsibility beyond that of merely exposing students to every possible image and to every point of view, expecting them to make fitting choices. Young adults require not only access to, but also guidance in discerning the adequacy of, images—language, concepts, theories, perspectives, and actions.

This is not to suggest that a responsible educator determines truth independently of the young adult and makes only one set of distilled images accessible. Quite the contrary. The educator makes available the full range of images that awakens the learner to competing claims. But the educator also makes vivid those images that the educator has found to provide the most fitting form for the composing of truth and meaning (while simultaneously teaching just how it is that such discernments are made).

Furthermore, the use of the plural when speaking of images fitting to truth appropriately suggests that truth can only be apprehended through multiple images. As I have said, each image that grasps truth also distorts that truth. It is only as forms struggle with each other that they correct each other. Again, however, by this I do not mean that the educator merely leads out toward the truth of relativism—thereby teaching unqualified relativism as the ultimate character of reality. The intention is rather to participate in the struggle between forms so as to lead out toward "right images"—a worthy place of commitment within relativism.

This is precisely what most students appear to seek; once they have seen relativism, the professor brings his or her "truth" to a shared conversation in which student and professor journey together toward a more adequate apprehension of truth. Perry observes that most students do not uncritically appropriate the professed values of educators. But students do ask for more "faculty-student contact," a request that he feels represents a desire to know the meanings faculty have composed—not so as to accept such meanings blindly, but rather as a way of saying, "If you have been able to compose a valid place of commitment, it gives me hope that I will be able to also."[23]

Second, images must be resonant with the student's experience. The power of an image that can shape a new faith is located in its fittingness to the truth of both mind and heart. This is to say that truth for a person, at least ultimate truth, is only that which involves his or her whole being.[24] And if an image is going to anchor the composing of a new reality, it must resonate in the feelings, history, and anticipated future of the young adult; it must have the capacity to affect, to touch, and finally, therefore, to pervade the being of the person. This means that either the educator will draw on the reservoir of images already planted in the experience of the learner or the educator will give the learner an experience of an image that brings the whole person into an encounter with the images the educator deems worthy. Jacques Barzun described something of what it means to create such an encounter with an image when he wrote:

How then do you pour a little bit of what you feel and think and know into another's mind? In the act of teaching it is done by raising the ghost of an object, idea, or fact, and holding it in full view of the class, turning it this way and that, describing it—demonstrating it like a new car or a vacuum cleaner. The public has an excellent name for this: "making the subject come to life." The student must see the point, must re-create Lincoln, must feel like Wordsworth at Tintern Abbey, must visualize the pressure of the atmosphere on a column of mercury. The "subject" should become an "object" present before the class, halfway between them and the teacher, concrete, convincing, unforgettable. This is why teachers tend so naturally to use physical devices—maps, charts, diagrams. They write words on the board, they gesture, admonish, and orate. Hence the fatigue and hence the rule which I heard a Dean enunciate, that good teaching is a matter of basal metabolism.[25]

To make images come alive, educators must intuitively and/ or systematically be informed by the insights from developmental psychosocial perspectives as tools for alerting themselves to the complex dynamics of human experience. An educator can never assume that each person or every group embodies the same readiness, questions, feelings, assumptions, images, sensitivities, awareness, or compositions of reality. Educators must recognize that the images they offer are being appropriated in the meaning-making process of each learner, often in vastly different ways. Educators live with the sobering truth that, for better or worse, they make connection with (or fail to make connection with) experience they have perhaps "outgrown," never experienced, or never even imagined. Yet it is the student's imagination that finally conditions the truth that will be "learned."

Professor Arthur McGill understood this well. During his illness a few months before his death, some of his students came to him hoping that they might be able to arrange for the publication of his lectures. They asked him if they could see his notes. He responded by saying that it was not his notes but their notes that were important, for it was what they had heard (perhaps in contrast to what he may have intended) that they apparently found meaningful enough to publish.[26] He knew that the learning of the student is finally composed by the student—or better, by the student in interaction with the educator.

Third, images that may serve young adult faith must have the capacity to grasp the "ideal." Educators of young adults have little choice about whether or not they will influence the recomposing of faith and the formation of the dream that will shape later adulthood, for this is the central agenda of young adults. To be a young adult is to search for the stuff in which to ground an emerging self and out of which to form a vision of the promise of life. Every insight and every discipline is subject to being appropriated ideologically for these purposes, despite the "objectivity" of the instructors. Not only philosophy or theology but every discipline of study may be appropriated in such a manner; one does not have to look far to find people who can explain the "whole of life" in terms of biology, economics, or psychology.

Thus, though dominated by positivism, the academy nevertheless serves as facilitator for the composing of ultimate meanings. What we mean to recognize here, first, is that ideas, of whatever sort, may be recruited by the young adult for the formation of faith. Ideas serve as images that shape experience into convictions of self, world, and ultimate reality.

William Barrett, in *The Illusion of Technique*, illustrates the power of ideas in the young adult life as he traces an experience of William James as it occurred in 1870, when James was twenty-eight.[27] Barrett writes of James: "He has left us an anonymous case in *The Varieties of Religious Experience* that is now taken to be largely a description of his own experience. Why this refuge in anonymity? Would it have seemed too mawkish . . . too unashamedly personal . . . ? In any case, the passage describes the kind of experience around which much of his philosophizing turns; long as it is, we need to give it in full":

Whilst in this state of philosophic pessimism and general depression of spirits about my prospects, I went one evening into a dressing room in the twilight to procure some article that was there; when suddenly there fell upon me without warning, just as if it came out of darkness, a horrible fear of my own existence. Simultaneously there arose in my mind the image of an epileptic patient whom I had seen in the asylum, a black-haired youth with greenish skin, entirely idiotic, who used to sit all day on one of the benches, or rather shelves, against the wall, with his knees drawn up against his chin, and the coarse grey undershirt, which was his only garment, drawn over him, enclosing his entire figure. He sat there like a sort of sculptured Egyptian cat or Peruvian mummy, moving nothing but his black eyes and looking absolutely nonhuman. This image and my fear entered into a species of combination with each other. *That shape am I*, I felt, potentially. Nothing that I possess can defend me against that fate, if the hour for it should strike for me as it struck for him. There was such a horror of him, that it was as if something solid within my breast gave way entirely, and I became a mass of quivering fear. After this the universe was changed for me altogether. I awoke morning after morning with a horrible dread at the pit of my stomach, and with a sense of insecurity the like of which I never knew before, and that I have never felt since. It was like a revelation; and although the immediate feelings passed away, the experience has made me sympathetic with the morbid feelings of others ever since. It gradually faded, but for months I was unable to go out in the dark alone.

We hear in this account the vulnerability of the young adult to the raw awareness of the stark and tragic dimensions of reality. Our psychological awareness also alerts us to the recognition that, as Barrett writes, "We witness here such a convulsion and seizure by the unconscious that consciousness and its ideas would seem by comparison to exert only a feeble and peripheral force." But then he continues, "On closer look, ideas play more of a role in this crisis than might first appear. It is hard for us today to recapture in imagination the stark and frightening power that the determinism embedded in physics had for the nineteenth-century imagination. 'The molecules blindly run,' the poet sang in his distress; and those molecules blindly moving would spin out our fate as they would, whatever we appeared to will in the matter. That idiot will be me, and there is nothing I can do, if the particles are already irreversibly spinning in that direction. The imagination cowered before this prospect. . . . And if this philosophical idea does not of itself beget the attack of acute depression, it nevertheless intensifies that depression because any way out seems to be barred beforehand. Ideas . . . can have a most potent connection with the will, in this case a negative and frustrating one" (p. 261).

Barrett then continues his tracing of the power of idea in James's life, noting a turning point recorded in James's diary in the spring of 1870:

I think that yesterday was a crisis in my life. I finished the first part of Renouvier's second *Essais* and see no reason why his definition of free will—"the sustaining of a thought *because I choose to* when I might have other thoughts"—need be the definition of an illusion. At any rate, I will assume for the present—until next year—that it is no illusion. My first act of free will shall be to believe in free will (p. 261).

Barrett observes: "In comparison with the murky and subterranean atmosphere of the previous excerpt, we are here in the daylight world of the mind and its ideas. Perhaps too much daylight; perhaps the note here is too selectively intellectual, and there were other subliminal and more obscure forces at work floating James past his blockage. We have, however, to follow him to the letter: It is an idea—in this case the idea of free will—that opens the door out of his darkness" (p. 261).

Barrett's point, and ours, is two-fold. First, he notices that in this composing of life at twenty-eight, James forged the knowing, commitments, and direction of the rest of his life. "For the rest of his days James remained sensitive to the desperation that lurks always at the core of even the best regulated lives. . . . James thereafter could never accept any idealistic philosophy that would make evil disappear through some ingenious feat of dialectic" (p. 261).

"The brief entries quoted from the journal . . . give us in compact outline the whole of the Jamesian philosophy that was to follow. The philosophy of The Will to Believe, twenty-seven years later, is already summed up in a single paragraph from the diary. Everything he was to write comes in some way out of the datum he had grasped in the crossing of this valley of the shadow" (p. 262).

The second point Barrett is illustrating with the life of James is also related to our concerns. Barrett is primarily concerned with the issues of freedom in the contemporary world, and sees that when the academy presents the notion of freedom in a detached manner to merely tease the student into thinking, the would-be teacher fails to recognize that a peculiar kind of unreality has infected the way in which reality is being presented in the classroom (p. 263). For, as he asserts, we learn about freedom in humiliation, harshness, lack, and struggle— we learn about freedom when the "question of freedom has turned into a cry for help" (pp. 263–4).

Barrett's analysis assists us in recognizing that images that capture the young adult imagination will promise a fitting embrace of the heights and depths of the human condition and are in this sense "ideal." The educator will self-consciously join the young adult's dialectic with promise—the dialectic between fear and trust, hope and despair, power and powerlessness, good and evil, the true and the false. The educator will join the imaginative, composing activity of the young adult so as to make accessible images of the "ideal," images that at once promise authenticity and consistency, images that provide a vehicle for the energy of the young adult who yearns to soar.

Such images will have two particular characteristics. They will grasp a sense of competence and excellence; they will also reveal the motion inherent in knowing—the struggling motion of which the young adult now has the capacity to be acutely aware.

Images that beckon the potential competence and inspire excellence enable the young adult to see beyond self and world as they presently are and to discern a vision of the potential of life—the world as it ought to be and the self as it might become. A virtuoso performance of a piano concerto; the skill and precision of a careful scientific experiment and the faithful interpretation of its results; the aesthetic inherent in the cogent formulation of an argument; the disciplined grace of a record-breaking athlete; the congruence between the professed philosophy of a professor and fateful and courageous moral choice by that same professor; the demonstration of a collaborative project, in which the interdependence of all contributions is recognized and each is celebrated as integral to the achievement of new truth—such images as these serve to beckon the potential competence of the young adult and to define excellence.

This is not to say, however, that a commitment to images of excellence must avoid inelegance. Steven Weinberg, winner of a Nobel Prize in physics for his contribution to unified field theory, arrived, by the end of an hour's lecture, at a formula seemingly problematic because of "its inelegance." He then, however, said that he suspected that the importance and truth of the trajectory he was pursuing had been avoided precisely because people resisted such inelegance.[28] A faithful commitment to truth pursued with excellence does not necessarily shun inelegance, nor does it shun the messiness of complexity, the humility required before mystery, or the seemingly endless character of suffering in the midst of "not knowing."

Therefore, if young adults are to be initiated into a conversation with truth that will lead toward a mature adult faith, they must be offered images dynamic enough to grasp the composing character of the motion of life and its transformations—particularly the dialectic between fear and hope, shipwreck and gladness, death and resurrection, bondage and freedom. Speaking from the perspective offered here, educators who do not offer an "imaginal complex" of central symbols that grasp the dynamic of dissolution and recomposition that is integral to knowing fail to provide a faithful image of the relationship of the person to truth. Crucial to the initiation of the young adult is the recognition of the finite nature of all constructions of knowledge (relativism)—and therefore the necessity of their eventual dissolution—*and* of the possibility of ongoing reconstruction toward more adequate knowing. This dynamic may be revealed in every discipline.

Rosemary Ruether, a noted Roman Catholic feminist theologian, recounts her discovery of this central dynamic through the teaching of Robert Palmer, a classicist. She writes:

Palmer was . . . more than faintly contemptuous of Christianity. . . . [It was] Palmer, the believing pagan, who first taught me to think theologically or, as he would have called it, "mythopoetically." Through him I discovered the meaning of religious symbols, not as intrinsic doctrines, but as living metaphors of human existence. I still remember the great excitement I felt in freshman Humanities when he said something that made me realize that "death and resurrection" was not some peculiar statement about something that was supposed to have happened to someone 2,000 years ago, with no particular connection to anyone else's life. Rather it was a metaphor for inner transformation and rebirth, the mystery of renewed life. He happened to be talking about Attis or Dionysos, not about Jesus. For the first time I understood a new orientation to Christian symbols that eleven years of Catholic education had never suggested to me. That was the beginning of my being interested in religious ideas in a new way.[29]

Or, as another (and more informal) example: I was talking

one day with a senior in college, Greg Spencer, a psychology major. He had learned a good deal about various developmental theories and their stages. But it seemed that the experience of college itself had conspired with such theories to teach something less systematic but also at the heart of the matter. Greg said, "You know, there are really just three stages in college. The first is when you arrive, and you look scared and you feel scared, but inside you're pretty sure that you know what life's all about. The second stage is when you know that you don't know, but you're pretty sure you'll know as soon as you've chosen your major, or gotten married, or at least when you're settled into a career. The third stage is when you know that you don't know what life is fully about, but you'll go on discovering it—and that that's the way it will always be."

The classics, the social sciences, engineering, anthropology, biology, physics—each discipline can make accessible the experience and corresponding images of the dissolution and recomposing of meaning.

The "hidden curriculum" of the academy, however, may be the most determinative bearer of images. Images are made accessible for the formation of young adult faith, not only through the explicit curriculum offered in the catalogue of course offerings, but in the more "hidden curriculum" embedded in the institution as a whole.[30] Every institution is itself a cluster of images that either teach a vision of excellence or make a compromise with mediocrity. And every institution offers, through the norms of its common life, an image that conveys how it is that people are to live with the reality of "shipwrecks"—the shipwrecks inherent in the motion of life itself.

It must be observed that the contemporary academy tends to "teach," through the prevailing ethos of its colleges and graduate schools, that professional competence in one's field of study, verified by certification from that institution, will enable one not only to transcend, but to avoid, "shipwreck," by ensuring economic success and social recognition (especially if the institution is prestigious).

There is ample evidence that such images are untrue. Faith anchored by these symbols will survive only under certain very limited conditions.[31] Such compositions of reality cannot hold up through the predictable threats and challenges that come to most adult lives. Such images fail to touch and engage the deepest yearnings of the human spirit; they fall short of grasping the richness and fierceness of the full force field of life. They do not lead out toward an adequate human future.

This is to say that if, in contrast, higher education is to initiate young adults into a self-conscious, realistic appraisal of the courage and costs of knowing, the institution must embody in its policies, practices, and prevailing attitudes a clear affirmation of the frustrations, fears, losses, confusions, and sometimes despair that can disorder the self on the journey toward truth. As a community of imagination the academy imagines and teaches either that meaning-makers and their apprehensions of meaning "stay intact" (read, "*should* stay intact") or that meaning and the selves who form it undergo dissolution in order to be more adequately recomposed.

Faith development theory invites educators and their institutions to acknowledge in the acts of our every day that when truth is being recomposed in the most comprehensive dimensions of self and world and "God," then necessarily the soul suffers disequilibrium in the service of a larger, more adequate knowing. This disordering activity may take inconvenient forms: trauma in a relationship, raising fundamental questions about the nature and worth of the self, a fascination with "extracurricular political activity," reordering one's notions of the character of the world so as to call into question the character of the academy and one's purpose in it, or an encounter with "the books," leading to an empty dismay and discouragement, swamping an earlier faith and its hope, and replacing it with a sense of futility that no lecture can "cure" but that an hour with a professor might comfort and inform.

This "instability" of the self is not outside the interests of the institution committed to truth, but integral to its central concerns. To seek life through learning is always in some sense to suffer; the capacity of the academy to imagine the reality of shipwreck, to serve as a holding environment, and to care about that pain is a measure of its commitment to truth.

REPATTERNING AND RELEASE OF ENERGY

As described in chapter 5, in the light of the new image and insight, a new energy becomes available, and a new patterning of the whole of one's knowing becomes possible. Perry illustrates this by telling about an experiment in which people who had studied Latin demonstrated a better ability to spell English, but *only* when they were specifically reminded that they knew Latin. The "implications" or repatterning that a stunning insight makes possible must usually be explicitly "taught."[32] And it is here that the reconnections with the whole of reality may be made.

A student remembers a chemistry teacher who continually repatterned his students' apprehension of the world because "with every fact he also taught a dream"; that is, he made the connections between the fact and what it might mean for the world. Many students feel that the content of the classroom has been sheared from the context of the world; when this is so, value judgments necessary for life in the world have been artificially removed from the discourse of the academy. This rupture may be healed wherever teachers attend to this moment of repatterning, inviting students through every subject and in every discipline to exercise not a modular but a whole imagination. Students represent this moment in the act of imagination when they ask, "But what does all this (our subjects, theories, methodologies, etc.) finally mean?" They are asking us to make the connections between the subject matter and the world of lived experience.

Conversely, "mere experience" does not constitute education. For students to have "experiences" is not enough. If an experience is to inform faith, there must be critical reflection on that experience, and it is the educator's responsibility to provide the space and the guidance for that to occur.

Educators of faith do not leave this moment in the imagination process to someone else. The educator who assumes self-conscious responsibility for the role that he or she may play in the life of the young adult is attentive to the integration of the curriculum—to how things cohere. Students need to be taught the relationship between courses (be they compatible or dissonant), as well as the insights of each particular course. One cannot assume that the student who is offered the smorgasbord of the contemporary university will alone be able even to recognize (much less adjudicate) the multiplicity of competing claims. Only as we pay attention to how each truth relates to another can we nurture the cautious confidence that the world may be understood.[33]

The "release of energy" that flows from the repatterning of the original conflict is integral to this moment and may be experienced, in part, as a sense of "celebration." Educators have too often failed to celebrate the resolution of conflict, the repatterning of perception, the arrival on a new shore, and/or have failed to offer a fresh challenge that both recognizes and extends the strength of a new insight. These two possibilities bring us to the last moment in the process of imagination.

INTERPRETATION

When a new image has given form to a new pattern of meaning, the process of imagination, of knowing, remains incomplete until it has found a public life. Everyone has had the experience of hearing something that seemed important and true and then, perhaps several days or weeks later, trying to tell someone else about it and finding oneself unable to remember quite what it was. This is liable to happen when one has not had occasion to express the insight for oneself. Moreover, it is a phenomenon that is intensified in young adulthood, when one has little confidence in a new way of knowing until the self-chosen (but essential) authority "out there" gives confirmation. The emerging, fragile self is intensely dependent upon such a community of confirmation to complete the act of imagination that constitutes a new faith.[34]

Thus a vital role is played by individuals and communities who are able to confirm the promise—or challenge the unfittingness—of what the young adult has (sometimes with great enthusiasm or terror) come to see. Further, this necessary interdependence in the determination of truth is an essential discovery for the young adult, if the omnipotence to which this era is particularly vulnerable is to be tempered. The young adult's confidence in his or her power to act is sponsored, and the young adult arrogance is chastened, in the discovery that the human community has an interest in and a claim upon what any one of its number has grasped of truth and meaning. Young adults require initiation into an awareness of their dependence upon a larger community for both the confirmation and contradiction of insight.

For many within the academy, there is only a minimal sense of a community—either of celebratory confirmation or of illuminating contradiction. The promise or even the possibility of a collegial community obviously comes under siege in an institution marked by competition as well as colleagueship and by the emergence of adversary politics among faculty, administration, staff, and students. Ironically, "community" is perhaps most difficult to create in the community college, in which the typical student and many faculty members are part-time and commuters (as is increasingly the case in the four-year college and in the university as well). Further, in the "community of scholarship," there is often a sense that academic structures pit student against student, and faculty member against faculty member. The prevailing forms for the moment of interpretation are term papers, grades, scholarly journals, and (sometimes) section meetings, seminars, and colloquia—each of which is vulnerable to the dynamics of competition, in contrast to confirmation or respectful, collegial critique.

It is significant, therefore, that the sociologist Daniel Bell has, nevertheless, stated:

For most people there are no distinctive places any more; patriotism does not provide you with a sense of identification; religious rites no longer give you a sense of anchorage. To some extent, for a lot of people the university has become, without its being explicated, the transcendental institution in society because it seems to promise the notion of community. It is a place in which people feel an attachment to something beyond themselves—scholarship, learning, books, ideas, the past. The university has some sense of reverence attached to it; it is a place where you have colleagues and engage in activities which are satisfying to you in a very emotional way.[35]

I am contending here that such a possibility of meaningful community within the academy is to be prized and nurtured out of a commitment to truthful faith. As we have seen, viable networks of belonging are essential to the formation and maintenance of faith for every person, and the re-formation of young adult faith *requires* a network of affiliation in which ontological dependence may be re-established. The emerging "young adult" of *any* chronological age requires a holding environment and a community of confirmation. Faculty, students, and administration must self-consciously attend to the nurturing of those connections that are the stuff of genuine communion-community, if truth at the level of ultimacy is to be recomposed. Attention to the quality of the social environment is not an expendable luxury. Rather, every classroom, residence hall, department, faculty meeting, athletic facility, student union, task force, campus religious center, college, and professional school is a setting in which a mentoring community of imagination may be formed.[36]

IMAGINATION AS PRAXIS

The question may be appropriately asked, "But how is this to be done?" The work of Thomas Groome is instructive.[37] Groome is a religious educator whose work has important implications for all educators. His approach to education transcends the dichotomy of theory and practice, or knowledge and life. He is seeking to promote a form of education that "leads out," not toward faith as mere intellectual assent to dogma, but rather toward a faith-knowing that is one with responsible, lived engagement of the whole person in the world. To do so, he posits not a "theoria" epistemology, which arises alone from reflection abstracted from life, but rather a "praxis" epistemology informed by Aristotle, Hegel, Marx, Dewey, Habermas, and Freire. A praxis form of knowing arises from the composing of the lived experience of the learner and a community. It includes critical reflection upon a shared Story or tradition of knowing, and upon a proposed future, or Vision. A praxis way of knowing or meaning-making takes place by means of critical reflection upon present action that is brought to articulation and named within a community context.

Something of the form that such an approach to the educational task may take is seen in Groome's outline of five pedagogical movements that, together, enable what he terms a "shared praxis" approach to education (chap. 10):

1. The participants are invited to name their own activity of knowing, as it arises from their own engagement in the world, in relation to a particular problem, issue, or topic (present action).
2. They are invited to reflect on why they do what they do, and what the likely and/or intended consequences of their actions are (critical reflection on one's own story and its vision).
3. The educator makes present to the group the community Story concerning the topic in hand and the response it invites (Story and its Vision).
4. The participants are invited to appropriate the Story to their lives, in a dialectic with their own stories (dialectic between Story and stories).
5. An opportunity is created to choose an action of personal and collective response for the future (dialectic between Vision and visions).

I do not have space to explore at length the implications of Groome's approach, nor to elaborate my perception of its extraordinary adequacy to the task of enabling faith development in the context of higher education. However, for the following reasons, I am convinced that a "shared praxis" approach offers educators who are concerned with issues of meaning and informed by a developmental perspective "a way to go."

This approach invites the educator to listen to the learner, thus making it possible to sense and to honor where the learner is in the meaning-making journey. Such listening may also help to sensitize the educator to the lived experience of the learner, so as to recognize which "conflicts" are already felt or are appropriate to the horizon of the learner's knowledge. This listening further enables the educator to anticipate what "images" may be most resonant in light of the learner's experience.

In this approach, the educator serves neither as infallible authority, nor simply as one with no more competence than another. The educator is a "guide" and the teller of the Story and its Vision—be it the Story of economics, the development of the French language, or the development of the understanding of microbiology and its consequences for lived action. Yet the authority (or emerging authority) of each learner is also honored. Furthermore, in that such a process involves a person's whole being, learning by "shared praxis" is not merely "cognitive" activity, but engages the affective dimension of being as well. Accordingly, whole patterns of knowing and meaning become engaged.

Above all, "shared praxis" appears to be a process that not only awakens the imagination but also corresponds with the transformative process of imagination I have been describing. It does so, first of all, by promoting and encouraging conscious conflict in each movement—by encouraging the learner's actions, stories, and vision to interact and inevitably conflict with those of the other learners, as well as with the Story and Vision of the community and culture. Groome has observed that in occasions of "shared praxis," the moment of "pause" occurs frequently as persons are invited to genuinely reflect on their own knowing/doing. Images become available in the telling of Story and story, and the sharing of Vision and vision may well propose new images of the "ideal" that can serve the formation of the young adult "dream." (All of this, of course, may occur in a variety of ways, through lectures, films, drama, demonstrations, travel, and so on.) Repatterning or reconstruction occurs as participants make fresh connections between stories, visions, and lived experience. The "shared praxis" group—be it a seminar, class, dorm discussion, task force, committee, trustee meeting, staff meeting, adviser-advisee appointment—potentially serves as a "holding environment" for the imagination process. As such, it may serve as a community for the moment of interpretation, critique, and confirmation.

Finally, a "shared praxis" approach recognizes that meaning-making, as a process, involves suffering and gladness. It is an approach to education that has the power to move beyond mere socialization and domestication. It invites people to come to a self-aware and responsible knowing, to their own self-conscious engagement in the imagination—the creation—of a world.

Something of how such an approach begins to take form is illustrated by Adrienne Rich in her account of "Teaching Language in Open Admissions" in New York City. She writes:

I decided to teach *Sons and Lovers*, because of my sense that the novel touched on facts of existence crucial to people in their late teens, and my belief that it dealt with certain aspects of family life, sexuality, work, anger, and jealousy which carried over to many cultures. Before the students began to read, I started talking about the time and place of the novel, the life of the mines, the process of industrialization and pollution visible in the slag heaps; and I gave the students . . . a few examples of the dialect they would encounter in the early chapters. Several students challenged the novel sight unseen: it had nothing to do with them it was about English people in another era, why should they expect to find it meaningful to them, and so forth. I told them I had asked them to read it because I believed it was meaningful for them; if it was not, we could talk and write about why not or how not. The following week I reached the classroom door to find several students already there, energetically arguing about the Morels, who was to blame in the marriage, Mrs. Morel's snobbery, Morel's drinking and violence—taking sides, justifying, attacking. The class never began; it simply continued as other students arrived. Many had not yet read the novel, or had barely looked at it; these became curious and interested in the conversation and did go back and read it because they felt it must have something to have generated so much heat. That time, I felt some essential connections had been made, which carried us through several weeks of talking and writing about and out of *Sons and Lovers*, trying to define our relationships to its people and theirs to each other.[38]

I am proposing, then, that the journey toward mature and adequate meaning, in the context of higher education, may best occur by means of the imagination, awakened by educators who are also spiritual guides and facilitated by administrators who enable the academy to become a community of imagination. Such a community would be engaged together in a process that might be described as multiple occasions of "shared praxis."

THE PROFESSOR AS SPIRITUAL GUIDE

When the academy serves as a community of imagination, initiating the young adult into a self-conscious composing of truth in its most comprehensive dimensions, the true professor serves, inevitably, as a spiritual guide. To speak of the professor as spiritual guide may well make any number of teachers and administrators uneasy. It is an especially problematic concept for public institutions in a culture committed to the separation of church and state. Furthermore, the notion of a professor's serving as spiritual guide may appear to stand in too sharp a contrast to the prevailing epistemological norms of the contemporary academy, as described earlier. I use this image, however, not so as to violate an appropriate distinction between political and religious power, but to emancipate professors from the inappropriate separation of self from truth.

The professor is an educator, one who has the responsibility of guiding toward right imagination; and right imagination is, as Coleridge saw, the activity of Spirit. Further, since the young adult is still appropriately dependent upon charismatic leadership, we must recognize that the professor leads out, in part, by beckoning the spirit—the animating essence—of the student. Hence, the encounter of student and teacher that serves the recomposing of truth at the level of ultimacy is a meeting of spirit with spirit.

We may be assisted in seeing how this is so by a re-examination of the word *professor*. A *professor* (which at an earlier time meant "church member") is, in its primary definition, a person who professes something, especially, one who openly declares his or her sentiments, religious belief, subject, and so on. Therefore, an educator-professor is one who leads out toward truth by professing his or her intuition and convictions of truth. This is not to say that the educator is given license to impose idiosyncratic or "private" truth upon the student. The responsible educator-professor is, in part, a bearer of tradition, participating with the student in a community's ongoing composing of wisdom. A community, in turn, not only consists of its living members, but extends to include its forebears. Scholarship is a disciplined engagement with sources that both include and go beyond one's immediate personal experience and that serve as part of the community of imagination—that is, as a community of confirmation and contradiction, contributing and critiquing images and capable of leading out toward the one reality there is. Goethe once said that a tradition is not inherited—rather, one must earn it. To engage in scholarship is to do just that. This is to value "objectivity" in a reformed sense: that is, to participate in a community's commitment to the shared discernment of truth understood as that upon which all minds can agree. The key word here (and the most challenging to the contemporary academy) is *all*, in that the community of discernment must include the full range of human experience across cultures and across time, if truth is to be perceived with as little distortion as possible.

However, the young adult does not participate significantly in the academy as a community of imagination unless led out by a scholarship also mediated by passion. Coleridge has grasped this dynamic in his description of the poetic imagination. He recognized that the image that potentially grasps truth remains a fixed, dead object until it is infused with the poet's own passion. Only then does the imagination become vital—full of life—and the poet serve to awaken those truths that lie slumbering in the dormitory of the soul. The poet remains "faithful to nature" (honoring objectivity)[39] while, at the same time, appropriating images and modifying them by a "predominant passion"—the poet's own spirit and apprehension of truth (p. 16). This passion "diffuses a tone and spirit of unity, that blends and (as it were) *fuses*, each into each, by the synthetic and magical power, to which we have exclusively appropriated the name of the imagination" (p. 12).

Coleridge valued George Fox because he "gave form to immediate feeling," thus performing the poet's role of giving form to affections, and bringing the "whole soul . . . into activity" (p. 11) by "creating the union of deep feeling and profound thought" (vol. 1, p. 59). The imagination of the poet, therefore, remains under the irremissive, though gentle, control of will and understanding, but its vocation above all is to make manifest "the original gift of spreading . . . the *atmosphere*, and with it the depth and height of the ideal world around forms, incidents, and situations, of which for the common view, custom had bedimmed the luster, had dried up all the sparkle and the dew drops" (p. 59).

Though we may wish to modify some of Coleridge's platonic and romantic metaphysics, he nevertheless compels attention to the critical insight that a passionate spirit of truth must infuse the forms of truth if truth is to thrive in the world. This understanding of the poetic imagination suggests that educators are "poets" who, by the guidance of their own passion (spirit), "represent familiar objects as to awaken in the minds of others a kindred feeling concerning them and that freshness of sensation which is the constant accompaniment of mental . . . convalescence" (p. 60).

Coleridge also wrote:

To contemplate the *Ancient* of days . . . with feelings as fresh, as if all had sprang forth at the first creative fiat characterizes the mind that feels the riddle of the world and may help to unravel it. (p. 59)

If the vocation of higher education is to feel the "riddle of the world and to help to unravel it," Coleridge invites educators to serve as "poets"—awakeners of imagination, professors whose spirits so infuse their subject matter that the spirit of the student is beckoned out and finds form.

Keniston observes that wholesome passion is rare in American life.

Passion is usually placed "out there"—in others, in the movies, in uncivilized countries, or even "out there" in some far corner of our psyches for which we feel neither kinship nor responsibility . . . The changed meaning of the word "passion" itself illustrates this disavowal: in colloquial speech, "passion" has become virtually synonymous with sexual excitation, and rarely means deep or ennobling feeling.

Of all the forces of human life, however, passion . . . is the least amenable to repression and the most prone to reassert itself in some other form. Pushed down, it springs up; denied in one form, it reappears in disguise; refused, it still makes its claim and exacts its price. When denied a central and conscious place alongside of intelligence, it becomes ugly and degenerates into mere instinct.[40]

Theodore White gives us an account of the fitting relationship of passion and intelligence and its significance for the young adult. He writes:

Yet the teacher who, more than any other, spun me off into history as a life calling was a young man who arrived at Harvard only at the beginning of my junior year: John King Fairbank, later to become the greatest historian of America's relations with China. Fairbank was then only twenty-nine—tall, burly, sandy-haired, a prairie boy from South Dakota; soft-spoken, with an unsettling conversational gift of delayed-action humor; and a painstaking drillmaster. . . . The tutorial system at Harvard was then in its early years, exploring the idea that each young mind needs an older mind to guide it. . . . But Fairbank approached me as if he were an apprentice Pygmalion, assigned a raw piece of ghetto stone to carve, sculpt, shape and polish. He yearned that I do well.

It was not only that I was invited to my first tea party at his home . . . nor that, by observation, I learned proper table manners at a properly set breakfast table. . . . It was his absolute devotion to forcing my mind to think that speeded the change in me. We would talk about China and he would tell me tales of life in Peking as chatter—but only after our work was done. . . . He would make the hardest work a joy, and his monthly assignments were written with a skill and personal attention. . . .

Yet though he molded me, he was pursuing his own cause, too—which was understanding the revolution in Asia in our time. . . . He was probably the only man in all Cambridge who recognized that the Long March of Mao Tse-tung, the year before . . . was epoch-making. Thus, then, in my senior year, young John Fairbank was allowed to teach a course—History 83b—on China from the death of Ch'ien-lung down to our times. It was a magnificent series of lectures, ground-breaking in intellectual patterns, and those few students who attended it caught the swell of what was happening in China and Asia from his wry, caustic, surgical stripping of myth from fact, noumena from phenomena, his separating Dr. Fu Manchu and *The Bitter Tea of General Yen* from what was really going on in China. His course reinforced what my father had told me of China and what I felt by instinct. It inflamed my itch to be off, away and out—to China, where the story lay.[41]

Some instructors do not share their passion and commitment, because in their own formation as educators, their vision was so disallowed that it has lost its voice. Others conscientiously resist having "too much influence," yet in so doing shrink from the power inherent in professorship. Indeed, the responsible professor does not seek a "cult following" built around his or her personality. But the point to be made here is twofold: First, the young adult (in contrast to the adolescent) does not seek a hero but a mentor, and in the mentoring relationship, it is the passion and the potential of the student that is finally what the relationship is all about. Note that Theodore White remarks that Fairbank "reinforced . . . what my father had told me and what I [White] felt by instinct." The mentor must "make sense" to the experience (past and potential) of the young adult. The images offered to the young adult must be "resonant." The mentor addresses, awakens, and empowers the dream of the potential self.

This is evident in one of our interviews with a college senior I will name Dan. When asked what had been important about a professor whom he had mentioned as significant, he responded:

She was a person who sort of . . . I talk about myself relatively easily, as in comparison with a lot of people I know have trouble. I don't. And I think she nurtured that a lot. I did that all the time when I was younger but I think she invited me to keep doing that and would give me back . . . here's the way I have to learn, you know, I throw something out and then let other people kick it around like a football then I can learn something from that rather than sort of zzzzzzzzzzzzz all the time.[42]

In the mentoring relationship the mentor has seen the potential of the student—usually beyond what the student yet dares to envision—and the mentor invites that potential into public life. Demaris Wehr, now a professor at Swarthmore College, expresses this in her account of being mentored in graduate school. She writes:

I had two experiences of being mentored during my Ph.D. program. . . . One mentor was a man and the other was a woman. At the time I didn't know that they were "mentors": I only knew that I worked especially hard for them. . . . His trust in my potential encouraged me to embark on the program in the first place. This man discerned gems in the rough, and he always treated me as if I were a gem and not especially rough. Thanks to his care and encouragement, I produced papers for him that were full of soul. They were not dry and academic (stale), but full of life and longing. They were honest. I secretly judged them inferior for these qualities, and quietly disdained my mentor somewhat because he always praised me highly for these papers. I recently resurrected one of them, written during my first year at graduate school, and was startled at the freshness, candor and insight in it. In retrospect, I would like to retrieve the lust for learning, the honesty, the longing that were in those early papers. Now that I *can* talk like an academic, I want soul. . . .

My woman mentor came the year after the man left. . . . She, it seems, also invested herself in me. . . . She wanted and expected my best efforts. I was afraid to turn in anything but my best, so I worked hard for her. I researched, organized, pored over texts. . . . and wrote less feelingly than before. This, too, was important. . . . She meant much to me, partly, because she was a woman with a husband and children and with others in her household. She held all these relationships together at the same time that she gave every evidence of being very learned and competent. She was an emulable model.[43]

Likewise, in a study of mentoring in the context of business, a protégée remembered a positive sense of "having to live up to being terrific."[44]

Mentoring can be powerful, but it must take into account the whole person if it is to be genuinely sponsoring, rather than destructive. In her novel *The Small Room*, May Sarton poignantly portrays the destructive pressure of a professor who passionately sponsors a brilliant mind, yet fails to see the whole student. When the student succumbs to the pressure and is caught plagiarizing "unnecessarily," a younger professor in the role of observer comes to discover the delicate balance that must be maintained between the professor, the subject matter, the potential intellectual achievement of the student, and the whole context of the student's life.[45] It is the whole life of the student that, rather than the mind alone, is being addressed and recomposed by the encounter with a professor who affirms the mind in the self. The whole fabric of a student's life, multiple dimensions of meaning, are being transformed when he or she is enlivened by new vistas of understanding and invited into and trusted in new arenas of competence.

The point here is that the student who responds to those who "make sense" at the level of ultimate truth rarely responds with the mind alone; he or she will respond with the whole self. This is not to say that students want to be "coddled," but students do want to be recognized as complex, whole human beings. A recent study by the Carnegie Council on Policy Studies in Higher Education found that a large majority of those studied agreed that undergraduate education would be improved if more attention were paid to the emotional growth of students. Of the seven areas of educational practice that were examined, there was most agreement about this item.[46]

It is my perception that a study of graduate students would yield similar results. I observe that the need of the young adult for sponsorship is least recognized at the graduate level, particularly in master's programs. Access to sponsorship typically depends upon the prior commitment of the student to a particular discipline (if not to a particular professor's work), and master's students are often still exploring, still seeking a fitting place for the integrity of the emerging self. Though culture often sends its searching young adults to graduate school, these undecided students do not typically receive the quality of attention professors reserve for "promising graduate students" who have "finished searching" and have committed themselves to a field. Yet even students who "go it alone"—a phenomenon increasingly characteristic of graduate students—are dependent upon whatever mentors (or mentoring elements) may happen to be available to them. All of this is to say that the one who teaches because he or she has something to profess will scarcely be able to avoid the role of spiritual guide. Thus, the issue resolves into one of what sort of guidance the professor will elect to provide. One place where the professor's stance toward reality is revealed to the student is in that apparently most innocuous of documents, the syllabus.

THE SYLLABUS: A CONFESSION OF FAITH

When I ask my students to read something for a class, they want to know *why*. And when they ask why, they want me to tell them about the person who wrote it, why he or she wrote it and, most of all, why *I* find it important. They want especially to know what in *my* experience leads me to think they should bother to read it.

Students will not sit still anymore while I argue that anyone who wants to be familiar with the "field" should know this book. They are drowning in things they "ought to know," as we all are. They sense already what it took me years to discover—that they will *never* know all the things somebody thinks they ought to know. Like me, they stagger under the daily surfeit of words we call the "information overload crisis." They wisely suspect that much of what they are supposed to "know" is useless information that has been magically transformed into awesome lore by those who control educational institutions and career advancement. But they do not want lore, they want testimony. . . .

What my students are saying, sometimes incoherently, is, "I don't want to master a field, nor do I want to leave all the decisions to experts and pros. What will help me survive, choose, fight back, grow, learn, keep alive? That I'll read or think about: anything else can wait."

The sentiments are not those of mere intellectual vagabonds growing up to be dilettantes. We are evolving a new way of organizing the life of the mind, and contrary to the criticisms, it does have a principle of selection and order. These students want to learn whatever will help them make sense of the world as they experience it and enable them to work for the changes they believe are needed. They will also gladly read something they know has made a real difference to someone they respect, be he or she faculty, student or anyone else.[47]

Professor Harvey Cox wrote this in 1973. If it sounds mildly foreign, this may be because the current so-called vocational-ism—the preoccupation of students with getting a job or preparing for a secure career—now somewhat masks or reorients the student's search for meaning in the curriculum. But the information overload crisis has not diminished, and students seemingly motivated by utilitarian concerns are in actuality often searching more frantically and despairingly for meaning. Students still urgently wonder, "How shall self and world be composed into a viable future?"

Once we recognize that the academy is a community of imagination, and that the professor serves as a spiritual guide, educators may appropriately recognize that, in a sense, a syllabus is appropriated by the learner as a "testimony," as a "confession of faith." We might say that in preparing a syllabus, educators confess what they believe to be of value—worthy images, insights, concepts, sources, and methods of learning that they have found to lead toward a worthy apprehension of truth. For in an interdependent universe in which all aspects of knowledge participate in the one reality there is and serve to give access to the character of its truth, we may say that each theory, course, and discipline discloses some aspect of this one reality. An educator who recognizes that the developmental tasks of the young adult require the recomposing of the whole of knowing seeks to teach through the integrity of the particular an accountability to the universal.[48] The educator who understands that every image may both disclose and distort the apprehension of all truth handles with care the language that mediates his or her discipline. Nancy Malone, a Roman Catholic educator, writes, "In a sacramental universe, to teach and study mathematics can be, and in fact is, as holy as to teach and study the Bible."[49]

It does not surprise me that, in my experience, the most effective educators are those who engage in their discipline (or administrative responsibility) because in the context of that discipline they have found access to transcendent meaning. In a world in which there is evidence in almost every news broadcast that matters of "scientific fact" are also matters of moral concern, reflective learners are increasingly compelled to require explicit access to connections professors have seen between the subjects they teach and life lived in the complexity, wonder, and terror of the everyday world.

What I am suggesting here is that students rightly intuit that it is not typically by mere happenstance that educators have given the energy of their lives to the discipline they teach. They have done so because, to some significant degree, they have found their discipline to be a worthy place of investment in their own composing of meaning—even in the composing of faith. Thus, the syllabus reflects only a portion of the professor's truth if it includes nothing more than a confession of some *aspect* of meaning (such as a particular discipline of study) and fails to include the educator's understanding of the relation between the discipline and the whole of meaning-making. When educators fulfill their vocation, and lead out the next generation by sharing the whole of their knowing, they do not have to be on an "ego trip"; one can so teach simply out of a humble recognition that "one generation owes the next the strength by which it can come to face ultimate concerns in its own way."[50]

Every generation of students has come seeking a path to a vision and vocation worthy of the potential of young adult faith. Roberto Unger, of the Harvard Law School faculty, spoke of the betrayal of this trust in the contemporary academy at a Critical Legal Studies Conference attended by law faculty from throughout the United States. After he had spent an hour and a half brilliantly describing and analyzing the post-Enlightenment divorce of legal method from a transcendant ethical vision, and calling for a reformulation of that linkage, I recall his closing by simply saying to his colleagues: The task is large and there are so few of us. But we know that we came to the study of law committed to the linkage between the practice of law and moral values. We found institutions prepared to flatter our vanity at the price of our self-respect. It is as though we found a priesthood that had lost its faith, tediously worshiping at cold altars. We find our intellectual work in the heart's revenge.[51]

*   *   *   *   *

Take Something Like a Star

O Star (the fairest one in sight),
We grant your loftiness the right
To some obscurity of cloud—
It will not do to say of night,
Since dark is what brings out your light.
Some mystery becomes the proud.
But to be wholly taciturn
In your reserve is not allowed.
Say something to us we can learn
By heart and when alone repeat.
Say something! And it says, "I burn."
But say with what degree of heat.
Talk Fahrenheit, talk Centigrade.
Use language we can comprehend.
Tell us what elements you blend.
It gives us strangely little aid,
But does tell something in the end.
And steadfast as Keats' Eremite,
Not even stopping from its sphere,
It asks a little of us here.
It asks of us a certain height,
So when at times the mob is swayed
To carry praise or blame too far,
We may choose something like a star
To stay our minds on and be staid.

Robert Frost[52]

8. Culture as Mentor

Our children cannot dream unless they live, they cannot live unless
they are nourished, and who else will feed them the real food without
which their dreams will be no different from ours?

—AUDRE LORDE

We have seen that the central task of young adulthood is to
discover and to compose a faith that can orient the soul to
truth and shape a fitting relationship between self and world.
We also have seen that as they engage that task, young adults
are dependent upon the mentorship of the adult world. Therefore, our attention is redirected, not only to examine the relationship between the young adult and higher education, but
also to reflect upon the larger cultural milieu in which the
young adult and the academy dwell. If the vocation of developmental theories is not to define, diagnose, categorize, and
dismiss, but rather to describe so as to understand and then
to ask, What do we now mean to each other? then the questions now before us are, What do young adults and the present
adult culture now mean to each other? and, Can a culture,
bereft of a worthy faith and vision, serve the mentoring role
upon which the young adult depends?

By "culture" here we mean "cultivation." A "culture" is
composed of the forms of life by which a people cultivate and
maintain a sense of meaning, giving shape and significance to
their experience. Culture is dependent upon the capacity of
human beings to learn and to transmit learning to succeeding
generations. Culture unfolds in its "politics"—the total complex of relations between people and their society—the myriad
of forms both mundane and sublime by which a people express their convictions of ultimate reality and thereby order
the life of their every day.[1] Every culture contains the seeds of

its own contradiction—its potential for healing and for self-destruction—in the particular forms of its traditions and in the promise and the vulnerability of its youth.

Assuming, then, that it is the nature of a culture to maintain and to cultivate the ultimate meanings by which a people live, we may say that the test of a culture is its capacity to nurture and to receive its idealistic young adults;[2]—or better, the test of a culture is its image of the future,[3] its capacity to imagine a survivable, desirable, and compelling future into which its young adults may be initiated.

Higher education is one expression of culture, one form of inculturation. Higher education has particular responsibilities for the enhancement and renewal of culture, nurturing the life of the mind, cultivating the will to truth, and continually examining conventional faith assumptions—thus serving as the nourishing soil for the seeds of contradiction upon which the ongoing vitality of a culture depends. The academy's competence in critical thought has, at its best, fostered the recognition that, though truth be one, we each only approximate it; we apprehend, but we never fully comprehend. Thus, critically aware souls have been given birth and set upon paths of continuing inquiry, manifesting, it is hoped, a lively and responsible imagination.

In the past, students and faculty alike have done their intellectual work within and on behalf of a relatively unified culture. Education occurred within an overarching canopy of significance, a shared context of meaning mediated by viable religious and political images. As American higher education evolved from its beginnings in Harvard College, a college grounded in the robust religious faith of the puritan immigrant vision, a "sanction of meaning, freedom, and hope were present in the life of virtually every college and university in America."[4] An assumed principle of ultimate meaning gave everything, including the university, a place in a shared sense of unifying pattern, even if the fabric was increasingly woven less from expressions of religious belief and more out of a confidence in social progress achieved by scientific and technological competence (and maintained at the cost of the marginalization or exclusion of minority voices and groups).

This shared sense of unifying pattern and purpose is no longer in place. The cultural shift is reflected in Theodore H. White's Class Day address at Harvard-Radcliffe in the spring of 1979. Referring to his own graduating class of '38, he said:

We were lucky . . . what we had going for us is something that you, alas, have not going for you. We had a world peopled with villains and heroes, a world where the clash between good and evil was so stark that there was very little doubt of the choice between Adolf Hitler and Franklin D. Roosevelt. . . . What a lovely moment it was to belong to a generation where there was no doubt in anyone's mind about what was right, what was wrong; a moment when you left Harvard proud of your country, of your university's creative contribution to the killing of the enemy, ready to give your life for our good against their evil. . . .

The difference between our jungle and the jungle you are entering is that we knew who our enemies were, and we were, if need be, willing to kill or be killed for clear cause. But now in the jungle you are entering, full of ghosts, guerrillas, and phantasmagoria, there is no way of distinguishing friend from foe—or, at least, being sure enough in your heart of what it is that is worth either killing or sacrificing for.[5]

Being sure enough in your heart of what is worth living and dying for is, indeed, a very different matter for the generations of students who dwell on the other side of Hiroshima and Nagasaki, Vietnam, and Watergate. Young adults must now search for meaning under a frayed and unraveling canopy. Bereft of a mentoring culture, these generations of young adults have, nevertheless, manifested intense, if tentative, probes toward meaning. Kenneth Keniston describes the young adults of the sixties and their response to history as commitment to a movement—a heady engagement in hard work toward social transformation.[6] Steven Tipton's study *Getting Saved from the Sixties* describes how, in the seventies, the young, radical vision of the sixties translated into marginal religious or quasi-religious movements.[7] Both Keniston and Tipton see these responses as experiments in the transformation of moral meaning, standing in continuity with a positive moral and utopian impulse in the American spirit. The impulse toward both social reform and spiritual reform has been a translation of hope and confidence into forms of meaningful action—even though partially adequate and seemingly marginal in their power to effect positive cultural transformation.

Arthur Levine, however, in his book *When Dreams and Heroes Died*, a careful study and report for the Carnegie Council on Policy Studies in Higher Education, presents a rather more sobering description of the mainstream of the post-Vietnam and Watergate undergraduate students as they moved into the eighties. He found the dominant characteristics of student social life to be diversity, individualism, escapism, and a search for something to believe in. "To escape an inhospitable world, students, like much of the rest of the country, are turning inward."[8] The consequence is a notable diminishment of altruism, and a prevailing "me-ism," encouraged by an individualistic and technological culture and manifested in the proliferation of "how-to" books that reflect a technology even of the self (perhaps epitomized in the title *How to Be Your Own Best Friend*).

Levine portrays a young adult generation whose dream is rooted primarily in issues of personal freedom. The salient feature of this generation of students is that they are reasonably optimistic about their individual futures but very pessimistic about the future of the country. Levine describes them as "going first class on the *Titanic*"—working hard to build an island of security in a world they expect to get worse and that they feel powerless to affect.[9]

This is reflected also in a study reported in *Fortune Magazine*, in which it was observed that the image of ultimacy for middle- and upper-class twenty-five-year-olds is the dream of a secure place at the top of the economic ladder; their fear is that the government, the poor, or the Russians will snatch that dream away. Meaning is to be found in securing a stimulating job that will provide the life-style reflected in the innumerable magazines they read. Commitments to either marriage or children are problematic—a consequence of their belief that they will have to look out for themselves. Yet they also long for a unifying purpose to sweep the nation, though they "are fuzzy about where they would stand and fight." Most interviewed described themselves as agnostic or privately spiritual. They tended to view life as "cyclical"—a sort of faith that there will be ups and downs. As one person put it, "I hate to say faith, but I have this feeling that whatever happens, I'll make the best of it."[10]

The consequence is termed (somewhat inappropriately) vocationalism, meaning, in this instance, an orientation to professions and careers in terms of their promise to provide an oasis of personal security in an increasingly threatening world. In a culture marked by the search for economic security, such altruism in young adults as does exist is blunted. Young adults, still dependent upon authority outside the self, are uncomfortable going against the norms and admitting their desire to serve other than personal goals. Young people are apt to say they are investing their energies in assisting the poor or the ignorant or the ill "because it will be a good experience," or because "it fits my interests and vocational direction."[11] There is little cultural permission to work and to serve so as to nurture, heal, and transform the world.

It must be noted that many factors contribute to this state of affairs. For example, middle-class youth in the United States do face a different economic future than did the generation of the fifties. Economists Frank Levy and Richard C. Michel calculate that the members of the generation that came of age in the mid-1970s could expect lower living standards than those of their parents, as a middle-class life-style now requires two middle-class paychecks. Levy and Michel, assessing the effect of changed economic conditions on changed politics, conclude,

"What we are witnessing may not be so much a shrinking of young conscience as a shrinking of young wallets."[12]

We will not discuss at length the question of the relationship between the wallet and the young conscience except to note the following: We have said that the particular potential of young adulthood lies, in part, in a relative freedom. Consequently, if young adults must bear real anxiety regarding their economic present or future, that freedom is diminished. Thus, though young visionaries have often "lived on nothing," many have done so with cultural support in that they have had at least some degree of choice made possible by alternative economic options ("I could get a well-paying job if I wanted one"). They have thereby had a base of economic security from which they could pursue their visions.

It is therefore instructive to examine how the phenomenon of a shrinking young conscience does and does not hold across ethnic and class lines. Sharon Bauer-Breakstone and her associates at the Bureau of Study Counsel at Harvard report that in a small but careful study of students of Asian, Afro-American, Hispanic, native American, and/or working-class backgrounds, the issues of commitment, so difficult to discern in the interviews of other students, stood out dramatically. "These students seem to be more in touch with value, care and personal engagement than many mainstream preprofessionals, apparently because of their strong community ties. Their explicit intent to 'serve my people' reminds us to evaluate other students' choices in a social context rather than hearing them as isolated existential decisions."[13]

That these students demonstrate a real hope that they will be able to reshape self and world may be because they have access to education and opportunity beyond what could be expected by earlier generations in their own families. Since this is not true for many other minority and/or working class young adults, we must look at the experience of others in order to examine the effect of the culture as a whole. In so doing, we find some tragic statistics.

Persons who might be presumed to be of "young adult" age (20–29) are more at risk for suicide than persons younger than they. White males are more apt to commit suicide during this period of their lives than at any other time. However, the incidence of suicide among blacks, traditionally considerably lower than among whites, has been rising steadily during the last decade and a half. In 1975 the rate of black suicide was still half the rate of the general population but represented a twenty percent increase over the 1970 figure. This alarming upswing is caused by young black men (ages twenty to thirty-five) killing themselves. Indeed, this is the only age/sex group whose rate is on a par with the white male rate, and in urban ghettos the rate is actually higher. Black females, also, are most at risk for suicide between the ages of twenty and thirty-five, though the actual rates remain slightly lower than for white females and the rate for all females (who typically express stress and alienation in other forms) remains lower than for males.[14]

Though the reasons for this increase are debated, an observation that is pertinent to the perspective we have developed here is that, according to one study, "the social ties of suicide attempters were greater than or equal to non-attempters . . . , but the personal integration of those ties into a coherent sense of Black identity has been less successful."[15] The reader may recall that I have suggested earlier that the primary task of the self-aware young adult is to secure the integrity of the self in the social world. The young adult self not only must have social ties but also must find a place in the social fabric that corresponds to, without violating, the integrity and promise of the emerging self. These statistics suggest that this task is particularly difficult for young adult males who are perhaps particularly vulnerable to being overindividualized and who, if also part of a minority group, may be placed at the margin of meaningful social connection and opportunity. The Bureau of Study Counsel work at Harvard and these suicide studies confirm the perception that the social dynamics of the young adult era are critical, capable of engendering life-affirming hope or truly life-threatening despair. Specifically, these studies point to the importance of the powerful role played by strong community ties that successfully recognize and anchor the young adult self in a sense of identity, belonging, and vocation.

Recognizing this, perhaps the most disturbing observation to be made is that "strong community ties" have become weakened for so many people at this time in our cultural history. The social contract between self and society has been dissolving. More sobering still is the further recognition that the dissolution of the social contract is, of course, the consequence of an even more profound dissolution—the unraveling of a shared faith, particularly the loss of confidence in a shared future worth discovering and serving. The social contract collapses when a people's faith—their Story and Vision—no longer serves personal and collective meaning-making at the level of ultimacy. Though the sentiment remains, we as a people no longer seem to be able to know with any felt certainty that it matters to be linked in fidelity to another—whether the other is friend, spouse, neighborhood, city, or nation.[16]

The collapse of a meaning that beckons beyond the parochial and utilitarian interests of the self alone becomes manifest in the inability of a culture to invest in the promise of the next generation, to believe in and to care for its youth. As a consequence, the composing of young adult faith becomes problematic, since a culture bereft of a worthy faith cannot serve the mentoring role upon which the young adult depends. Care, commitment, and hope seem to be replaced by mere coping, and it has been said that cynicism has become a national credo.[17] While the culture seems to sway between nostalgia and faith in technology, young adults stand in need of a mentoring ethos that beckons them to dream, to believe, and to serve.

The erosion of collective faith and the consequent loss of the culture's ability to serve as mentor has been precipitated by several forces which prevail in the contemporary world. Perhaps the most far-reaching is that, as a result of modern technology, particularly the development of the communication industries, the cultures of the world are colliding. Every culture is now confronted by the finite nature of its own composition of reality, as it dwells uneasily in an intensifying relationship with surrounding cultures and competing formulations of ultimate truth. In this new cultural pluralism, every authority to which faith may appeal is relativized, and previously composed symbols of transcendent meaning no longer have a collective resonance, as the "collective" is at once relativized and enlarged.

George Rupp, engaging precisely this set of conditions and their consequences for theological reflection, carefully notes that pluralism and the relativizing of authority are not without antecedents in other periods of history. He asserts, however, that "the pervasive and self-conscious awareness of pluralism characteristic of contemporary culture and the attempt to analyze the relativism implied in that awareness have fewer precedents."[18] In the growing awareness of a plurality of claims for allegiance, even within traditions, a great diversity of views is increasingly accessible to the individual, confounding assumed conventional faith and frustrating the task of composing responsible, self-aware commitments. This pertains to every dimension of knowing, be it "mundane" or ultimate.

In the context of such pluralism, every aspect of life choice is expanded (though not as dramatically so for the lower class). As Keniston has observed, "A medieval lad might choose between priesthood and peasantry, and this single choice almost entirely defined the rest of his life: his residence, his work, his marriage, his religion, his friends, and his values. But our society offers no such 'packaged deals,' no prefabricated and pre-assembled adulthoods which can be donned like a suit of clothes."[19] (A possible exception is the "package deal" that conventional marriage and childbearing still assumes for many women, but this "package" also is coming unwrapped in the disequilibrium of a shifting culture.)

This plurality of choice obtains also for the composing of ultimate meaning in religious terms. As Rupp states: "Perhaps the most crucial result [of the awareness of a pervasive pluralism] is that reflective believers or devotees are increasingly in the position of self-consciously having to fashion their own interpretations of the institutional forms, ritual actions, images, and ideas mediated through the tradition to which they are committed. Reflective believers are, in short, involved in the enterprise of theology or religious philosophy."[20] Everyone must become his or her own theologian in a new and disorienting array of faith choices.

Ironically, however, even as the fragmentations of pluralism multiply, an intuition of the interrelatedness of the whole of life is being manifested. In the light of growing ecological and economic awareness and of nuclear threat, not only young adults, but also older adults, are increasingly aware of the interdependence of all life—and not as a mere sentiment, but as a stark and complex reality. It is a reality that is also overwhelming. "Life intuited as a whole" now has, as its transcendent referent, not an abstract "world," but a complex and fragile planet floating in a sea of space that threatens to become a war zone. Therefore, the need to "intuit life as a whole" brings many people either to the coping mode of "modular" faith or to a powerlessness born of their awareness of overwhelming complexity. This is to say that contemporary complexity swamps the patterns of traditional faith, fragmenting conventional meaning. Culture undergoes shipwreck. In the relativizing of every authority, the human community in the contemporary world becomes, as it were, an emerging young adult.

To suggest that present cultural experience may be described as the sort of "shipwreck" that marks young adulthood is to appropriate as metaphor the model of the journey toward mature adult faith that I have developed here (see chapter 5).[21] The use of metaphor is, as discussed earlier, dependent upon recognizing the limits of any model or metaphor to interpret the richness of any life phenomenon. Models are deliberate simplifications, abstracted from the concrete. When models are appropriated as metaphors, they may at once disclose and obfuscate the richness of a phenomenon. Metaphors are useful only if they enable us to see aspects of reality that we would otherwise misunderstand.

Recognizing the limits of any metaphor, I do, nevertheless, suggest that the model of the journey of faith in adulthood developed here be appropriated as one complex image that may assist us in imagining our way through the present maze of pluralism and relativism. If psychological developmental theory brought into dialogue with a generic understanding of faith reveals something of the character of the motion of life itself, then the dynamics we find descriptive of personal transformations in faith may offer us insight into the character of the larger currents of life which they share.

We may then suggest that in the unprecedented interaction of multiple cultural shifts, the relativizing of all knowledge is occurring on a global scale. An emerging fragile but increasingly self-aware world culture stands as a "young adult" on a new threshold of knowing and being. Like the young adult, it must compose a new faith—a new sense of "self," "world," and "God."

This young-adult world is vulnerable—and also full of promise. In its dependence upon available authority, it may be exploited by "false imagination." This is to say that, as are all young adults, the emerging young adult world is vulnerable to such images as are available to the collective imagination. Likewise it is vulnerable to the abuse of any leadership that would appropriate religious language to create, maintain, and enforce a false reality (even a traditional one) rather than to disclose reality itself. But the young adult world may also be nurtured by "right imagination"—by Spirit. There is the possibility that a new and more adequate pattern of life and meaning may be composed so as to renew the whole human family.

This means that a young adult world now depends upon the mentorship of those who can embody the promise of a new world culture, adults who are able to sustain an awareness of multiple communities and tolerate, if not embrace, the felt tensions between inevitable choices. Such adult faith would be robust enough to engage the world with a confident ability to act, yet also be capable of responsiveness—participating responsibly in an interdependent process of transformation of self and other toward a yet larger communion, toward a more profound imagination of the interdependence of all life, toward a more mature faith.

If the social contract is to be recomposed, there is a need for leadership that will self-consciously participate in the formation of a new faith in which to ground it. This will require participation in a new act of imagination, critically reappropriating traditional symbols and giving birth to new images and insight.[22] As Whitehead saw so clearly, "Those societies which cannot combine reverence to their symbols with freedom of revision, must ultimately decay either from anarchy, or from the slow atrophy of a life stifled by useless shadows."[23]

Specifically, a faith that embodies the truth of interdependence as it now breaks in upon us requires that a language of interdependence must be reborn. Images of interdependent power must be made accessible to give form to and anchor our emerging intuitions of the ultimate character of reality.

Every institution increasingly feels the need for such images. People everywhere are engaged in the composing of comprehensive and more complex meaning. Reflection on the character of ultimate reality is becoming as difficult to avoid in the physical sciences and the business community as it is in theology and in religious communities.

It is the case, however, in a religiously pluralistic and secularized culture, that in every institution there are many competing languages of ultimacy. Therefore, if the institutions of culture are to address the whole of the reality that now breaks in upon us, the prevailing norms must be able to legitimate the naming—the imagining—of ultimate meanings in a plurality of languages. Only as form engages form will symbols emerge that are powerful enough that we may imagine a new, life-bearing pattern by which the human family may be recomposed.

Religious language—language that has the power "to shape into one"—must be a part of such an interdisciplinary, "multilingual" dialogue, not only because it may provide access to wisdom previously disclosed in the human story, but also because in the interchange it may itself be transformed so as to serve the promise of a new culture. When religious language enters into such dialogue, it must be recognized that every symbol, word, and ritual carries the integrity of the particular and therefore is to be engaged with reverence; simultaneously it must be held accountable to the universal and therefore must be brought under review.[24]

Yet it is precisely this tension between the integrity of the particular and accountability to the universal that confounds us and shapes our resistance to using explicit faith language in a pluralistic context. We know that it is only together that we can survive and that therefore we need a language of ultimacy we can share. We fear, however, that if we disagree at the level of ultimacy we are truly divided. Yet *any* language that functions religiously (including secular faith languages) holds our ultimacy and is, therefore, inevitably "loaded"—full of passion and spirit, full of the whole of our understanding and being, full of faith. We cannot discuss it dispassionately. Some measure of conflict is inevitable, until only by such process "initially competing claims recognize their mutual limitations."[25] Nevertheless, the courage to critically engage languages of faith will be essential to people and institutions who would offer leadership to a "young adult world" composing a new and more adequate apprehension of reality as a whole, an apprehension by which we could reorder our very lives.

A faith development perspective assists us in understanding

the character of this task. When the activity of faith is recognized as a human universal, dependent upon the role of finite images to name apprehensions of ultimacy, then we may begin to hear religious imagery, or imagery that functions religiously, in a new way. The recognition of faith as, in part, the universal task of making meaning holds the promise of enlarging our participation, compassion, and commitment in the central conversation all human beings share. To see with the eyes of faith is to see that all human beings share in the dialectic between self and other, power and powerlessness, truth and untruth, fear and confidence, hope and despair, good and evil, belonging and alienation, doubt and conviction—and that all human beings yearn to shape into one the polarities, the disparities, the terrors, and the hopes that address us within the one reality there is.

As a "young adult world" stands on a threshold of promise and vulnerability, this dialectic of faith is the infrastructure of the ambivalence, wariness, and fierce ideologies that mark this age. Rather than despair that our myths, dreams, and forms of religious faith are now in disarray and often seem empty of meaning as they are now relativized by a larger, confounding awareness, we may instead increasingly discover that perhaps the motion of life itself is at work in the ongoing act of creation.

This possibility is recognized in the ancient wisdom of a Sufi meditation upon the central symbol of Muslim faith, "There is no god, but God." Again we draw on the scholarship of Wilfred Smith, who writes:

I would mention . . . one other interpretation of the "no god, but God" phrase, one that again has been put forward by some of the mystics. This one has not been widespread, even among those; yet I mention it because I personally find it attractive, and it shows the kind of thing that can be done. This particular view is in line with the general position taken by the mystics that the religious life is a process, a movement in faith. According to this interpretation, then, the statement that "there is no god but God" is taken in stages. No one, this reading suggests, can legitimately and truly say "God" who has not previously said, and meant, "no God." To arrive at true faith, one must first pass through a stage of unbelief. "There is no God": this comes first, and must be believed through in all sincerity, and all terror. A person brought up in a religious tradition must have seen through that tradition, its forms and fancies, its shams and shibboleths; . . . must have learned the darkness of atheism and have experienced its meaninglessness and eventually its dread. Only such a person is able to go on, perhaps only years later, to a faith that is without superficiality and without merely cheap second-hand glibness. If one has said, "There is no god" with the anguish of genuine despair, one may, then, . . . go on to say, " . . . but God," and say it with the ecstasy of genuine insight.[26]

Many young adults and the young adult world in which they are coming to adulthood are perhaps undergoing the experience of unqualified relativism—the experience of "no god." The central formulations of faith—stories, symbols, rituals, religious and political myths—are unable to meditate meaning with sufficient power to anchor trust and compose commitment. We need a new faith, or more fitting connections need to be drawn between the traditional forms of faith and contemporary life. If faith is to be re-formed, if a trustworthy recognition of a fitting pattern of the interrelationships of life is to be woven, a mentoring environment must be created. Our interdependent young adult world is dependent upon older adults who respond to the invitation of this age to become mentors to a world.

In chapter 6, we recognized the power of a professor to serve as a mentor, as a spiritual guide. The true professor serves as mentor by bringing passion—the power of Spirit— to the image or insight that is transforming. If adult culture is to participate in the motion of life, which seems to be taking us individually and as a people to and across a new threshold in history, then adult culture must reconnect with its essential, vitalizing spirit so as to mentor the future.

How is this to be done? I am discovering that it is important for adults, particularly at times of potential transformation—those developmental openings termed mid-life crisis, and so on—to remember, reclaim, and renew their young adult dream.

Based on my understanding of developmental psychology and faith, I hypothesized some years ago that the "dream" forged in the cauldron of the young adult lives of the sixties might resurface. Though it appeared that the sixties generation had re-joined the establishment and had, in large measure, resumed "business as usual," it was my hypothesis that if national and international events coincided with the mid-life transitions of this sixties generation, we might see a "faithful remnant"—those who had not forgotten the dream of peace and the hope of a new relationship to the earth and to all who inhabit it, and who, in fact, still maintained a commitment to invest the energies of the self in that dream.

I believe that we saw the resurfacing of that dream in the march for peace and against nuclear proliferation in June of 1982. The dream resurfaced, and with a more mature power. Three quarters of a million people came and went from New York, and there were no major injuries. The demonstration was intentionally quiet, and there were instances of police thanking the demonstrators for coming. There was a sense that "we haven't forgotten; we know how to do this; we're needed again—and we're ready to go."

I was sharing these same observations and reflections with a group I was addressing a year ago, a group that included many older adults in their sixties and seventies. One woman responded by saying, "Yes, and 'the dream' resurfaces again when one is sixty. Some of us are ready to make good on the promises we made in the Roosevelt era." This year, when I was speaking again to the same group, I remarked that I had quoted this woman during the previous year without knowing her name and would appreciate her making herself known to me. At the end of the day a woman came to me and said, "I am not the person you spoke of, but I think I do know who said that. She is not here today, because she is in Nicaragua.''

When, in later adulthood—be that thirty-five, forty, fifty, sixty, or beyond—the young adult dream comes under re-examination and review, several dynamics must be at work. If the young adult dream is to have mature power and serve the full potential of self and world, then the dream must be *critically* re-appropriated. When these dreams, as it were, "bubble up" in the later transitions of life, their yet-unrealized potential is dependent upon the person's willingness to wrestle with them. They resurface, in any case, forcefully enough so as not to be easily ignored, but they can be either muzzled or welcomed. When they are welcomed, they must then be re-known, and the formative power they held, for better or for worse, must be recognized. The young adult dream that dwells in the older adult was formed in interaction with a particular historical era that is no more; it was formed in a particular place and circumstance in the individual's journey that has now passed. What was worthy and full of promise must be reclaimed, and what was limited and limiting—even destructive to the self and others—must be grieved for and relinquished. The wounds in which it was embedded, and the wounds it created, must be healed.

This is neither an easy nor a quick process. On the night Mondale and Ferraro were defeated in their race for the presidency, Larry Daloz, forty-four years old and a former Peace Corps volunteer, wrote in his journal:

It took me a long time to get to sleep, then I woke up and couldn't get to sleep again. The turmoil is terrific, and I need to do something about it.

There's enormous anger beneath it—and despair and frustration. There's also a lot of fear. I'm not sure where my next income is coming from—for taxes, insurance, food, or (hah!) children's education. Not a little of that is fueled by seeing the vision of all my contemporaries, of the whole nation (all fifty states!) racing ahead on the big "me-first" gravy train. . . . I staked my future on the hope that there would be money around for people like me who wanted to be able to earn a living while doing something for human beings besides get rich at their expense. . . .

But it is profoundly about a dream. I've felt hints of this for months lately, but this election is the ritual that is finally driving it home to me. The dream that sustained me, that lured me down this track that I once thought to be the main line and has turned out to be a dead-end spur, the dream of being a part of an unflaggingly virtuous and ultimately successful effort to bring about a better world, the dream is dead. That's what the despair is about. What makes it so hard is that it was the whole first half of my adult, working life! It's not that I think it was wrong—more that we have lost. And lost badly. And what has won I find agonizingly banal—worse—destructive, self-centered, self-righteous, and uncaring. . . .

What have we lost to? I'm still not sure. My head feels as though I just caught a solid right cross to the temple. I can't see well enough to focus on who hit me. We lost because apparently the people are now so thoroughly enmeshed in their own need. . . . The world has grown so complicated for our poor minds that principle cannot be distinguished from platitude. . . . But it's so hard to sustain a dream for twenty years. If we must be our own Gods, whence the strength?

All the while I'm writing this, I can hear a tiny voice talking about how I have to pick up and start again from here. I know that, and I know I will; that's the way I work. But I'm not done yet with my past. There's still a lot left to be worked through. It's not time yet to do that. I need, somehow, to purge myself of the whole dream first. It didn't work. Either it was too far out of whack with the world's capacity to make it happen, or it was too viciously opposed from directions I didn't understand well enough. . . . But it didn't happen, that's plain. And I need to let go of it.

Last night, on National Public Radio (a fragment of the dream that is dying too), I heard a commentator wryly describing a group he called the "MUDPIES," (stands for something about middle-class something) contrasting them with the YUPPIES. MUDPIES, he said, are the true '60s children who actually got out there and did something—Peace Corps, civil rights, Vista—and who haven't sold out. YUPPIES, on the other hand, are simply shallow echoes, children of the 70s who picked up some of their older siblings' values but then escaped with them to the woods and ultimately back to suburbia. The emphasis remains on the "upwardly-mobile" rather than on their vision of a possible future. It was a distinction that rang true . . . if also a bit hollow against the din of election results. . . .

But at least it reminded me of my own tribe. It's a tribe I saw part of last week when my name appeared in tiny print on a Mondale ad that a group of ex-Peace Corps Volunteers had put together. I think a lot of my despair and frustration comes of feeling, yes, my dream shattered, but also my tribe is decimated . . . The Jackson people were having all the fun last summer because they can work solely with their dream; we Hart people are constrained by the possibility that we might win. Because of that division, the agonizing gap between the vision and the creation, we all lost.

When this sort of re-examination of the dream takes place, there is the possibility that the early adult dream can be transformed into adult vision and a deepened passion; these then become the stuff that can, in turn, beckon the promise of the next generation of young adults. (Indeed, Daloz, an educator, is just completing an important book on mentoring.)[27]

When a culture's dream has exhausted its initial energy, a culture too needs a re-examination of its ideology and a reawakening of passion and imagination. This requires a recovery of spirit, a reconnection with the master currents of the soul. It requires the reassembling of the tribe—perhaps fewer, perhaps not held together so tightly, but a network of belonging, trust, and commitment in which a positive vision can thrive.[28] The renewal of adult commitment also requires a renewal of the search for right images, images more fitting to our ongoing collective experience. As has already been suggested, such images will have the capacity to give form to excellence (now more richly and compassionately understood), to the "ideal" (now understood in more complex ways), and to the motion of life—the necessity for both holding on and letting go (now more trusted). Thus will the mature adult also be able to hold and embody the wisdom of interdependence (now more self-consciously experienced).

This capacity for movement into a more self-conscious inter-dependence is perhaps the most significant strength that the mature adult has to offer to a young adult world.[29] We have exhausted the capacity of the image of the autonomous individual to serve as an image of mature adulthood. Independence alone cannot represent the character of a mature culture in the contemporary world. A deeper truth and a more adequate apprehension of reality seeks to take form among us. Those who would mentor the future will seek less to serve as individual heroes and heroines and to serve more as demonstrations of community. Young adults in his era intuitively know this and are drawn, not to individuals alone, but to communities that demonstrate a renewed vision of human possibility.

We see this recognition of the importance of interdependence in the base community movement in Latin America and the Green Movement in Europe and even, to a lesser degree, in the evangelical and fundamentalist movements in North America.[30] We see an interdependence of new knowing in the women's movement, in the civil rights movement (particularly as it takes the form of "rainbow" coalitions), in the struggle to maintain the fragile coalition of the United Nations, in "new age communities," in "co-ops," in the renewal movements of traditional religious orders, and in some new religious movements. The intuition that we need a new articulation of the interdependence of all life is seeking to find form. This is affirmed and celebrated when well-fed children in the United States sing in behalf of hungry children in Africa, "We are the world; we are the children; we are saving our own lives." In them a new consciousness may be taking form, cultivated by adult mentors who seek to recognize that life itself is at stake in the possibility of moving beyond competition between mere "egos" toward a more profound imagination.

In our political life, the press toward a more profound recognition of the interdependent reality in which we dwell is expressed in the issues of inclusion and entitlement. Though these issues ebb and flow, their persistence is a manifestation of a master current that seeks to re-join our exclusive ethic of competition, fairness, and detached justice with an ethic of connection, responsibility, and love.[31] This motion is a motion toward wisdom, toward maturity as a culture and as a world, toward the self-conscious recognition that the one who is "other" is the one to whom, inextricably, the self is related in the ecology of mutual interdependence that we all share.

A WORD TO THE RELIGIOUS COMMUNITY

It has been observed that students tend to become more "secular" during their college or university experience.[32] One university student wrote to her grandfather, "I didn't stop believing all at once; nor was it a steady continuous process. It was like a graph tracing the ups and downs of a gradually declining stock."[33] As she tells her story, one senses that as she encountered a larger world and grew in her capacity to think critically, there were fewer and fewer strong and fitting connections between the religious faith of her childhood and the experience of her life. She noticed. This is not to say that she ceased to be spiritually sensitive. In fact she would slip into the university chapel, which was "huge, dark, and cavernous . . . early in the mornings . . . or in the late afternoon, and just sit by myself. . . . Sundays I go to services . . . becoming more depressed . . . watching all those people invoking 'our help in ages past, our hope for years to come.' What help? What hope? 'The dead shall be raised?' Dad, do you really believe that? I'm fascinated by people who are able to open themselves to all the experiences life has to offer, accepting the harshness, pain, and tragedy without becoming callous or without withdrawing. Because of some elusive sustaining quality they call faith, they seem to retain their . . . humor, their humanity, and find strength to continue to fight for what they believe in. . . . I am intrigued, seduced, skeptical" (p. 29).

Like this young woman, many persons searching for faith

simply do not find a correspondence between the word, symbol, and ritual of religious life and the reality of the world in which they must dwell. If the institutions of religion are to offer leadership in the formation of a mentoring ethos for a young adult world, then the religious community must recognize that countless people have a sense of having outgrown religion in order to be truthful and faithful.[34] Religious language does not "shape into one" the disparate elements of their experience. And it is not the case that they must simply "return to the fold."

Yes, some will "return to the fold," seeking meaning on the other side of "shipwreck" or simply seeking protection in complicated times—a seeking finally betrayed when met by a faith community that cannot move into that very complexity. Others, particularly young adults, will return, as expected, "when they have children." Indeed, the religious community will do well to note that young adulthood is typically the time of the initial formation of the family; and it has been said that it is as the new parent first holds the infant that the parental soul most yearns for the "ideal" and seeks a worthy "dream." Thus children are a reason why some seek out religion, but children alone cannot secure the religious loyalty of critically aware young adults who can only set their hearts (and the hearts of their children) on that which can claim real trust and express real integrity. This is also the case for those adults who return to religion after "shipwreck" in the varied forms of doubt, divorce, and defeat.

Only if religion can demonstrate a robust capacity to "make sense" in the reality of lived experience will a young adult world recognize religious institutions as contexts for the recomposing of a faith to live by. This requires careful, critical interrogation, reappropriation, and lived engagement with the central symbols of religious faith, joining ancient insight to the issues of nuclear war, racial and economic injustice, changing sexual roles and mores, political complexity and cynicism, personal discouragement and despair, and the hunger for comfort, belonging, beauty, challenge, and delight—all the issues which shape the young adult's everyday world.[35]

This is to begin to reflect on the question, What do established religion and a young adult world now mean to each other? I suggest that just as a consciousness of the needs of young adults may serve to renew older adults, the consciousness of the needs of a young adult world may serve to reawaken religion to its deepest vocation. At a time when even highly educated people seek an oasis of security in a world they feel powerless to affect, religion will either serve as a mere haven or renew its own vocation. The vocation of religion is finally to witness to an understanding of reality in which souls have a vocation and to give form to that vocation.[36]

By *vocation*, I do not mean mere "vocationalism" as discussed earlier. Rather, I mean that the purpose of religion is to reveal a consciousness of being created for and beckoned into faithful participation in the delight, demands, and sacred mystery of the everyday. I mean by *vocation* a recognition that the essence of religious sensibility is the dependence upon more than ourselves—and the simultaneous recognition that we are needed. To recognize the interdependence of all life is to recognize that life depends on us, even as we are absolutely dependent. Frederick Buechner has provided a useful definition of vocation that reflects this double dimension.

It comes from the Latin *vocare*, to call, and means the work one is called to by God.

There are all different kinds of voices calling you to all different kinds of work, and the problem is to find out which is the voice of God rather than of Society, say, or the Superego, or Self-Interest.

By and large a good rule for finding out is this. The kind of work God usually calls you to is the kind of work (*a*) that you need most to do and (*b*) that the world most needs to have done. If you really get a kick out of your work, you've presumably met requirement (*a*), but if your work is writing TV deodorant commercials, the chances are you've missed requirement (*b*). On the other hand, if your work is being a doctor in a leper colony, you have probably met requirement (*b*), but if most of the time you're bored and depressed by it, the chances are you have not only bypassed (*a*) but probably aren't helping your patients much either.

Neither the hair shirt nor the soft berth will do. The place God calls you to is the place where your deep gladness and the world's deep hunger meet.[37]

The deep hunger of a young adult world is for a dream that reveals the work that we are called to by God. The deep gladness of the religious faith community is to be found in a vocation formed in response to that hunger. When the dominant image of the future is a mushroom cloud, a young adult world asks religious institutions to pose an alternative imagination and to serve as mentoring communities.[38] The religious community can offer access to images of promise, for it knows the way of shipwreck, gladness, and amazement. But religion can only mentor the future when it does not obscure this knowledge by confining it in Authority-bound forms. Religion that effectively mentors young adults is ever a pilgrim in faith, open to doubt and ambiguity, leading out with an authority, not of assumed established structures, but rather of competent, committed, passionate visions—as Jews and Christians have expressed it, a vision of the Kingdom, or better, a vision of the Commonwealth of God.

Culture is dependent upon the competence of religion to form and to practice the images and rituals that have the power to beckon, hold, sustain, and renew the promise of emerging life and to nurture it into forms of justice and love.[39] This means offering leadership in the ongoing weaving of faith as the fabric of life itself—pulling through the true and bright threads of the past to make it strong, yet exercising the courage to weave more complex patterns than we have known before.[40]

Religion has historically, in fact, demonstrated a certain genius for mentoring young adults. Traditionally religious orders in particular provided for young adults an identity, a community of confirmation, a mentor, a mentoring community, images of the "ideal," of excellence, and of personal and social transformation. Religious orders asked for commitment to a task that one was "called to by God." Religious orders at once stood over-against society to critique and save it and provided a recognized role within society. Religious vision and commitment offered a way into the future that could capture the imagination of the young adult soul, and religious orders self-consciously accompanied the yet dependent young adult on the journey toward mature adult faith. It may be observed that missionary movements and the so-called new religious movements represent similar dynamics (as do the military and the Peace Corps, though with some significant differences).

If religious formation is again to beckon young adults in this culture, it may require the very sort of critical reflection we have been suggesting here: a rich dialogue between the Story of religious communities and a Vision of the needs of the world as it could become. Critically aware young adults may require new translations of "obedience"; forms of religious community may need to reflect more interdependence (community) and less hierarchy (Authority-bound structures); and the purposes and practices of religious vocation must appear to respond to "the world's deep hunger" while demonstrating a style of life and a joy that reflects "the heart's deep gladness." Further, the whole self must be addressed in a way that promises belonging, vocation, and wholeness, albeit in a variety of forms.

As a specific example, in the contemporary world, the linking of religious vocation with one particular form of sexual expression is dubious. In Christianity, for Roman Catholics, vowed celibacy is a condition of formal religious vocation. Likewise, Protestant churches have tended to divide young adults into groups labeled married and single. In so doing, the religious community has defined participation in the religious life by forms of marital status rather than first by "the work that God calls us to do." Though issues of sexual identity and interpersonal intimacy are integral to young adult formation, they are most meaningfully addressed within the confidence and trust that one participates first in the creative and redemptive activity of God—a vocation requiring the interdependent faithfulness of all persons, single, married, or vowed to celibacy.

This is to say that religious leadership needs to recover and teach the disciplines by which both particular religious cultures and the larger culture may distinguish between the habits of the culture that lead to isolation and deadness and those that lead to communion and aliveness.[41] This suggests a renewal of spiritual life that is not escapist but flows from a renewed engagement with the life of the *polis* (the body politic) and the *cosmos* (the natural environment).[42] Such a renewal includes the discipline of theology—that is, critical reflection upon what we mean by "God" and, therefore, how we may recognize "idols," the products of the erroneous imagination. However, this discipline shall not be thought of as the function only of "experts" (professional theologians). Rather, it is the work of the whole community of faith.

That young adults become natural theologians has been acknowledged by religion. Throughout our history, religious faith communities have not simply sent young adults "off to college" but have recognized the mentoring responsibility of religion by establishing not only religious orders, but also colleges, seminaries, universities, and campus ministry centers. These institutions have a venerable history of making accessible to young adult souls a set of images and symbols that generations before them have found worthy for the composing and recomposing of faith, thereby initiating young adults into a community's vision of faithful adulthood.[43] The motivations have been at least two: One has been a commitment to the formation of young adults into a disciplined discernment of truth as a profoundly religious activity. The other, however, has been, in effect, a protectionism that has not encouraged the journey from Authority-bound, dependent, and dualistic faith to an inner- or interdependent form of faith. The boundaries between these motivations have often, of course, been less than clear,[44] so that, though some schools represent essentially one or the other of these types, today many "religiously affiliated" schools find it difficult to know how to maintain both religious faith commitments and academic integrity.

Sharing in the vulnerability of all academies to departmentalizing and competition, these schools likewise may have few occasions for a collective and critical engagement with issues of ultimate meaning, occasions when the faith of both faculty and students might be recomposed. It is sometimes the case that the primary images of ultimacy taught through the hidden curriculum of the religiously affiliated school are essentially the same as in other institutions: upward mobility, certified by a college or university degree, will ensure professional achievement and protect from shipwreck. Yet it is the opportunity and privilege of the faculty of these schools to self-consciously, collectively, and critically sponsor inquiry into the issues of the contemporary world that concern us ultimately and to do so in such a way as to accompany the young adult in a critical and compelling re-examination of the traditions of faith, discovering together those images that have the capacity to sustain and to enhance the promise of life for all. It has been said that tradition and conscience are the wings given to the soul to reach the truth.[45] Religiously committed schools may profess a tradition in a manner that stifles the moral imagination or nourishes a vitality that awakens the critical conscience of the young adult, creating the most profound conditions of the search for truth.

All of what I have suggested here finally necessitates an openness to critical, creative dialogue with every religious tradition in the service of a renewed religious imagination. Religiously committed institutions must now engage the full range of religious experience in which contemporary young adults search for faith—creating dialogue with religions other than their own that now inevitably shape the confusion and hope of the young adult. Given a shrinking planet and a religiously pluralistic culture, young adults now wander and wonder among many religious traditions. Particularly as young adults are initially exploring beyond the safe harbor of their own religious port, new vessels may extend their experience of the faith journey and offer a new perspective from which to reflect upon and to know one's own heritage. In any case, young adults increasingly seek mentors who know that in an ecumenical world the flow of images is richer for all of us but who at the same time can assist in distinguishing between the forms that lead to life and the forms that distort and destroy.

Finally, and above all, religious vision must be re-joined with act. This means that because faith must be embodied, religious people must reveal the power of their Story and Vision in the forms of their common everyday life. Only then does a new generation of young adults find in religion the satisfaction of its search for vivifying images by which to name self, world, and God. The "real food" by which young adults will be nourished is an image of the future—the Commonwealth of God and a vocation within it—that is demonstrated in the lives of faithful and mentoring adults.

Miguel de Unamuno has suggested that the temple is the place where we go to weep in common.[46] The faith community can serve as a place where the pain and hurt of contemporary life is comforted and where collective sin is acknowledged and lamented. But the religious faith community must also serve as an open, public space[47] where we not only weep in common but also imagine together. The young adult needs the religious community, like the academy, to be a community of imagination. In fact, the young adult and the academy might rightly discover that the faith community demonstrates what the discipline and practice of such a community might be, so as to offer leadership to both the young adult and the academy. Mike Bloy wrote, "It is precisely the presence of faithful Jews and Christians in academic institutions, openly living the richly communal life God has given them, which can bring a steady, healing challenge to the demonic forces of atomistic individualism which more and more possess academic life." He then observes that such communities are marked by spiritual discipline, moral engagement, theological reflection, and collegial leadership.[48]

All of this is to suggest that there is a potential, though still inadequately realized, for renewal of dialogue between religion and the academy, institutions necessarily interdependent in their responsibility for the formation of faithful truth.[49]

YOUNG ADULTS AND MENTORS: PARTNERS IN CREATING THE FUTURE

But if either culture in general, or higher education and religion in particular, is to mentor the faith that will ground a positive human future, we must renew the dialectic with the promise of the young adult. It is in the restored motion of self and other, adult and young adult—a motion seeking form in fitting images—that we reorder and strengthen the shape of our hope.

In the interdependence of meaning-making, the mentor needs the protégé as much as the protégé needs the mentor. The generativity of the adult is dependent upon meaningful, faithful connection with the next generation. To accompany the young adult in faith can mean a reawakening of one's own potential for compassion, excellence, and vocation. A recognition of the promise of the young adult may have the power to beckon the spirit and the dreams of weary, routinized, cynical, numbed adults, who may respond with a renewal of passion and vision so as to serve as a beacon for the future. History, as well as psychological theory, shows that young adults have a particular capacity to see that beacon. By embodying both passion for the ideal and a willingness to give energy only to what appears worthy, young adults, in both their promise and their vulnerability, hold the power to give form to emerging possibilities for all life—a power dependent upon the faithful imagination of older adults who embody a generous, mature, and mentoring adulthood.

APPENDIX A

Faith Stages by Aspects

ASPECT STAGE	A. Form Of Logic (Piaget)	B. Perspective Taking (Selman)	C. Form of Moral Judgment (Kohlberg)	D. Bound of Social Awareness	E. Focused Authority	F. Form of World Coherence	G. Symbolic Function
I.	Preoperational	Rudimentary empathy (egocentric)	Punishment-reward	Family, primal others	Attachment/dependence relationships. Size, power, visible symbols of authority	Episodic	Magical-Numinous
II.	Concrete Operational	Simple perspective taking	Instrumental hedonism (Reciprocal fairness)	"Those like us" (in familial, ethnic, racial, class, and religious terms)	Incumbents of authority roles, salience increased by personal relatedness	Narrative-Dramatic	One-dimensional; literal
III.	Early Formal Operations	Mutual interpersonal	Interpersonal expectations and concordance	Composite of groups in which one has interpersonal relationships	Consensus of valued groups and in personally worthy representatives of belief, value, traditions	Tacit system, felt meanings, symbolically mediated, globally held	Symbols multi-dimensional, evocative power inheres in symbol
IV	Formal Operations (Dichotomizing)	Mutual, with self-selected group or class— (societal)	Societal perspective. Reflective, relativism or class-biased universalism	Ideologically compatible communities with congruence to self-chosen norms and insights	One's own judgment as informed by a self-ratified ideological perspective. Authorities and norms must be congruent with this.	Explicit system, conceptually mediated, clarity about boundaries and inner connections of system	Symbols separated from symbolized Translated (reduced) to ideations Evocative power inheres in *meaning* conveyed by symbols.

V.	Formal Operations (Dialectical)	Mutual with groups, classes and traditions "other" than one's own	Prior to society, Principled higher law (universal and critical)	Extends beyond class norms and interests. Disciplined ideological vulnerability to "truths" and vulnerability to "truths" and "claims" of outgroups and other tradition.	Dialectical joining of judgment, experience, processes, with reflective claims of others and of various expressions of cumulative human wisdom	Multi-systemic symbols and conceptual mediation	Postcritical rejoining of irreducible symbolic power and relational meaning. Evocative power inherent in the reality in and beyond symbol *and* in the power of unconscious processes in the self.
VI.	Formal Operations (Synthetic)	Mutual with the commonwealth of being	Loyalty to being	Identification with the species. Transnarcissistic love of being	In a personal judgment informed by the experiences and truths of previous stages, purified of egoic striving and linked by disciplined intuition to the principle of being.	Unitive actuality felt and participated unity of "One beyond the many"	Evocative power of symbols actualized through unification of reality mediated by symbols and the self.

Source: James Fowler, *Stages of Faith: The Psychology of Human Development and the Quest for Meaning* (San Francisco: Harper & Row, 1981), pp. 244-5.

APPENDIX B

Faith Development from Adolescence to Mature Adulthood

	Adolescent (Conventional)		Young Adult	Adult	Mature Adult
Form of Cognition	Authority-bound Dualistic	Unqualified Relativism (Transitional)	Probing Commitment	Tested Commitment	Confirmed Commitment
Form of Dependence	Dependent/Counter-Dependent		Fragile Self-Dependence	Confident Self-Dependence	Interdependence
Form of Community	Conventional	Diffuse	Ideologically Compatible Communities (Mentoring)	Self-Selected Class or Group (Within world-as-it-is)	Open to "others"
Form of Self	Derivative		Self-Aware (Ambivalent)	Self-Reflective (Centered)	Wise-hearted
Locus of Authority	"Those Who Count" (Outside the self)		Spokespersons or Group Procedures (Validated by self)	Self (Validated by group)	Dialectic between self and selves in other groups
Form of Logic	Early Formal Operations		Full Formal Operations (Dichotomizing; Collapsing)	Full Formal Operations (Dichotomizing; Maintaining tension)	Full Formal Operations (Dialectical-Paradoxical)
Form of World Coherence	Tacit System		Explicit System ("Over-against")	Explicit System (World engaging)	Multi-Systemic
Terms of the Structure of the World	Interpersonal		"Ideal"	Pragmatic/Ideal	Integration of Pragmatic & Ideal
Form of Role-Taking	Mutual ("Third-person perspective")		Mutual (Within "ideal" community)	Mutual (With awareness of groups other than one's own)	Mutual (With groups other than one's own)
Form of Moral Judgment	Conventional (Objective truth-interpersonal-social system)		Explicit/Ideal (Contextual Relativism)	(Ethical Responsibility—Gilligan) (Principled Ethical—Kohlberg)	
(Fowler Stage)	Three		Three-Four	Four	Five

Sharon Parks–The Critical Years: The Young Adult Search for a Faith to Live By

Notes

INTRODUCTION

1. Meaning is, broadly speaking, the awareness of connectedness, importance, and "felt significance" among perceived objects both external and internal and is, narrowly speaking, the attribution of positive value to a particular configuration of attitudes, ideals, and connections that stand close to the center of one's identity and provide the key to judging importance in relation to time, persons, and events. Adapted from William R. Rogers, "Defense and Loss of Meaning" (Paper delivered to the Society for the Scientific Study of Religion, Philadelphia, 1976), p. 8.
2. William Perry, private communication. See also Robert Kegan, *The Evolving Self: Problem and Process in Human Development* (Cambridge: Harvard University Press, 1982), p. 11.
3. "New England's First Fruits," quoted in S. E. Morrison, *The Founding of Harvard College* (Cambridge, Mass., 1935, p. 168.) *See also* Perry Miller, *The New England Mind: The Seventeenth Century* (Cambridge: Harvard University Press, 1939), pp. 75–76

CHAPTER 1—THE ELUSIVENESS OF ADULTHOOD

1. Robert T. Gribbon, "Will They Come Back When They're Thirty Years Old?" *Alban Institute Action Information*, Mount St. Alban, Washington, D.C., Mar.–Apr. 1981.
2. Erik Erikson wrote: "In postulating a 'latency period' which precedes puberty, psychoanalysis has given recognition to some kind of psychosexual moratorium in human development—a period of delay which permits the future mate and parent first to go to whatever 'school' his [or her] culture provides and to learn the technical and social rudiments of a work situation. The libido theory, however, offers no adequate account of a second period of delay, namely prolonged adolescence. Here the sexually matured individual is more or less retarded in his [or her] psychosexual capacity for intimacy and in the psychosocial readiness for parenthood. This period can be viewed as a *psychosocial moratorium* during which the young adult through free role experimentation may find a niche in some section of his [or her] society, a niche which is firmly defined and yet seems to be uniquely made for him [or her]." *Identity: Youth and Crisis* (New York: Norton, 1968), p. 156. The concept of regression was used by Kohlberg to describe phenomena observed in later adolescence. See Lawrence Kohlberg and Carol Gilligan, "The Adolescent as a Philosopher: The Discovery of the Self in a Postconventional World," *Daedalus*, vol. 100,

no. 4 (Fall 1971). The term *equilibrated transitional* appeared in James W. Fowler, "Faith and the Structuring of Meaning" (Paper delivered at the convention of the American Psychological Association, Symposium on Faith and Moral Development, San Francisco, August 26, 1977), p. 20.

3. Within the discipline of constructive-developmental psychology, Carol Gilligan has most forcefully drawn attention to the importance of being alert to the power of "discrepant data" to serve as a methodological principle by which distorting research assumptions might be addressed. See Carol Gilligan, *In a Different Voice: Psychological Theory and Women's Development* (Cambridge: Harvard University Press, 1982). See also chap. 3, this work.

4. Douglas C. Kimmel, *Adulthood and Aging* (New York: Wiley, 1974), p. 12.

5. Daniel Levinson, *The Seasons of a Man's Life* (New York: Knopf, 1978), p. 28.

6. See Bernice L. Neugarten, "Adult Personality: Toward a Psychology of the Life Cycle," in *Middle Age and Aging: A Reader in Social Psychology*, ed. Bernice L. Neugarten (Chicago: Univ. of Chicago Press, 1968).

CHAPTER 2—MEANING-MAKING: AN ACTIVITY OF FAITH

1. The first four definitions offered in *Webster's New World Dictionary*, 2d college ed., s.v. "faith" are "(1) unquestioning belief that does not require proof or evidence; (2) unquestioning belief in God, religious tenets, etc.; (3) a religion or a system of religious belief (the Catholic *faith*); (4) anything believed." Only the final two definitions depart from the sense of faith as belief, defining faith as "(5) complete trust, confidence, or reliance; (6) allegiance to some person or thing." The synonym offered for faith is *belief*.

2. Wilfred Cantwell Smith, *Belief and History* (Charlottesville, Va.: University Press of Virginia, 1977), pp. 41–45.

3. William F. Lynch, *Images of Faith: An Exploration of the Ironic Imagination* (Notre Dame, Ind.: Univ. of Notre Dame Press, 1973), p. 9. According to Viktor Frankl, "The human being's search for meaning is a primary force in his or her life and not a 'secondary rationalization' of instinctual drives. . . . There are some authors who contend that meaning and values are 'nothing but defense mechanisms, reaction formations and sublimations.' But as for myself, I would not be willing to live merely for the sake of my 'defense mechanisms,' nor would I be ready to die merely for the sake of my 'reaction formation.' Human beings, however, are able to live and even to die for the sake of their ideals and values! A poll of public opinion was conducted a few years ago in France. The results showed that 89% of the people polled admitted that human beings need 'something' for the sake of which to live. Moreover, 61% conceded that there was something, or someone, in their own lives for whose sake they were even ready to die. I repeated this poll at my clinic in Vienna among both the patients and the personnel, and the outcome was practically the same as among the thousands of people screened in France; the difference was only 2%. In other words, the will to meaning is in most people *fact*, not

faith" (language modified to be inclusive). *Man's Search for Meaning: An Introduction to Logotherapy* (New York: Washington Square Press, 1959, 1963), pp. 154–55.

4. Lynch, *Images of Faith*, p. 125.

5. Charles Spezzano, "Prenatal Psychology: Pregnant with Questions," *Psychology Today*, May 1981, pp. 49–57.

6. H. Richard Niebuhr, also pointing toward this sense of faith as primal promise, writes: "There is in the background of existence whether as memory of childhood, or as platonic recollection of something heard in another existence, or as an echo of an inner voice, the sense of something glorious, splendid, clean, and joyous for which this being and all being is intended. . . . This promise of life is the promise of glory and splendor." But, he then writes, "to our personal life which begins with such a sense of promised brightness there comes, whether in childhood or adolescence or later, the great disillusionment." "Faith on Earth," quoted in James W. Fowler, *To See the Kingdom: The Theological Vision of H. Richard Niebuhr* (Nashville: Abingdon Press), 1974, p. 223.

In religious ritual marking the birth of a child, Jewish and Christian communities of faith gather around the new little one and, in a variety of forms, address the child as child of the covenant or child of the promise. The community of faith thereby affirms its own discovery that on the other side of chaos the promise is restored. James Fowler, building on the insights of Erik Erikson, George Herbert Mead, and Harry Stack Sullivan, has also recognized the foundations of faith in the mutuality achieved in a relationship marked by trust in a primary giver of care. As the infant comes to trust and rely upon the consistency and care of the parent, he or she also comes to feel a sense of trustworthiness in the self, which becomes a harbinger of a later ability to commit the self and to invest loyalty. James W. Fowler, "Faith and the Structuring of Meaning," in *Toward Moral and Religious Maturity*, (Morristown, N.J.: Silver Burdette, 1980), p. 54.

7. Erik Erikson, *Childhood and Society*, 2d ed. (New York: Norton, 1963), pp. 247–51.

8. Jim Fowler and Sam Keen, *Life Maps: Conversations on the Journey of Faith*, ed. Jerome Berryman (Waco, Tex.: Word Books, 1978), pp. 17–21, and James W. Fowler, *Stages of Faith: The Psychology of Human Development and the Quest for Meaning* (San Francisco: Harper & Row, 1981), p. 24 ff., and chap. 12. See also H. Richard Niebuhr, *Radical Monotheism* (London: Faber & Faber, 1943), p. 45.

9. H. Richard Niebuhr, *Radical Monotheism*, p. 24.

10. Ibid., p. 25. Wilfred Smith perceives that, from this broad phenomonological perspective of faith, a "true atheist" would be one "who loves no one and whom no one loves; who does not care for truth, sees no beauty, strives for no justice; who knows no courage and no joys, finds no meaning, and has lost all hope." *Faith and Belief* (Princeton: Princeton University Press, 1979), p. 20.

11. See Sharon Lea Parks, "Faith Development and Imagination in the Context of Higher Education" (Th.D. diss., Harvard University, 1980), p. 42. Note also that the potential of "polytheism" to serve a positive

psychological function is not addressed here, nor is the question of whether "monotheism" is necessarily an exclusive dynamic or a dynamic dependent upon fullness and inclusion. See James Hillman, *Re-Visioning Psychology* (San Francisco: Harper & Row, 1977).

12. Smith, *Faith and Belief*, p. 13.

13. H. Richard Niebuhr, *Radical Monotheism*, p. 29.

14. Ibid., pp. 24–39. Standing in this same intellectual tradition, Gordon Kaufman writes: "God has been a center of devotion and service which could draw selves and communities out of themselves, thus overcoming the warfare of a thousand centers each attempting to order everything in its own terms, and opening up human life to structures of order and meaning otherwise outside its reach." *The Theological Imagination: Constructing the Concept of God* (Philadelpha: Westminster Press, 1981), p. 36.

15. For the phrase "both ultimate and intimate" I am indebted to James Luther Adams (Invocation at the ordination of Suzanne Spencer, King's Chapel, Boston, April 1985).

16. H. Richard Niebuhr, W.C. Smith, and James Fowler are all ambiguous on this point. They appropriate the word *faith* to connote all human "sense-making"; they also appropriate the word *faith* to point specifically toward meaning-making that is transcendent in character, the organizing of one's sense of ultimacy. (Note that this point is related to the tension discussed earlier between transcendence and immanence.) Niebuhr recognizes faith as a human universal, in that all human beings are engaged in composing the canvas of existence. Smith follows, suggesting that "in this sense perhaps no human being is, ever has been utterly without faith although some have in despondence come at times close to that bleakness." *Faith and Belief*, p. 20; see also p. 13. But Smith also specifically speaks of faith as "a capacity to live at a more than mundane level; to see, to act, to feel, in terms of a transcendent dimension" (p. 12). Fowler also represents both impulses. On one hand, he speaks of the fiduciary structures that permeate all of human knowing and being—faith is a human universal in the sense that all human beings must construct a "world." Yet he also speaks of faith as "the binding of the self and the transcendent . . . the awareness, the intuition, the conviction of a relatedness to something or someone more than the mundane." And further, "Faith is the knowing or construing by which persons apprehend themselves as related to the transcendent." Fowler, "Stages in Faith," in *Values and Moral Development*, ed. Thomas C. Hennessy, S.J. (New York: Paulist Press, 1976), p. 175. It is perhaps best to say that "faith" is manifest in even "mundane" forms, but our concern here is with the recognition of faith in its transcendent and transforming dimensions. The tension that is integral to understanding faith as a human universal lies in the questions, If one composes a faith that is trustworthy, is it true? If one composes an ultimacy that is not trustworthy, is it faith? Smith describes faith in its fullest manifestation as "a quality of human living. At its best it has taken the form of serenity and courage and loyalty and service: a quiet confidence and joy which enables one to feel at home in the universe, and to find meaning in the world and in one's own life, a meaning that is profound and ultimate and is stable no matter what may happen to oneself at the level of

immediate event. Men and women of this kind of faith face catastrophe and confusion, affluence and sorrow, unperturbed; face opportunity with conviction and drive; and face others with a cheerful charity." *Faith and Belief,* p. 12.

17. Smith, *Faith and Belief,* p. 61.

18. (Language modified to be inclusive.) Ibid., pp. 65–66. For implications for education in communities of faith, see Sara Little, *To Set One's Heart: Belief and Teaching in the Church* (Atlanta: John Knox Press, 1983), chaps. 2, 3.

19. Reflecting this recognition of the relationship between action or behavior and faith, Richard R. Niebuhr writes: "So wherever and whenever we see persons giving themselves for that which is greater than themselves and greater than all the particular forces impinging upon them, there we meet faithful [faith-full] human beings" (language modified to be inclusive). *Experiential Religion* (New York: Harper & Row, 1972), p. 39.

20. See ibid., p. 42. Fowler is fully cognizant of this. He writes: "We choose and act (and/or find explanations or rationales for our acts) with reference to our assumptions or convictions about the character of power and value in an ultimate environment." "Stages in Faith," p. 178. But he has focused on faith as composing ultimate meaning. He has not given as much attention to faith as act. Nor has he made much effort to distinguish between them. But in the total gestalt of human faith, it is important to recognize the observable act—be it mundane or heroic—as a crucial dimension. For an extended discussion of faith as act and its implications for religious education see Thomas H. Groome, *Christian Religious Education: Sharing Our Story and Vision* (San Francisco: Harper & Row, 1980).

21. Lynch, *Images of Faith,* p. 39.

22. "The Furies insert themselves in a terrible way into human affairs precisely where the greatest faith has been violated, where a mighty word has been given but is now betrayed. In every case the Fury attacks the violator of a *word* written out in the most primitive and earthly forms of nature, the form of mother, who is word to her child, the form of wife, the form of friend, the form of father. All these forms are words carved out in the deepest realities of nature itself, making promises without opening the lips and demanding belief for very survival's sake. . . . The energy and power of human faith become visible in the size of this fury. We tend to reduce faith to a sweet pious dimension, weak rival and challenger of knowledge. We know it better than that through its embodiment in fury. And through its incarvement, without words, in the very deepest structures of human life. Aristotle knew this well in *The Poetics* when he chose these violations of kinship and fidelity as the most tragic forms of tragedy. They are." Ibid., pp. 39–40.

23. Richard R. Niebuhr, *Experiential Religion,* pp. 42–43. See also Miguel de Unamuno, *Tragic Sense of Life,* trans. J. Flitch (New York: Dover, 1954; first published 1921), chap. 8.

24. Ibid., pp. 91–104.

25. The tragic outcome of some individual lives challenges a notion of faith as a dynamic of shipwreck, gladness, and amazement. My own reflections on this matter in relation to young adulthood are tugged into discipline and mystery by the suicide of one of my close friends when we were

twenty-eight. The question that suffering and death poses to us is, Is there a frame of meaning large enough and adequate enough to embrace and hold suffering and death? Moreover, it is the threats to meaning that confront us on the scale of collective experience that most challenge any cursory affirmation of the dynamic described here as faith. Specifically, the task of making meaning at the level of shared human experience has been almost overwhelmingly confounded by the suffering of Jews and others in the holocaust in Europe, and compounded further by the recognition that this holocaust represents other "holocausts" in other times and places. Yet it is holocaust sufferers themselves who confront us with some of the most compelling examples of the capacity of the human spirit to reconstitute meaning of the most profound integrity. Viktor Frankl, a holocaust survivor, has written, "But not only creativeness and enjoyment are meaningful. If there is a meaning in life at all, then there must be a meaning in suffering. Suffering is an ineradicable part of life, even as fate and death. Without suffering and death human life cannot be complete." *Man's Search for Meaning*, p. 106. See also the writings of Elie Wiesel; *An Interrupted Life: The Diaries of Etty Hillesum*, trans. Arno Pomerans (New York: Pantheon Books, 1983); and William R. Rogers, "Order and Chaos in Psychopathology and Ontology: A Challenge to Traditional Correlations of Order to Mental Health and Ultimate Reality, and of Chaos to Mental Illness and Alienation," in *The Dialogue Between Theology and Psychology*, ed. P. Homans (Chicago: University of Chicago Press, 1968).

26. James Carroll, *A Terrible Beauty* (New York: Newman Press, 1973), p. 102.
27. William F. Lynch, *Images of Faith*, p. 25.
28. "Affection . . . refers to a much more encompassing phenomenon of the life of the mind in the body, a phenomenon that the German language designates by the word *Stimmung*, which the English language can best render as attunement. The attunement of the self is the basic and all-including frame of mind that gives to the whole of personal existence its determinate quality, color, and tone. An affection, so conceived, is not a specific response to a stimulus or object. . . . Rather, it tempers the rapid succession of stimulae and responses in personal existence and superimposes on them a degree and quality of *order*" (emphasis added). Richard R. Niebuhr, *Experiential Religion*, pp. 44–45. It is also to be noted that Robert Kegan and James Fowler have each insisted that "in faith the 'rational' and the 'passional' are fused." Fowler and Keen, *Life Maps*, p. 37.
29. See Robert Kegan, *The Evolving Self: Problem and Process in Human Development* (Cambridge: Harvard University Press, 1982), pp. 121–32.

CHAPTER 3—DEVELOPMENTAL THEORIES: INSIGHTS INTO THE MOTION OF FAITH

1. Robert Ellsberg, ed., *By Little and by Little: The Selected Writings of Dorothy Day* (New York: Knopf, 1983).
2. Laura Wood Roper, *FLO: A Biography of Frederick Law Olmsted* (Baltimore: Johns Hopkins University Press, 1973), p. 37.

3. *Webster's New Collegiate Dictionary*, "psych– or psycho–: Greek, from *psyche*, breath, principle of life, soul, or spirit." See also Bruno Bettleheim, *Freud and Man's Soul* (New York: Knopf, 1983).

4. The fact that developmental psychology has been established by two "grandfathers" should appropriately invoke a feminist suspicion and critique. The field has been dominated by male theorists and suffers from the distortion inevitably arising when theories of human experience are composed by persons of a single gender. The most influential address to this distortion to date is the work of Carol Gilligan and her associates. See *In a Different Voice: Psychological Theory and Women's Development* (Cambridge: Harvard University Press, 1982). *See also* Mary Belenky, et. al; *Women's Ways of Knowing: The Development of Mind, Voice and Self* (New York: Basic Books, 1986). Developmental psychology has yet to be as adequately critiqued through the categories of race and class. See John Broughton, "The Political Psychology of Faith," in *Faith and Development: Critical Reflections on James Fowler's Theory of Faith Development*, ed. Dykstra and Parks (Religious Education Press, forthcoming).

5. Daniel Yankelovich and William Barrett, *Ego and Instinct: The Psychoanalytic View of Human Nature* (New York: Vintage, 1971), p. 21, quoted in Gil Noam, Lawrence Kohlberg, and John Snarey, "Steps Toward a Model of the Self," in *Developmental Approach to the Self*, ed. B. Lee and G. Noam (New York: Plenum Press, 1984).

6. Erik Erikson, "The Eight Ages of Man," *Childhood and Society*, 2d ed. (New York: Norton, 1963), chap. 7. See also a fictional conversation between Erikson, Piaget, and Kohlberg in James W. Fowler, *Stages of Faith: The Psychology of Human Development and the Quest for Meaning* (San Francisco: Harper & Row, 1981), chap. 6.

7. For a helpful discussion of Kant's influence on Piaget, see Gabriel Moran, *Religious Education Development: Images for the Future* (Minneapolis: Winston Press, 1983), pp. 47–58. For a rich discussion of the evolution of social science, past and future, see Alexandra Hepburn, "The Interpretive Turn in Social Science" (Ph.D. diss., University of Penn., 1982).

8. Emily Souvaine, Lisa Laslow Lahey, and Robert Kegan, "Life After Formal Operations: Implications for a Psychology of the Self," in *Beyond Formal Operations*, ed. E. Langer and C. Alexander (New York: Oxford University Press, forthcoming), p. 8.

9. The differences in the experience of the child and the adolescent are shaped, in part, by their differing capacity to hold the perspective of another. An achievement of concrete operational thought is the capacity to take the perspective of another, a feat that Robert Selman terms "second person perspective taking." But the child cannot hold his or her *own* perspective while taking the perspective of another. The development of formal operational thought creates the capacity or structure by which it is possible to do "third person perspective taking"—holding in mind the perspective of two or more points of view simultaneously as from the position of a third person. See Robert L. Selman, *The Growth of Interpersonal Understanding: Developmental and Clinical Analyses* (New York: Academic Press, 1980), pp. 23–47.

10. Jean Piaget, "Time and Intellectual Development," in *The Child and Reality: Problems of Genetic Psychology*, trans. Arnold Rosin (New York, Grossman,

1973), chap. 1. See also Gil Noam, "Stage, Phase, and Style: The Developmental Dynamics of the Self," in *Moral Education*, ed. M. Berkowitz and F. Oser (New Jersey: Earl Baum Assoc., 1985).

11. Robert Kegan, "There the Dance Is: Religious Dimensions of a Developmental Framework," in *Toward Moral and Religious Maturity*, (Morristown, N.J.: Silver Burdette, 1980), p. 407. See also *The Evolving Self: Problem and Process in Human Development* (Cambridge: Harvard University Press, 1982).

12. "It may well also be the essence of what we really mean by 'understanding,' to 'stand *under*,' to hold or suspend, rather than to be 'caught in,' or 'a part of.' This motion is the basic 'logic of development,' a question of to what extent the elements of one's knowing and experiencing are *taken as object* and so can be reflected upon, and to what extent one is *subject to* them in one's knowing and experiencing." Souvaine, Lahey, and Kegan, "Life After Formal Operations," p. 2.

13. Carol Gilligan, *In a Different Voice*. See also chap. 5, this work.

14. Lawrence Kohlberg, *The Philosophy of Moral Development: Moral Stages and the Idea of Justice* (San Francisco: Harper & Row, 1981), esp. chap. 5 and pp. 409–412.

15. Carol Gilligan, "Remapping the Moral Domain: New Images of Self in Relationship" (Paper presented at the conference "Reconstructing Individualism," Stanford Humanities Center, Feb. 18-20, 1984). The example from the children's play was given to Gilligan by Anne Glickman, mother of the boy.

16. Kegan, "There the Dance Is," p. 409.

17. Ibid., p. 410. See also Kegan, *The Sweeter Welcome: Voices for a Vision of Affirmation: Bellow, Malamud and Martin Buber* (Needham Heights, Mass.: Wexford Press, 1977).

18. James W. Fowler, *Stages of Faith: The Psychology of Human Development and the Quest for Meaning* (San Francisco: Harper & Row, 1981). See also Jim Fowler and Sam Keen, *Life Maps: Conversations on the Journey of Faith*, ed. Jerome Berryman (Waco, Tex.: Word Books, 1979).

19. William G. Perry, *Forms of Intellectual and Ethical Development in the College Years: A Scheme* (New York: Holt, Rinehart & Winston, 1968). See also Sharon Bauer-Breakstone, "Seeing Students from Diverse Backgrounds Through the Perry Lens, and Vice Versa" (Unpublished paper, Bureau of Study Counsel, Harvard University, June 1983).

20. See David Bakan, *The Duality of Human Existence* (Chicago: Rand McNally, 1966), pp. 4–5.

CHAPTER 4—THE JOURNEY TOWARD MATURE ADULT FAITH: A MODEL

Edgar Lee Masters, *Spoon River Anthology* (New York: MacMillan, 1976), p. 65.

1. This "strand" image, which Selman attributes to Jane Loevinger, is a theoretical approach that "construes ego development as consisting of various conceptual domains, each with its own set of interrelated stages. . . . The notion of different concept domains does not imply that

ego development occurs without some unifying, binding force." Robert Selman, "Social Cognitive Understanding: A Guide to Educational and Clinical Practice," *Moral Development and Behavior*, ed. T. Lickona (New York: Holt, Rinehart & Winston, 1976), p. 316.

2. William G. Perry, *Forms of Intellectual and Ethical Development in the College Years: A Scheme* (New York: Holt, Rinehart & Winston, 1968).

3. Quotation from author's research interviews, available with permission from Whitworth College Library Archives, Spokane, Washington.

4. Perry, *Intellectual and Ethical Development*, pp. 79–88. The fact that in the present situation there are a growing number of students for whom this way of composing truth has not yet even taken form must be acknowledged as a matter of growing concern. Lee Kenefelkamp, a primary interpreter and elaborator of Perry's research and study, observes that "the integrity of American higher education is grounded firmly in its responsiveness to new and diverse populations. Each major sociological expansion in society has resulted in new students entering the college population." But the newest type of "new student" is in the lower one third of academic ability and the majority of these "new students" are white. "They are primarily students from lower socio-economic families having no previous history with higher education. They come to us succeeding best at concrete learning tasks, failing frequently at abstract tasks such as reading about, talking about, writing about theoretical subject matter. They have high needs for structure, personal attention, immediate feedback on performance, and education to directly result in vocational choice and economic improvement. They come, in short, to campus and faculty environments that do not know who they are." L. Lee Kenefelkamp, "Faculty and Student Development in the 80's: Renewing the Community of Scholars," *Current Issues in Higher Education*, no. 5 (1980), p. 15. Faculty seeking to better understand and respond to these students may find it useful to recognize that they do not need so much to be initiated into critical thought as to be sponsored into more reflective thought and to be nurtured into communities of loyalty and shared purpose. See also Robert Kegan, *The Evolving Self: Meaning and Process in Human Development* (Cambridge: Harvard University Press, 1982), chap. 6.

5. Jim Fowler and Sam Keen, *Life Maps: Conversations on the Journey of Faith*, ed. Jerome Berryman (Waco, Tex.: Word Books, 1979), p. 61.

6. For the term *unqualified relativism*, I am indebted to George Rupp. See George Rupp, *Beyond Existentialism and Zen* (New York: Oxford University Press, 1979), chap. 1. See also Kieran Egan's discussion of the curricular implications of what he terms the "ironic stage." *Educational Development* (New York: Oxford University Press, 1979), chap. 4.

7. Perry, *Intellectual and Ethical Development*, p. 33.

8. Ibid., pp. 109–33.

9. Robert Rankin, "Beginning," in *The Recovery of Spirit in Higher Education: Christian and Jewish Ministries in Campus Life* (New York: The Seabury Press, 1980), p. 10.

10. Fowler and Keen, *Life Maps*, pp. 82–83.

11. Robert Kegan, "There the Dance Is: Religious Dimensions of a

Developmental Framework," in *Toward Moral and Religious Maturity*, ed. Vergote (Morristown, N.J.: Silver Burdette, 1980), p. 408.

12. See Robert Kegan, *The Evolving Self*, p. 44.

13. The reader will note that this volume addresses the mind-heart dualism but often assumes, yet does not directly address, the body/embodied dimension of human personality. This undoubtedly, in part, reflects the body-spirit dualism that prevails in much of Christian culture. Beverly Harrison reviews the fallacies and dangers of the traditional body-spirit or heart-mind dualisms that fail to recognize persons as fully embodied, psychosexual, spiritual unities. "We are not split, 'compounds' of mind and emotion or body and spirit. Our emotions mediate our basic interactions with world. Our minds are an integrated aspect of our body-systems, shaped by the matrix of our sensuous being in the world" (p. 147). Pervasive sex-negativity in the Christian tradition has left us with a great deal of bodily repression. "With bodily repression comes a *loss of a sense of our connectedness* to the rest of nature, the cosmos, and to each other" (p. 148). Thus, our ability to affirm the integration of our selves precedes our ability to participate in mature interrelationships. See Beverly Wildung Harrison, "Human Sexuality and Mutuality," *Christian Feminism*, ed. Judith L. Weidman (San Francisco: Harper & Row, 1984), pp. 141–157. See also Tu Wei-ming, "The Confucian Perception of Adulthood," *Daedalus* Spring 1976, p. 115.

14. See Robert Jay Lifton and Richard Falk, *Indefensible Weapons: The Political and Psychological Case Against Nuclearism* (New York: Hasic Books, 1982), esp. chap. 10.

15. Frederik Schleiermacher perceived the feeling of absolute dependence to be the essence of religious sensibility. See *The Christian Faith*, ed. H. R. Mackintosh and J. S. Stewart (Philadelphia: Fortress, 1977). In the initial study that led to the thesis presented here, the author, with David Erb and Timothy Tiemans, engaged in a pilot study, a part of which included a consultation with William Weyerhaeuser. He, building on the thought and work of John Finch, offered the original version of the language of development in terms of dependence. See William Weyerhaeuser, "One Person's View of Conscience with Special Reference to His Therapy" (Ph.D. diss., Fuller Graduate School of Psychology, 1975).

16. To speak of authority "outside the self" is not to appear to counter the insight termed introjection of primary objects, particularly as understood in the object-relations school of psychology. Quite the contrary, in this era of development it is precisely the dynamic of introjection of which the individual is quite unaware, as he or she may assume that they are acting on the basis of their own choice rather than as influenced by those persons upon whom their personality formation has been dependent. See Ana-Maria Rizzutto, *The Birth of the Living God* (Chiago: University of Chicago Press, 1979).

17. For the image of "pushing away from the dock" I am indebted to my colleague David Erb.

18. William R. Rogers. "Dependence and Counterdependency in Psychoanalysis and Religious Faith," *Zygon*, vol. 9, no. 3 (Sept. 1974), p. 197. Rogers also notes that "the interesting thing about counter-dependence is that it

implicitly affirms realistic contexts in which there is genuine dependence."
He further argues that it is neurotic denial of such genuine dependence
that is expressed in the overprotestations of "independence" or autonomy
in our culture. Yet the counterdependence of the adolescent-becoming-
adult is not necessarily neurotic; it is, on the contrary, an appropriate
movement necessary to preparing to venture out into the seemingly deep
water of knowing for oneself what or what more is dependable and
trustworthy.

19. William R. Rogers, "Dependence and Counterdependency," p. 191. See
    also Takeo Doi, M.D., *The Anatomy of Dependence*, trans. John Bester
    (Tokyo, New York, and San Francisco: Kodansha, 1973), and Martin
    Bauermeister, "Dependence," *International Journal of Offender Therapy and
    Comparative Criminology*, vol. 26, no. 2 (1982), pp. 138–44.

20. James W. Fowler, *Stages of Faith: The Psychology of Human Development and
    the Quest for Meaning* (San Francisco: Harper & Row, 1981), pp. 197–98.

21. Parker Palmer, *The Company of Strangers: Christianity and the Renewal of
    America's Public Life* (New York: Crossroad, 1980).

22. Dwayne Huebner, "Toward a Political Economy of Curriculum and Human
    Development," *Curriculum and Instruction*, ed. Giroux, Penna, and Pinar
    (Berkeley, Calif.: McCutchan, 1981), p. 129.

23. James W. Fowler, "Stages in Faith," in *Values and Moral Development*, ed.
    T. Hennessy, S.J. (New York: Paulist Press, 1976), p. 184.

24. Robert Kegan, *The Evolving Self*, p. 90.

25. Dwayne Huebner, "From Theory to Practice: Curriculum," interview by
    William B. Kennedy, *Religious Education*, vol. 77, no. 4 (July-Aug. 1982),
    pp. 363–74. See also Walter Brueggemann, Sharon Parks, and Thomas
    Groome, *Act Justly, Love Tenderly, Walk Humbly: An Agenda for Ministry*
    (New York: Paulist Press, 1986), chap. 2.

26. See Kegan, "There the Dance Is," pp. 411–12.

27. Robert Selman, *The Growth of Interpersonal Understanding: Developmental
    and Clinical Analyses* (New York: Academic Press, 1980).

28. Fowler and Keen, *Life Maps*, p. 63.

29. See Sharon Lea Parks, "Communities as Ministry: An Exploration of the
    Role of Community in Undergraduate Faith Development," *NICM* Journal,
    Winter 1977.

30. Ronald Marstin, *Beyond Our Tribal Gods: The Maturing of Faith* (Maryknoll,
    N.Y.: Orbis Books, 1979).

31. Kegan, "There the Dance Is," pp. 411–12.

32. Marstin, *Beyond Our Tribal Gods*, p. 37.

33. Gordon Allport, "The Quest for Religious Maturity," *Waiting for the Lord:
    33 Meditations on God and Man*, ed. Peter A. Bertocci (New York: Macmil-
    lan, 1978), p. 60.

34. St. Paul, 1 Corinthians 12:12.

35. Linda Barnes (Unpublished lecture, Harvard Divinity School, 1984). See
    also Tu Wei-ming, "The Confucian Tradition: A Confucian Perspective on
    Learning to be Human," in *The World's Religious Traditions: Current Per-
    spectives in Religious Studies* (Edinburgh: T. & T. Clark, 1984), chap. 2.

36. (Language modified to be inclusive.) Earl Balfour in Belle Valerie Gaunt

and George Trevelyan, *A Tent In Which to Pass a Summer's Night: An Anthology for a New Age* (London: Coventure, 1977), p. 6.

CHAPTER 5—YOUNG ADULT FAITH: PROMISE AND VULNERABILITY

1. Lawrence Kohlberg, "Continuities in Childhood and Adult Moral Development Revisited," in *Life-Span Development Psychology: Personality and Socialization*, ed. Kohlberg and Turiel (New York: Academic Press, 1973). For a later analysis of these concerns, see Anne Colby, "Evolution of a Moral-Developmental Theory," *New Directions for Child Development*, no. 2 (1978).
2. Erik H. Erikson, *Identity: Youth and Crisis* (New York: Norton, 1968), p. 155.
3. Ibid. Such "identity" is an extraordinary achievement, because "it helps simultaneously in the containing of the post-pubertal id and in the balancing of the then newly invoked super-ego as well as appeasing the often rather lofty ego ideal—all in the light of a foreseeable future structured by an ideological world image."
4. Erik H. Erikson, *Childhood and Society*, 2d ed. (New York: Norton, 1963), pp. 261–63.
5. See Jane Loevinger, *Ego Development* (San Francisco: Jossey-Bass, 1976), p. 19.
6. Quotation from author's research interviews.
7. Jim Fowler and Sam Keen, *Life Maps: Conversations on the Journey of Faith*, ed. Berryman (Waco, Tex.: Word Books, 1978), p. 70.
8. Kenneth Keniston, *Youth and Dissent: The Rise of a New Opposition* (New York: Harcourt Brace Jovanovich, 1960), p. 7.
9. Clues or discrepant data confounding Fowler's formulation of stage four (Individuative-Reflective) were identified by Fowler himself. He wrote: "Frequently the transition from Stage 3 to Stage 4 is a somewhat protracted affair. The transition may begin around ages 17-18, though we rarely find well-equilibrated Stage 4 characteristics before the early twenties. It is not uncommon to interview adults at all ages who are best described as 3-4 transitional types and who give evidence of having been there for a number of years." *Life Maps*, p. 70. He also noted that "we find a quite large group of adults in our sample who are best described as 'equilibrated transitionals' between the Synthetic (stage 3) and Individuative (stage 4) stages." He suggests that "this may say something about the 'modal' [average acceptable] faith development stage encouraged in contemporary American society." James W. Fowler, "Faith and the Structuring of Meaning" (Paper delivered at the Convention of the American Psychological Association, San Francisco, Aug. 26, 1977), p. 20. See also note 18.
10. (Language modified to be inclusive.) Keniston, *Youth and Dissent*, p. 8.
11. Ernest L. Boyer, Jr., *A Sailor's Journal* (Volant, Penn.: Napier Press, 1974), pp. 19–20.
12. Keniston, *Youth and Dissent*, p. 8.
13. William G. Perry, Jr., *Forms of Intellectual and Ethical Development in the College Years: A Scheme* (New York: Holt, Rinehart & Winston, 1968), pp.

134–76. (This is not to negate the obvious fact that, for example, many young adults are parents—a commitment that is not "negotiable" in any fundamental sense. This is only to recognize that the extension of the life span and the educational needs of a postindustrial culture have altered the assumptions by which such commitments are engaged. For example, young adults may be parents but not self-supporting in the traditional sense. The phenomenon of "probing commitment" is affecting assumptions around marriage, family, and work patterns.)

14. Boyer, *A Sailor's Journal*, pp. 27–28. See also Ernest Boyer, Jr., *A Way in the World: Family Life as Spiritual Discipline* (San Francisco: Harper & Row, 1984).

15. Keniston, *Youth and Dissent*, pp. 8, 9.

16. Howard Brinton, *Quaker Journals* (Wallingford, Penn.: Pendle Hill, 1972), pp. 6–68. It is also interesting to note that the average age at which Quakers made the decision to be "at one" (marking the end of young adulthood) was twenty-six.

17. Keniston not only uses the term *youth* to designate the psychosocial stage I prefer to term *young adult*, he also uses the term *young adult* to describe those who are "apprentices to the existing society"—those who appear to settle down in the expected fashion. His use of the term *young adult* seems to describe those who move from adolescence into an "adulthood" marked by conventional forms of faith. Kenneth Keniston, *Youth and Dissent*, pp. 17–18.

18. Quotation from author's research interviews.

19. "The original mentor appears as an old man in Homer's *Odyssey*. A former companion and trusted friend of Odysseus, he remained behind to look after the great warrior's interests and to care for his son, Telemakhos. Mentor thus is a designated authority figure, a stand-in for the father. More to the point, however, his is the form chosen by Athena, goddess of wisdom, for her human manifestation. It is in the guise of Mentor that she urges the young Telemakhos to set out on a voyage in search of his father, and ultimately on a quest for a new and fuller identity of his own. The journey will be difficult, she warns him, but she will help, and he has 'a fair chance of winning through.' "

"So Mentor was half-man, half-God, half-male, half-female, believable yet unreachable. As wisdom personified, Mentor was the paradoxical union of both goal and path." Laurent A. Daloz, "Mentors: Teachers Who Make a Difference," *Change* (Sept. 1983), pp. 24–27.

20. John Henry Newman, so convinced of the power of the social environment to train, mold, and enlarge the mind, proposes that if he had to choose between a school without residence hall life and one with only the life of the residence hall, he would choose the latter, where "the conversation of all is a series of lectures to each." *The Idea of a University* (Notre Dame, Ind.: University of Notre Dame Press, 1982), pp. 109–111.

21. Robert Graham Kegan, "Ego and Truth: Personality and the Piaget Paradigm" (Ph.D. diss., Harvard University, 1977), p. 16.

22. Keniston, *Youth and Dissent*, pp. 18–21.

23. Fowler described stage 4 as "dichotomizing." Dichotomizing is a style of formal operations that has an either-or quality. Tensions (such as those

between individuality vs. belonging to community or the relative vs. the absolute) tend to be collapsed in one direction or the other. (Fowler, "Stages in Faith: The Structural Developmental Approach," *Values and Moral Development*, ed. T. Hennessy (New York: Paulist Press, 1976), p. 184. See also Fowler, "Faith Development Theory and the Aims of Religious Socialization," *Emerging Issues in Religious Education*, ed. Durka and Smith (New York: Paulist Press, 1976), p. 11.) I am proposing that the "dichotomizing" form of logic of Fowler's stage 4 may be of a "collapsed" character only in young adulthood or Fowler's "early stage 4."

24. Quotation from author's research interviews.

25. This is the form of faith resonant with Erikson's description of his stage of "generativity vs. stagnation." *Childhood and Society*, pp. 266–68.

26. In the initial formulation of his theory, Fowler was influenced by Robert Bellah's essay "Religious Evolution," in *Beyond Belief* (New York: Harper & Row, 1970), chap. 2. To the degree that personal faith development may indeed be parallel to the development of collective religious consciousness as Bellah described it, it is important to examine the essay vis-à-vis the modifications of faith development theory suggested here. We note that in Bellah's theoretical construct his "stages" also are transformations representing "differentiation between experience of self and the world that acts upon it." And if his "primitive" stage, which is both "fluid in its organization" and "mythical par excellence," corresponds with Fowler's first two stages, then Bellah's scheme seems to correspond with the sequence described here more adequately than Fowler's initial conception. Bellah's "archaic religion," with its complex of gods, priests, and sacrifice, hierarchically arranged, bound into one world, and merged with other social structures resulting in a social conformity reinforced by religious sanction, seems to parallel our description of "adolescent faith." The potential multiplication of cults and conflicting gods possible in "archaic religion" leads to "historic religion" as surely as the same in adolescent experience leads to young adulthood. "Historic religion," which denotes the breaking of cosmological monism, is the first clear conception of a core self facing a reality over-against the self, a dualism expressed in the separation of politics (the world-as-it-is) from religion (ideal faith), and in the sense that the "ideal life" is the separated life—all seem congruent with the young adult era proposed here. Bellah's "modern religion" (which I find much more problematic) nevertheless seems to correspond with "mature adult" faith. It does so in its collapse of dualism, its multiplex character, its completion of the centering of the self and its transcendence of any single religious group.

27. Erikson, *Insight and Responsibility* (New York: Norton, 1964), p. 126. Note that Erikson makes this comment in relationship to "adolescence." However, the statement seems less fitting to what Erikson would agree to term early adolescence, thus justifying our using it in relationship to young adulthood.

28. Daniel Levinson, *The Seasons of a Man's Life* (New York: Ballantine Books, 1979), pp. 91–97.

29. Keniston, *Youth and Dissent*, p. 9. "Admirers and romanticizers of youth tend to identify youth with virtue, morality, and mental health. But to do

so is to overlook the special youthful possibilities for viciousness, immorality, and psychopathology. . . . The fact that youth is a time of psychological change also inevitably means that it is a stage of constant recapitulation, re-enactment, and reworking of the past. This reworking can rarely occur without real regression, whereby the buried past is re-experienced as present and, one hopes, incorporated into it. Most youthful transformation occurs *through* brief or prolonged regression, which, however benignly it may eventually be resolved, constitutes part of the psychopathology of youth. And the special compulsions and inner states of youth—the euphoria of omnipotentiality and the dysphoria of estrangement, the hyperconsciousness of consciousness, the need for constant motion, and the terror of stasis—may generate youthful pathologies with a special virulence and obstinacy." pp. 18–19. *See also* David Dean Brockman, M.D., ed., *Late Adolescence: Psychoanalytic Studies* (New York: International Universities Press, 1984).

30. Carol Gilligan, "Moral Development," in *The Modern American College*, ed., Arthur W. Chickering and Associates (San Francisco: Jossey-Bass, 1981), pp. 139–57. This course was a characteristic effort on Kohlberg's part to apply theory to the real human community. Kohlberg hypothesized that the ethical principles characterizing his theory of the highest stages (structures) of moral reasoning (represented by Kant's moral imperative) would be able to meet and address the "adolescent's awareness of the limitations and hypocrisy of conventional moral thought." He intended the course to lead freshmen "in Socratic fashion toward the discovery of its solution in moral principles upon which all 'rational men could agree' " (p. 146).

However, as reported by Gilligan, "the course . . . did not lead, in any consistent way, to the development and stabilization of principled moral judgment described by the Kohlberg model [see appendix A, column C]. Instead, relativism appeared both more tenacious and complex than had originally been assumed. The relationship between relativistic and principled thinking resisted the simple logic of Kohlberg's stage sequence and instead complicated the understanding of moral development at its higher stages. Though some students progressed as Kohlberg had predicted, "these students seemed often to have avoided rather than confronted relativism, while the relativists conversely resisted the solution that principles offered to the problem of moral judgment" (p. 147).

"Rather than being dispelled by an understanding of moral principles, relativism instead generated questions about the adequacy or the applicability of the principles themselves" (p. 148). The conception of relativism as a transitional problem in the developmental shift from Kohlberg's conventional to principled stages did not fit these data. This transition (between Kohlberg's stages 4 and 5) appeared regularly to follow, as well as to precede, the attainment of principled thinking (p. 153). Students questioned the principles "not in their utopian conception, but rather in their practical construction—in their application to the reality of the actual moral dilemma, to what one student called 'the dilemma of the fact' " (p. 149). "The assumption of 'all other things being equal' tangled with the awareness that in reality they never were" (p. 148). Indeed, Gilligan asserts the following: although the Kohlberg stage sequence did not impart a clear developmental ordering to the changes in moral reasoning in these students, Perry's scheme (modified to fit moral judgment data) did (p. 153). For "Kohlberg, principled moral judgement *solved* the problem of moral relativism, for Perry, relativism *found* the problem in principled moral judgment" (p. 153).

This study also helps us to recognize that if "principled moral reasoning" (i.e., Kant's categorical imperative) is a structure of thought, it may conversely be a content of thought, that is, a particular philosophy of moral decision making. Given that "principled moral reasoning" both preceded and followed relativism, "principled moral reasoning" may apparently serve as content held by the structures of either adolescent, young adult, or tested adult commitment—but it will "mean" something different at each place. As such, the language of "principled moral commitment" could appear either before, in the midst of, or after the encounter with relativism and the exploration of commitment.

Gilligan's map of the journey of moral development as described by this study traces a journey from "objective truth" through "contextual relativism" to "ethical responsibility."

31. Carol Gilligan, "Moral Development," p. 150.
32. Fowler has described moral reasoning in his individuating stage (stage 4) as "reflective relativism or class-biased universalism." These designations suggest both the experience of relativism and the "ideal" quality characteristic of the young adult. Fowler and Keen, *Life Maps*, p. 99.
33. Gilligan, "Moral Development," p. 145.
34. Ibid., p. 155. See also John Michael Murphy and Carol Gilligan, "Moral Development in Late Adolescence and Adulthood: A Critique and Reconstruction of Kohlberg's Theory," *Human Development*, vol. 23 (1980), pp. 77–104.

CHAPTER 6—IMAGINATION: THE POWER OF ADULT FAITH

1. As quoted by H. Richard Niebuhr in *Radical Monotheism and Western Culture* (London: Faber & Faber, 1943), p. 41. Suzanne K. Langer, *Philosophy in a New Key: A Study in the Symbolism of Reason, Rite, and Art* (Cambridge: Harvard Univ. Press, 1942), pp. 40–41. Miguel de Unamuno, *Tragic Sense of Life*, trans. J.E. Crawford Flitch (New York: Dover, 1954; first published 1921), p. 20. William James, *The Varieties of Religious Experience: A Study in Human Nature* (New York: New American Library, Mentor, 1958), p. 397.
2. Philip Wheelwright, *The Burning Fountain* (Bloomington: Indiana University Press, 1954), pp. 8–16.
3. Suzanne Langer, *Philosophy in a New Key*, p. 40.
4. Jean Piaget. *Six Psychological Studies*, ed. David Elkind (New York: Vintage Books, 1968), pp. 88–92. See also James E. Loder, *The Transforming Moment: Understanding Convictional Experiences* (San Francisco: Harper & Row, 1981), pp. 40–41, 128–29. Loder perceives his "transformational logic" as the pattern that governs the stage transition process, but does not seem to extend it to the activity between stages, or "the motion of life itself."

5. Immanuel Kant, *Critique of Practical Reason* (1788), trans. L. Beck (Indianapolis: Bobbs-Merrill, 1956), pp. 3–19, 92–93. Pure reason, reason in its theoretical and speculative employment, cannot know matters of "eternal truth"—God, immortality, etc. Practical reason, reason in its practical employment, may only postulate (rather than know) freedom, immortality, self, world, and God, but must do so because one must determine the legitimacy of one's acts in the context of the phenomenal world in which actions have consequences.

6. A.D. Lindsay, *Kant* (London: Ernest Benn, 1934), pp. 95, 275. Kant perceived that imagination can contemplate but cannot know the sublime. However, as the imagination strains to its utmost to know the sublime, the imagination has a sense of being unbounded. It thereby activates practical reason, which then deduces the nature of the sublime (pp. 247–51). Lindsay suggests that Kant did not extend the role of imagination because he never saw that freedom and necessity somehow had to be reconciled within reason itself (p. 288).

7. Coleridge remarked in a notebook entry: "How excellently the German *Einbildungskraft* expresses this prime and loftiest faculty, the power of coadunation, the faculty that forms the many into one—*in-eins-bildung!*" Quoted in Ray L. Hart, *Unfinished Man and the Imagination: Toward an Ontology of Rules and Rhetoric* (New York: Herder & Herder, 1968), p. 338.

8. For this particular interpretation of Coleridge's thought I am indebted to Linda L. Barnes.

9. William F. Lynch, *Images of Faith: An Exploration of the Ironic Imagination* (Notre Dame, Ind.: University of Notre Dame Press, 1973), p. 119.

10. "FANCY on the contrary, has no other counters to play but with fixities and definites. The fancy is indeed no other than a mode of Memory emancipated from the order of time and space; while it is blended with, and modified by that empirical phenomenon of the will, which we express by the word CHOICE. But equally with the ordinary memory the Fancy must receive all its material ready made from the law of association." Coleridge, *Biographica Literaria*, ed. J. Shawcross (Oxford: Oxford UniversityPress, 1907) vol. 1, p. 202.

11. Lynch, *Images of Faith*, p. 63.

12. Samuel Taylor Coleridge, *The Friend*, 2 vols., ed. B. Rooke (Princeton: Princeton University Press, 1969), vol. 1, p. 177.

13. Samuel Taylor Coleridge, "The Statesman's Manual," in *Lay Sermons*, ed. R. White, vol. 6 of *The Collected Works*, ed. Kathleen Coburn (Princeton: Princeton University Press, 1972), pp. 59–61.

14. Ibid., p. 69. Coleridge continues, " 'and a pure influence from the glory of the Almighty; which remaining in itself regenerateth all other powers, and in all ages entering into Holy Souls maketh them friends of God and prophets' (Wisdom of Solomon, c. vii)." By "Sense" Coleridge denoted the imitative power, which is both voluntary and automatic. Coleridge, *Biographic Literaria*, vol. 1, p. 193. Sense is "Whatever is passive in our being, . . . all that the person is in common with animals, in *kind* at least . . . sensations, and impressions . . . *recipient* property of the soul, from the original constitution of which we perceive and imagine all things under the forms of space and time." (Language modified to be inclusive.

The reader will find quotations from Coleridge to follow customs of his day in style of writing, to be preserved as far as present printing practices will allow.) Coleridge, *The Friend*, vol. 1, p. 177. "Understanding" he perceived (with Kant) as the "regulative, substantiating and realizing power." Coleridge, *Biographica Literaria*, vol. 1, p. 193. Understanding is "the faculty of thinking and forming judgments on the notices furnished by the sense according to rules existing in itself which constitutes its true nature." Coleridge, *The Friend*, vol. 1, p. 177.

15. Northrop Frye describes the maturing of the imagination when he writes: "To the individual visionary the upper limit of Beulah is the limit of orthodox vision, and as far as a church of any kind will take him [or her]. It is a state in which nature is seen as beatified, God as a father, man as a creature, and the essence of mental life as the subjection of reason to mystery. It is, or may be a state of genuine imagination, but, because still involved with nature and reason, with a Father God, and perhaps a Mother Church, it is imaginative infancy, the child's protected world. Many visionaries remain in this state indefinitely, but those who reach imaginative puberty become aware of an opposition of forces, and of the necessity of choosing between them. Ahead of them is the narrow gap into eternity, and to get through it they must run away from their protecting parents, like Jesus at twelve, and become adult creators themselves. They must drop the ideas of a divine sanction attached to nature, of an ultimate mystery in the Godhead, of an ultimate division between a human creature and a divine creator, and of recurrent imaginative habits as forming the structure, instead of the foundation, of the imaginative life. . . . Imaginative puberty may occur at any time, or never, in a person's life." (Language modified to be inclusive.) *Fearful Symmetry: A Study of William Blake* (Princeton: Princeton University Press, 1947), pp. 389–90.

16. Coleridge, *Biographica Literaria*, vol. 1, p. 202.

17. Winnicott has addressed this paradox by observing that the child composes that which the child finds. D.W. Winnicott, *The Maturational Processes and the Facilitating Environment* (New York: International University Press, 1965), p. 181. See also Ana-Maria Rizzuto, *The Birth of the Living God: A Psychoanalytic Study* (Chicago: University of Chicago Press, 1979).

18. Winnicott, *The Maturational Processes*, p. 246.

19. Loder, *The Transforming Moment*, pp. 31–35.

20. Ibid. p. 32.

21. Coleridge, "Theory of Life," as quoted in Owen Barfield, *What Coleridge Thought* (Middleton, Conn.: Wesleyan University Press, 1971), p. 155.

22. Coleridge, *The Friend*, vol. 1, p. cii.

23. Wheelwright, *The Burning Fountain*, p. 79.

24. Gaston Bachelard, *The Poetics of Space*, trans. M. Jolas (Boston: Beacon Press, 1969), p. 39. See also Richard R. Niebuhr, *Experiential Religion* (New York: Harper & Row, 1972), pp. xi–xiv.

25. Wheelwright, *The Burning Fountain*, p. 82.

26. Loder, *The Transforming Moment*, p. 53.

27. Winnicott has used the term *holding environment* in his discussion of the mother and the infant. *The Maturational Processes*, p. 43–46. Kegan has appropriated this concept to describe the necessary conditions of relation upon which human development depends in every developmental era.

Robert Kegan, *The Evolving Self: Problem and Process in Human Development* (Cambridge: Harvard University Press, 1982), pp. 115–16.

28. Bachelard, *The Poetics of Space*, p. xviii. Coleridge described this moment of intellection by using the images of the waterbug and the snake—images incorporating pause as a factor of locomotion. Coleridge, *Biographica Literaria*, vol. 1, pp. 85–86.

29. Loder, *The Transforming Moment*, p. 32. Here Loder draws on Harold Rugg, who described this moment as allowing the "transliminal mind to be at work. The true locus of the creative imagination is the border state that marks off the conscious from the nonconscious. This is the stage between conscious alert awareness, about which Dewey wrote for fifty years, and the deep nonconscious in which Freud was intensely absorbed. James was aware of it, calling it 'the fringe,' 'the waking trance.' Others spotted it long ago. Galton names it 'antechamber'; Varendonck, 'foreconscious'; Schelling, 'preconscious'; Freud, 'subconscious'; more recently Kubie, 'preconscious'; and Tauber and Green, 'pre-logical.' This is the Taoists' state of 'letting things happen,' where daydreaming and reveries go on, where Whitehead's prehension and Wild's intuition, as primal awareness, function; where we know before we know we know . . . the true creative center. . . .

"I think of it as 'off-conscious,' not unconscious, for the organism is awake, alert, and in control." Harold Rugg, *Imagination* (New York: Harper & Row, 1963), pp. 39–40.

30. Coleridge, *Biographia Literaria*, vol. 1, p. 167.

31. Virginia Woolf, *A Room of One's Own* (New York: Harcourt Brace Jovanovich, 1929), pp. 5–6.

32. Loder, *The Transforming Moment*, p. 36.

33. Horace Bushnell, "Dissertation on Language," in *God in Christ* (Hartford, Conn.: Brown & Parsons, 1976), pp. 20–21.

34. Ibid., p. 24–25. Bushnell extends this premise even to conjunctions: "So the conjunction *if*, is known to be the imperative mood of the verb *to give*, and is written in the Old English, *gif*, with the particle *that* after it. 'I will do this *gif that* (if) you will do the other' " (p. 27).

35. Ibid., p. 23. "The Latin word *gressus*, for example, is one that originally describes the measured tread of dignity, in distinction from the trudge of the clown, or footpad. Hence the word *congress* can never after, even at the distance of thousands of years, be applied to the meeting or coming together of outlaws, jockeys, or low persons of any description. It can only be used to denote assemblages of grave and elevated personages, such as councillors, . . . ambassadors, potentates" (p. 51).

36. Ibid., p. 52 or 53. Note that *conception* (*con-capio*), meaning "to take up with" or "to hold together," may be thought of as "form only." Concepts are "formal" modes of thought refined and abstracted from the "gross material" of image.

37. Ibid., pp. 81–82, 80.

38. See Gordon Kaufman, *The Theological Imagination: Constructing the Concept of God* (Philadelphia: Westminster Press, 1981), esp. chaps. 1, 10; and Sallie McFague, *Metaphorical Theology: Models of God in Religious Language* (Philadelphia: Fortress Press, 1982).

39. Langer, *Philosophy in a New Key*, pp. 40–41. Langer uses *symbolization* to

connote all the activity of the imagination, at the level of sense and understanding. "Symbolization is pre-rationative, but not pre-rational. It is the starting point of all intellection in the human sense, and is more general than thinking, fancying, or taking action. For the brain is not merely a great transmitter, a super switchboard; it is better likened to a great transformer. The current of experience that passes through it undergoes a change of character, not through the agency of sense by which the perception entered, but by virtue of a primary use which is made of it immediately: it is sucked into the stream of symbols which constitutes a human mind." Langer, *Philosophy in a New Key*, p. 42. It is Coleridge who reserves symbols for the grasping of complex pattern, as when he writes that imagination is "that reconciling and mediatory power, which incorporating the reason in images of the sense and organizing (as it were) the flux of the sense by the permanence and self-circling energies of reason, gives birth to a system of symbols." Coleridge, "The Stateman's Manual," p. 26. It is this sense that Langer echoes when she identifies symbols as having to do with a relationship. "Meaning is not a quality, but a *function* of a term. A function is a *pattern* viewed with reference to one special term around which it centers; this pattern emerges when we look at the given term *in its total relation to the other terms about it*. The total may be quite complicated." Langer, *Philosophy in a New Key*, p. 55.

40. Quoted in Owen Chadwick, *The Secularization of the European Mind in the Nineteenth Century* (New York: Cambridge Univ. Press, 1975), p. 209. See also Harvey Cox, *Religion in the Secular City: Toward a Postmodern Theology* (New York: Simon & Schuster, 1984), chap. 17.

41. H. Richard Niebuhr, *The Meaning of Revelation* (New York: Macmillan, 1952), p. 93.

42. Alfred North Whitehead, *The Aims of Education and Other Essays* (New York: The Free Press, 1929), p. 25. He continues, "A Religious education is an education which inculcates duty and reverence" (p. 26).

43. Loder, *The Transforming Moment*, p. 55.

44. Ibid., p. 33.

45. This phrase is from a lecture by Richard R. Niebuhr and is, I think, perhaps a paraphrase from Coleridge (to whom it was attributed): "with feelings as fresh as if all had then sprang forth at the first creative fiat." *Biographia Literaria*, vol. 1, p. 59.

46. Lynch, *Images of Faith*, p. 63. See also Miguel de Unamuno, *Tragic Sense of Life*, pp. 192–93.

47. Loder, *The Transforming Moment*, p. 56. Note that the sequence of moments as presented here does not presume that the process always begins with conscious conflict. It may begin, for example, with an "image" or an "interpretation," but once the process is entered it drives toward completion.

48. Northrop Frye, "The Expanding World of Metaphor," *Journal of the American Academy of Religion*, vol. 53, no. 4, p. 591.

49. Loder also alerts us to the "seduction of the depths," indicating that "depths" are as "capable of error and distortion, seduction, and corruption as are the routinized patterns of behavior that others use to keep them from ever exploring matters of depth. The creative process surely *has* a depth dimension but it is *not* validated thereby." (Unpublished draft ms).

50. H. Richard Niebuhr, *The Meaning of Revelation*, pp. 95–109.
51. Patricia M. Sparks, *The Female Imagination* (New York: Avon Books, 1976), p. 4.
52. Barfield, *What Coleridge Thought*, p. 155. Barfield suggests that this detachment, when it occurs in a self-conscious will, is the nature of "apostasy" or "original sin." In the following passage, Coleridge elaborates the same: "The ground work, therefore, of all true philosophy is the full apprehension of the difference between the contemplation of reason, namely that intuition of things which arises when we possess ourselves, as one with the whole, which is substantial knowledge, and that which presents itself when transferring reality to the negations of reality, to the ever-varying framework of the uniform life, we think of ourselves as separated beings, and place nature in antithesis to mind, as object to subject, thing to thought, death to life." Coleridge, *The Friend*, vol. 1, p. 520.
53. H. Richard Niebuhr, *The Meaning of Revelation*, p. 96.
54. Ibid., p. 80.
55. (Language modified to be inclusive.) Ibid., p. 107. For further discussion of the dynamics of revelation and the quest for the moral life see Craig Dykstra, *Vision and Character: A Christian Educator's Alternative to Kohlberg* (New York: Paulist Press, 1981), esp. chap. 3.
56. Mary Moschella (Baccalaureate Address, Harvard Divinity School, June 8, 1983).
57. Robert Jay Lifton, *The Broken Connection: On Death and the Continuity of Life* (New York: Simon & Schuster, 1979), p. 39.

CHAPTER 7—HIGHER EDUCATION: A COMMUNITY OF IMAGINATION

1. Daniel Levinson, *The Seasons of a Man's Life* (New York: Ballantine Books, 1979), pp. 73–111.
2. See Richard A. Morrill, *Teaching Values in College* (San Francisco: Jossey-Bass, 1980), pp. 59–62.
3. Wilfred Cantwell Smith, review article: *The University: The Anatomy of Academe*, by Murray G. Ross, *Dalhousie Review*, Halifax, vol. 57 (1977), p. 546.
4. James Laney, Address to the Harvard Alumni Association, Apr. 1984. See "The Education of the Heart," *Harvard Magazine*, Sept.–Oct. 1985.
5. George Rupp, *Beyond Existentialism and Zen* (New York: Oxford University Press, 1979), pp. 8–9.
6. Thomas H. Groome, *Christian Religious Education: Sharing Our Story and Vision* (San Francisco: Harper & Row, 1980), pp. 4–7.
7. For the notion of education as initiation into a conversation I am indebted in part to R. S. Peters, "Education as Initiation," in *Philosophical Analysis and Education*, ed. Reginald D. Arehambault (London: Routledge & Kegan Paul, 1965), pp. 87–111. And the concept of education as conversation is helpfully articulated by Michael Oakeshott: "As civilized human beings, we are the inheritors, neither of an inquiry about ourselves and the world, nor of an accumulating body of information, but of a conversation, begun in the primeval forests and extended and made more articulate in the

course of centuries. It is a conversation which goes on both in public and within each of ourselves. Of course there is argument and inquiry and information, but wherever these are profitable they are to be recognized as passages in this conversation, and perhaps they are not the most captivating of the passages. . . . Conversation is not an enterprise designed to yield an extrinsic profit, a contest where a winner gets a prize, nor is it an activity of exegesis; it is an unrehearsed intellectual adventure. . . . Education, properly speaking, is an initiation into the skill and partnership of this conversation in which we learn to recognize the voices, to distinguish the proper occasions of utterance, and in which we acquire the intellectual and moral habits appropriate to conversation. And it is this conversation which, in the end, gives place and character to every human activity and utterance. *Rationalism in Politics and Other Essays* (London: Methuen, 1962), pp. 198–199, quoted in Paul H. Hirst, "Liberal Education and the Nature of Knowledge," in *Philosophical Analysis and Education*, ed. Arehambault.

8. Derek Bok, *Beyond the Ivory Tower: Social Responsibilities of the Modern University* (Cambridge: Harvard University Press, 1982), p. 308.

9. Alvin Kernan, "The Image of Wholeness," *The Chronicle of Higher Education*, Nov. 28, 1977.

10. Ibid.

11. William G. Perry, *Forms of Intellectual and Ethical Development in the College Years: A Scheme* (New York: Holt, Rinehart & Winston, 1970), p. 33.

12. Michel Foucault, *The Archaeology of Knowledge and the Discourse on Language* (New York: Pantheon Books, 1972), pp. 218–19.

13. James E. Loder, *Religious Pathology and Christian Faith* (Philadelphia: Westminster Press, 1966), p. 18.

14. Derek Bok, *Beyond the Ivory Tower*, pp. 61–66 ff.

15. For a somewhat different appropriation of this term, see Ruben Alves, *Tomorrow's Child: Imagination, Creativity, and the Rebirth of Culture* (New York: Harper & Row, 1972), p. 35.

16. Everett Mendelson, lecture to Science, Technology and Values Discussion Group, Massachusetts Institute of Technology, 1983.

17. See William F. Lynch, *Images of Faith: An Exploration of the Ironic Imagination* (Notre Dame, Ind.: Univ. of Notre Dame Press, 1973), p. 8.

18. Harold Loukes, *Friends and Their Children: A Study in Quaker Education* (London: George G. Harrap, Friends Home Service Committee, 1969), p. 93. This same recognition is evident in the suggestion that students major in a problem area, such as health, the cities, hunger and nutrition, criminal justice, or the environment, and minor in a discipline like economics, sociology, biology, art, or English. Arthur Levine, *When Dreams and Heroes Died: A Portrait of Today's College Student* (San Francisco: Jossey-Bass, 1980), p. 140.

19. For reflection on the issue of the size of contemporary institutions of higher education in America, see Virginia B. Smith and Alison R. Bernstein, *The Impersonal Campus: Options for Reorganizing Colleges to Increase Student Involvement, Learning, and Development* (San Francisco: Jossey-Bass, 1979).

20. See Parker Palmer, "Contemplation and Action in Higher Education: An

Interpretation," in *The Recovery of Spirit in Higher Education*, ed. Robert Rankin, pp. 103–22.

21. Parker Palmer, *To Know as We Are Known: A Spirituality of Education* (San Francisco: Harper & Row, 1983), p. 80.

22. For the notion of "accessibility" as a task of education I am particularly indebted to Mary Boys, *Biblical Interpretation in Religious Education* (Birmingham, Ala.: Religious Education Press, 1980), pp. 285–86.

23. William G. Perry (Lecture, Harvard University, 1979).

24. Søren Kierkegaard, *Concluding Unscientific Postscript*, trans. D. Swenson (Princeton: Princeton University Press, 1941), p. 169 ff.

25. Jacques Barzun, *Teacher in America* (Indianapolis: Liberty Press, 1981; originally published 1945), pp. 42–43.

26. See *Harvard Divinity Bulletin*, Sept.–Oct. 1980, p. 5.

27. William Barrett, *The Illusion of Technique* (New York: Anchor Books, 1978), pp. 262–64.

28. Steven Weinberg, "Observable Traces of Extra Dimensions," lecture, Harvard University, May 3, 1984.

29. Rosemary Radford Ruether, "Beginnings: An Intellectual Autobiography," in *Journeys*, ed. Gregory Baum (New York: Paulist Press, 1975), pp. 40–41.

30. See Lawrence Kohlberg, "The Moral Atmosphere of the School," *Readings in Moral Education*, pp. 149–63.

31. This is the "henotheistic faith" described in chapter 2. H. Richard Niebuhr, *Radical Monotheism and Western Culture* (London: Faber & Faber, 1963), pp. 27–28.

32. This same concept is sometimes referred to as transfer of training. See Gardner Murphy and Joseph K. Kovah, *Historical Introduction to Modern Psychology*, 3rd ed., chap. 15 (New York: Harcourt Brace Jovanovich, 1949), pp. 222–36.

33. Alvin Kernan, dean of graduate studies at Princeton, has observed that although "other institutions no longer seem to organize the vast conflicting ranges of knowledge . . . the academy satisfies the almost metaphysical need for cosmic orientation, by providing reassurance that although the old certainties have been battered almost to oblivion, we still have or someone conceivably might have a grasp on the outlines of reality and a method for getting on with the work of understanding ourselves and the world. . . . It is also, I think, the confidence that such knowledge gives that finally marks and strengthens those who have really deeply absorbed what the university has to say about a cautious confidence that the world is ultimately understandable." "Images of Wholeness," *The Chronicle of Higher Education*, Nov. 28, 1977.

34. The critical importance of the moment of "interpretation" in the learning process is reflected in studies of women's development in which "finding a voice" is a way of expressing one's own sense of growth. See Mary Belenky et al., *Women's Ways of Knowing: The Development of Mind, Voice, and Self*, (New York: Basic Books, 1986).

35. Daniel Bell, *Daedalus* (Fall 1969), p. 1040, as quoted in *Students, Religion, and the Contemporary University*, ed. C. Minneman (Ypsilanti, Mich.: Eastern Michigan University Press, 1970), p. v.

36. See Zelda F. Gamson et al., *Liberating Education* (San Francisco: Jossey-Bass, 1984).

37. Thomas H. Groome, *Christian Religious Education: Sharing Our Story and Vision* (San Francisco: Harper & Row, 1981).

38. Adrienne Rich, "Teaching Language in Open Admissions," in *On Lies, Secrets, and Silences* (New York: Norton, Inc., 1979), p. 65. For further discussion of curricular patterns appropriate to developmental needs see Michael Basseches, *Dialectical Thinking and Adult Development* (Norwood, N.J.: Ablex, 1984), Kieran Egan, *Educational Development* (New York: Oxford University Press, 1979), and Zelda Gamson et al., *Liberating Education*, esp. chaps. 2, 7.

39. Samuel Taylor Coleridge, *Biographia Literaria*, ed. J. Shawcross, 2 vols. (Oxford: Oxford University Press, 1907), vol. 2, p. 5.

40. Kenneth Keniston, *The Uncommitted: Alienated Youth in American Society* (New York: Dell, 1960), pp. 338–39. See also Nancy Malone, "On Being Passionate: Reflections on Roman Catholic Approaches to Spirituality," in *The Recovery of Spirit in Higher Education*, ed. R. Rankin (New York: Seabury, 1980), pp. 58–67.

41. Theodore H. White, *In Search of History: A Personal Adventure* (San Francisco: Harper & Row, 1978), pp. 49–51. Evidence that such a "spiritual guide" has always been needed (as well as to some degree lacking) in the context of higher learning is revealed in the following report written in 1868 by Ralph Waldo Emerson on behalf of the Visiting Committee to Harvard College. In the portion transcribed below, the Visiting Committee recommends establishing a "Library Counselor."

"The first use of a college library is to be irresistibly attractive to young men. In daily experience it is not so. Young men go in and then go out of it repelled by the multitude of books which only speak to them of their ignorance,—their very multitude concealing from the gazing youth the one or the few volumes which are there waiting for him with the very information or leading he wants. Could some kind scholar take pity on his sincere curiosity, and by a little discreet [word omitted] guide him to the class of works and presently to the precise author who has written as for him alone. Could not a gentleman be found to occupy a desk in Gore Hall [library] as the *Library Counselor*, to whom the Librarian could refer inquiry on authors and subjects? We are aware that such selection would be a delicate point,—easy to miss,—and that it requires a man of sympathy, a lover of books and readers of books, to fulfill the design. Every one of us has probably known such persons, but it will commonly happen that they are of such condition or pre-engagements as not to be thought of as candidates.

"The suggestion was made in conversation at the last meeting of the Committee but found such favor that it was directed to be embodied in the report." Harvard Archives, Report of the Visiting Committee, 1868 (in Emerson's own hand), pp. 452–54.

42. Quotation from author's research interviews.

43. Demaris Wehr, "Being Mentored" (unpublished paper, Swarthmore College, 1985). The significance of faculty in the experience of students and particularly the significance of women faculty as "role models, reaffirming

or stimulating achievement aspirations and solidifying occupational choices"
for career-salient students is reported in a study of women at Barnard
between 1979 and 1983. See also Mirra Komarovsky, *Women in College:
Shaping New Feminine Identities* (New York: Basic Books, 1985); Laurent A.
Daloz, *Effective Teaching and Mentoring: Realizing the Transforming Power of
Adult Learning Experiences* (San Francisco: Jossey-Bass, 1986).

44. Agnes K. Missirian, *The Corporate Connection: Why Executive Women Need
Mentors to Reach the Top* (Englewood Cliffs, N.J.: Prentice-Hall, 1982), p. 47.
45. May Sarton, *The Small Room* (New York: Norton, 1961).
46. Arthur Levine, *When Dreams and Heroes Died*, p. 77. See also Lansing
Lamont, *Campus Shock: A Firsthand Report on College Life Today* (New York:
Dutton, 1979).
47. (Language modified to be inclusive as per the present practice of the
author.) Harvey Cox, *Seduction of the Spirit* (New York: Simon & Schuster,
1973), pp. 100–101, 103–4.
48. See Sharon D. Welch, *Communities of Resistance and Solidarity: A Feminist
Theology of Liberation* (Maryknoll, N.Y.: Orbis Books, 1985), pp. 81–84.
49. Nancy Malone, "On Being Passionate," p. 66.
50. Erikson, *Insight and Responsibility* (New York: Norton, 1964), p. 133.
51. See also Roberto Mangaberira Unger, "The Critical Legal Studies Movement," *Harvard Law Review*, Jan. 1983.
52. Robert Frost, *The Poetry of Robert Frost*, ed. E. Lathem (New York: Holt,
Rinehart & Winston, 1969), p. 403.

CHAPTER 8—CULTURE AS MENTOR

Audre Lorde, *Sister Outsider: Essays and Speeches by Audre Lorde* (Trumans-
burg, N.Y.: The Crossing Press, 1984), p. 38.
1. Clifford Geertz, *The Interpretation of Cultues* (New York: Basic Books, 1973),
p. 312.
2. Erik Erikson, *Insight and Responsibility: Lectures on the Ethical Implications
of Psychoanalytic Insight* (New York: Norton, 1964), p. 127.
3. Fred L. Polak persuasively contends that the history of civilizations may
be interpreted in terms of the nature of a civilization's image of the future.
The Image of the Future, vol. 1 (New York: Oceana Publications, 1961),
p. 15–56.
4. Richard E. Wentz, "The Sanctions of Celebration," in *Students, Religion,
and the Contemporary University*, ed. C. Minneman (Ypsilanti, Mich.: Eastern Michigan University Press, 1970), p. 99.
5. As quoted in the *Radcliffe Quarterly*, vol. 65, no. 3 (Sept. 1979), p. 2.
6. Kenneth Keniston, *Young Radicals: Notes on Committed Youth* (New York:
Harcourt, Brace & World, 1968).
7. Steven M. Tipton, *Getting Saved from the Sixties: Moral Meaning in
Conversion and Cultural Change* (Berkeley: University of California
Press, 1982).
8. Arthur Levine, *When Dreams and Heroes Died: A Portrait of Today's College
Student* (San Francisco: Jossey-Bass, 1980), p. 21. This report is based

upon studies conducted under the auspices of the Carnegie Commission and Carnegie Council on Policy Studies in Higher Education, including national surveys of undergraduates in 1969 and 1976 and a 1978 survey of nearly six hundred schools, representing a cross-section of American higher education, on institutional and student changes since 1969. In addition, during visits in 1979 to twenty-six colleges and universities reflecting the diversity of this nation's institutions of higher education, a round table discussion was conducted with a varied group of undergraduates. A ranking student government official or the student newspaper editor was interviewed as well. In addition, extensive use was made of the Cooperative Institutional Research Program's annual studies of college freshmen.

9. Levine reports: "The fact of the matter is that almost half of all college students feel helpless to control the world in which they live. Forty-nine percent agree that an individual can do little to bring about change in our society (Carnegie Surveys, 1976). . . . Only one out of three students would influence social values and one out of seven cares to grapple with political structures." Levine, *When Dreams and Heroes Died*, p. 113. For an educational response see Cheryl Hollmann Keen, "Sources and Supports for a Sense of Global Responsibility in College Students and Adults," Ed.D. diss, Harvard University, 1981.

10. *Fortune Magazine*, Apr. 7, 1980, pp. 74–84.

11. See Levine, *When Dreams and Heroes Died*, pp. 137–38.

12. Frank Levy and Richard C. Michel, "Are Baby Boomers Selfish?" *American Demographics*, Apr., 1985, p. 41.

13. Sharon Bauer-Breakstone, "Seeing Students from Diverse Backgrounds Through the Perry Lens, and Vice Versa" (Unpublished paper, Bureau of Study Counsel, Harvard University), p. 5.

14. Mustapha Khan, "A Critical Review of Recent Literature on Suicide among Young Black American Men" (Unpublished paper, Harvard University, January 1984); also *Vital Statistics of the U.S.* vol. 2, "Mortality," U.S., Department of Health and Human Services National Center for Health Statistics, 1979; and U.S. Department of Health and Human Services National Center for Health Statistics, Hyattsville, Maryland, 1984. *See also* Elsie J. Smith, "The Black Female Adolescent: A Review of the Educational, Career and Psychological Literature," *Psychology of Women Quarterly*, Vol. 6 (3) Spring 1982.

15. R. Zuker and A. Kirk, "Some Sociopsychological Factors in Attempted Suicide among Urban Black Males," *Suicide and Life-Threatening Behavior*, vol. 2, pp. 76–86.

16. See Robert N. Bellah et al., *Habits of the Heart: Individualism and Commitment in American Life* (Berkeley: Univ. of California Press, 1985).

17. "A majority of adult Americans now believe that what they think does not count for much; that the people running the country do not really care what happens to them; that public leaders do not know what they are doing; that the rich get richer and the poor get poorer; and that government wastes a lot of money. Since 1964, the percentage of people reporting such opinions has seen a dramatic increase." Levine, *When Dreams and Heroes Died*, p. 10.

18. George Rupp, *Beyond Existentialism and Zen: Religion in a Pluralistic World* (New York: Oxford University Press,. 1979), p. 10.

19. Kenneth Keniston, *The Uncommitted: Alienated Youth in American Society* (New York: Harcourt, Brace & World, 1965), p. 251.

20. Rupp, *Beyond Existentialism and Zen*, p. 12.

21. This use of model as metaphor is similar to the use of typologies that Rupp proposes as a method of discerning truth within the pluralism of competing worldviews. Typologies, by means of which multiple perspectives and their interaction within a single tradition or culture may be described, provide a way of understanding the more complex interactions between different traditions (p. 13). "If one abstracts from specific images, conceptions, institutions, and rituals, there may in short be greater commonality in systematic commitments or tendencies between some adherents of different traditions than among the full variety of perspectives within a single tradition" (p. 14). Rupp states clearly the limits of typologies: "Those limitations derive from the fact that types are abstractions. To abstract or generalize from concrete and particular data may be illuminating. . . . But abstractions also distort data insofar as their status as abstractions is obscured or overlooked. For instance, a generalized type may be employed to indicate systematic common ground between a particular Buddhist and a particular Christian perspective. This procedure does not, however, entail the contention that there are no differences between the two positions or that the type can replace both positions. Instead, as a deliberate simplification of experience . . . every typology patently presupposes the complex dynamics of the concrete and varied traditions from which it is abstracted" (p. 24).

22. See Margaret R. Miles, *Image as Insight: Visual Understanding in Western Christianity and Secular Culture* (Boston: Beacon, 1985).

23. Alfred North Whitehead, *Symbolism: Its Meaning and Effect* (New York: Macmillan, 1927), p. 88.

24. Sharon D. Welch, *Communities of Resistance and Solidarity: A Feminist Theology of Liberation* (Maryknoll, N.Y.: Orbis Books, 1985). pp. 81–84.

25. John Stuart Mill, "Coleridge," *Essays on Ethics, Religion and Society by John Stuart Mill*, ed. J. Robson (Toronto: University of Toronto Press, 1969), p. 122.

26. (Language modified to be inclusive.) Wilfred Cantwell Smith, *The Faith of Other Men* (New York: New American Library, 1963), p. 63.

27. Laurent A. Daloz, *Effective Teaching and Mentoring: Realizing the Transforming Power of Adult Learning Experiences* (San Francisco: Jossey-Bass, 1986).

28. See James P. Keen, "Global Issues, Citizen Responsibility and Community Life: A New Synthesis for Social Education" (Ed.D. diss., Harvard University, 1979).

29. See Letty Russell, *The Future of Partnership* (Philadelphia: Westminster, 1979).

30. See Harvey Cox, *Religion in the Secular City: Toward a Postmodern Theology* (New York: Simon & Schuster, 1984).

31. See Paul Tillich, *Love, Power, and Justice: Ontological Analyses and Ethical Applications* (London: Oxford Univ. Press, 1954).

32. See Alexander W. Astin, *Four Critical Years: Effects of College on Beliefs,*

Attitudes, and Knowledge (San Francisco: Jossey-Bass, 1977), pp. 67–71, 77–79.

33. Harriet Harvey, *Stories Parents Seldom Hear: College Students Write About Their Lives and Families* (Delacorte Press/Seymoure Lawrence, 1983), p. 38.

34. Ana-Maria Rizzuto's work as a psychoanalyst and researcher is of enormous usefulness in understanding some of the dynamics by which faith is formed and translated across the life span. Informed by the object-relations school of psychology, she describes the formation of the initial God representation (image) in the child. She finds that like the teddy bear that serves as a transitional object in the development of the very young child, even so is one half of the image of God formed from the primary relationships the child has "found" in life, whereas the other half comes from the child's capacity to "create" a God according to his or her needs (p. 179). She then observes that the image of God "remains a potentially available representation for the continuous process of psychic integration" (p. 180), but "if the God representation is not revised to keep pace with changes in self-representation, it soon becomes asynchronous and is experienced as ridiculous or irrelevant or, on the contrary, threatening or dangerous" (p. 200). *The Birth of the Living God: A Psychoanalytic Study* (Chicago: University of Chicago Press, 1970). See also, John McDargh, *Psychoanalytic Object Relations Theory and the Study of Religion: On Faith and the Imaging of God* (Lanham, MD: University Press of America, 1983) and John H. Westerhoff III, *Will Our Children Have Faith?* (New York: Seabury, 1976).

35. See Richard R. Niebuhr, *Experiential Religion* (New York: Harper & Row, 1972), pp. 23, 112–24.

36. See James W. Fowler, *Becoming Adult, Becoming Christian: Adult Development and Christian Faith* (San Francisco: Harper & Row, 1984).

37. Frederick Buechner, *Wishful Thinking: A Theological ABC* (New York: Harper & Row, 1973), p. 95.

38. See Walter Brueggeman, *The Prophetic Imagination* (Philadelphia: Fortress Press, 1978); Gordon D. Kaufman, *Theology for a Nuclear Age* (Philadelphia: Westminster Press, 1985); Urban T. Holmes III, *The Future Shape of Ministry* (New York: Seabury, 1971), esp. chap. 11.

39. See Don Browning, *The Moral Context of Pastoral Care* (Philadelphia: Westminster Press, 1976).

40. Vivienne Hull, "A Wedding Meditation" (Unpublished paper, Chinook Learning Community, Clinton, Washington, 1983).

41. See Margaret R. Miles, *Fullness of Life: Historical Foundations for a New Asceticism* (Philadelphia: Westminster Press, 1981).

42. Sam Keen, *The Passionate Life: Stages of Loving* (San Francisco: Harper & Row, 1983), p. 5.

43. See David Riesman, *On Higher Education: The Academic Enterprise in an Era of Rising Student Consumerism* (San Francisco: Jossey-Bass, 1980), pp. 162-78.

44. For several observations regarding the effect of religiously affiliated schools, see Astin, *Four Critical Years*, pp. 235–36.

45. Bill Moyers, "A Walk Through the Twentieth Century with Bill Moyers," Public Broadcasting System, Sept. 22, 1984.

46. Miguel de Unamuno, *Tragic Sense of Life* (New York: Dover, 1954; originally published 1921), p. 17.

47. See Parker J. Palmer, *The Company of Strangers: Christians and the Renewal of America's Public Life* (New York: Crossroad, 1983).

48. Myron B. Bloy, Jr., "The Ministries of Faith Communities: an Interpretation," in *The Recovery of Spirit in Higher Education*, ed. Rankin (New York: Seabury, 1980), pp. 211–14.

49. See Sharon Parks, "Pastoral Counseling in the University," *Handbook of Pastoral Care*, ed. Parsons, Capps, and Wicks (New York: Paulist Press, 1985), pp. 388–405.

Index

Academic objectivity, 134–135, 150, 166, 175–176. *See also* Relativism; Truth
Academy. *See* Higher education
Accommodation, 35, 100
Act, faith as, 21, 94, 111, 144, 204
Adams, James Luther, 212
Administrators, in higher education, 2, 60, 97, 140–141, 161, 165, 174
Adolescence, 4, 34, 64, 75, 83, 86; emergence as stage, 78–79; identity in, 76, 80; late, 6; prolonged, 3, 75, 78, 80–81. *See also* Young Adult
Adulthood: defined as mode of meaning-making, 6; and developmental psychology, 6, 37; expectations of, 4, 7, 41, 85, 177, 187–188, 202–205; when it begins, 1–7, 74, 75–78. *See also* Young Adult; Tested Adult; Mature Adult
Affect, 8, 37, 52–53, 55, 60, 88, 90, 120, 149, 167, 214; and cognition, 36; in dependence, 53; motion of, 60–61; ordering power of, 26, 41, 214. *See also* Dependence, Despair, Furies, Gladness, Grief, Joy, Passion, Suffering
Allport, Gordon, 69
Amazement metaphor, 25–27
Ambivalence, as characteristic, 82, 83, 87, 90, 92, 98, 99, 109, 190
⸻dices, 206–208
⸻ faith, 40–41, 206–207
⸻ ⸻–35, 110
⸻ ⸻: locus of, 85–86,
⸻ 70–71,

Barzun, Jacques, 149
Basseches, Michael, x, 232
Bauer-Breakstone, Sharon, x, 182, 216
Belenky, Mary, 215, 231
Belief, xv, 9, 10–13, 103, 197
Bell, Daniel, 161
Bellah, Robert, 222, 234
Beyond the Ivory Tower (Bok), 140–141
Biological maturation, 30, 35, 46
Birth, 14, 211
Body-spirit dualism, 218
Bok, Derek, 140
Boyer, Ernie, Jr., 81, 83
Boys, Mary, 231
Bounds of social awareness, 64, 66
Brinton, Howard, 84–85
Broughton, John, 215
Browning, Don, 236
Brueggemann, Walter, 219, 236
Buber, Martin, 40, 107
Buddhist vision, 71
Buechner, Frederick, 199
Bushnell, Horace, 122–124

Canopy of significance, 21–22, 178–179
Carroll, James, 214
Catholic Worker Movement, 28–29
Charismatic leadership. *See* Mentor; Professor
Christianity. *See* Religion
Cognition, 33–36; and dependence, 69; form of, 43–53, 208; form of Logic, 206–207
Cogwheeling of generations, 32
Colby, Anne, x, 220
Coleridge, Samuel Taylor, 112, 113–117, 118, 120, 128, 137–138, 142, 166, 167–168, 227
Commitment, 2, 3, 70, 95, 192, 208; probing, 82–84; in relativism, 49–50, 138, 148; tested, 84, 93; convictional, 50–53

Community: of confirmation, 88, 160, 164, 166; of contradiction, 160, 164, 166, 177–178; conventional, 64, 70, 95, 208; diffuse, 64–65, 70, 95, 208; form of, 61–69, 70, 89–96; 208; ideologically compatible, 89, 90–91, 93, 95, 208; of imagination in higher education 139–165; mentoring community, 89–91; network of belonging, 90, 99, 161, 201; open to other, 66–69, 70, 94, 208. *See also* Holding environment; Religious communities

Commonwealth of God, 97, 200

Complexity, 50–51, 67, 79, 109, 118, 124, 139, 154, 175, 194, 198, 200 global, xvii, 185, 186–187

Composing: of "explicit system," 50; mind, 47; meaning, 37; truth, 41, 45, 48–50. *See also* Faith; Meaning-making; Imagination; Symbolization

Concept, 227

Concrete operations, 33–34

Confident, adult as, 88, 93–94, 95, 208. *See also* Tested adult

Conflict. *See* Conscious conflict

Confucian teaching, 71, 218

Conscious conflict, 117–120; in higher education, 141–145. *See also* Ambivalence; Suffering

Constructive-developmental theory, 40, 41, 46, 63, 109; and faith, 39–40, 105

Contemplation. *See* Pause

Content, of structure, xvi, 34, 45, 68, 101–106, 109–112. *See also* Image

Context of rapport, 145. *See also* Community; Holding environment

Conventional: community, 64, 70, 90, 95, 208; faith, 41, 75, 208; morality, 104; stage, 55; world, 48;

Convictional commitment, 50–51, 95, 208

Cosmos, 16, 22

Counterdependence, 55–57, 70, 79–80, 95, 208, 218–219

Cox, Harvey, 173–174, 228, 235

Crimes of passion, 23

Critical reflection, 2, 41, 68, 75, 79–80, 159, 178, 188, 192, 198; emergence of, 46–50, 76–77. *See also* Conscious conflict; Dream; Ideal; Vision

Culture, xii, 177–205

Curriculum, xvi, 159, 174. *See also* Hidden curriculum; Syllabus

Cynicism, 13, 68, 184, 198, 105, 205

Daloz, Larry, x, 193–195, 221, 233

Day, Dorothy, 28–29, 31, 41–42

Deep self, 59

Dependence, 5, 14, 53, 63, 69, 71, 133, 160, 218; form of, 53–61, 70, 85–88, 95, 208. *See also* Trust

Despair, xv, 30, 99, 104, 145, 151–152, 154, 157, 183, 190, 198. *See also* Suicide

Development, defined, 31; motion of, 38; in response to interaction, 36, 38

Developmental psychology, xvi, 3, 6, 31–42; and feminist critique, 215; as motion, 37. *See also* Constructive-Developmental theory

Dewey, John, 33

Dichotomizing, 91–93, 98, 221–222. *See also* Ambivalence

Differentiation, of self-other, subject-object, 36-37

Diminishment, experience of, 25

Discipline, 42, 142, 144, 145, 150, 155, 174, 201

Discrepant data, 4, 91

Doubt, 48, 77, 145, 179, 190, 198

Dream, formation in young adulthood, 97–98, 139, 150, 153, 158, 164, 180–181, 193, 198, 199; reexamination of in later life, 192–195

Dualistic position, 44–47, 48, 64, 70, 95, 208

Dykstra, Craig, x, 215, 229

Easter, 26

Egan, Kieran, 232

Einbildungskraft, 113, 130, 189

Education, 125; as initiation and conversation, 229–230; *See also* Higher education

Emerson, Ralph Waldo, 232

Emotion. *See* Affect; Dependence; Despair; Furies; Gladness; Grief; Joy; Passion; Suffering

Epistemology, 112, 134–139. *See also* Cognition; Reason; Relativism; Truth

Enlightenment, The, 112–116, 175
Environment and cognition, 35–36. *See also* Community; Holding environment
Equilibrated transitional, 3, 210
Equilibrium, in developmental process, 35, 38
Erb, David, ix, xiii, 218
Erikson, Erik, 14, 32–33, 39, 40, 75–76, 77, 80, 97, 209, 222
Ethic of connection, 196
Evil, 105, 144, 190; and imagination, 128–129
Explicit system, 50, 70, 95, 206–207, 208

Faculty, xvii, 12–13, 41, 146, 148, 158, 202. *See also* Administrators; Mentor; Professor
Fairbank, John King, 169, 170
Faith, xv, 9–27, 31, 41, 71, 108, 187, 197, 212; as act, 21, 111, 144, 204; and belief, 10–13; in constructive-developmental perspective, 39; as dialogue with promise, 26, 153–154; doubt of itself; 77; journey toward mature adult faith, 70, 95, 208; as suffering, 21–27; as trust, 19–21, 26, 43; as truth, 19–21; young adult, 78–100
Faith development, 157, 189; stages of, 40–41, 206–207, 208
Fanciful, in contrast to imagination, 114, 225
Feelings. *See* Affect
Fiddler on the Roof, 22
Finch, John, 218
Formal operational thought, 34, 76, 206–27, 208
Fowler, James, ix, xvi, 16–17, 40–41, 50, 51, 55, 64, 66, 73, 82, 85, 91, 206–207, 208, 210, 211, 212, 213, 214, 215, 220, 221–222
Fox, George, 167
Fragile, young adult as, 88, 89–90, 94, 95, 208
Frankl, Viktor, 210, 214
Freedom, 49, 96, 98, 152–153, 155, 178, 182; and constraint, 62
Freud, Sigmund, 32, 57, 215
Frost, Robert, 176
Frye, Northrop, 127–128, 226

Furies, 23, 213
Future, xvii, 7, 139, 157, 184, 191, 195, 200, 204, 205

Gamson, Zelda, 232
Gilligan, Carol, 38–39, 57–58, 101–105, 208, 209–210, 215, 223–224
Gladness metaphor, 25, 26–27, 199–200
God, 16–20, 53, 111, 124, 128, 130, 133, 199, 202; and journey toward faith, 70; "no God, but God," 190–191; tribal, 68. *See also* Theists
Gribbon, Robert, 209
Grief, 16, 25, 193
Groome, Thomas, 161–164, 213, 219, 229

Harrison, Beverly, ix, 218
Harvard College, xvi, 169, 178–179, 182
Harvey, Harriet, 236
Heart-mind dualism, 149, 218
Hedonism, 104, 105
Hegel, G.W.F., 137
Heinz Dilemma, 102–103
Hidden curriculum, 156, 203
Higher education, xiii, xv, xvii, 2, 9, 12, 73, 131–132, 133–176; adulthood in relation to, 5, 7; and culture, 177–181; ethical development in, 41, 139–141; religiously committed schools, 202–203. *See also* Community; Curriculum; Professor
Holding environment, 120, 145, 158, 161, 164, 226–227. *See also* Community
Holmes, Oliver Wendell, 50–51
Holmes, Urban T., 236
Holocaust, 139, 214
Huebner, Dwayne, x, 62
Hull, Vivienne, ix, 40

Ideal, characteristic of young adult faith, xiii, 96, 103, 104, 105, 108–109, 153–154, 178, 205, 208; and images, 150–151, 164, 195
Ideas, power of, 151–153
Identity, 75–78, 220. *See also* Self
Ideology, 90–91, 99–100, 104–105, 190, 206–207, 208

The Illusion of Technique (Barrett), 151
Image, 35, 105, 110, 122–126, 195; as
  finite, 123–124, 128–129; and
  higher education, 147–158; of
  ultimacy, 180–181, 188; *See also*
  Imagination; Metaphor;
  Symbolization
Imagination, 106, 111–132, 187–188;
  and Coleridge, 113–116;
  confrontive, 118–119;
  Einbildungskraft, 113; five moments
  within, 117–132; in higher
  education, 139–165; and Kant, 113,
  225; neglect of, 111–112; as praxis,
  161–165; stylistic, 119
Immanent, faith as, 19, 22, 212
Inner-dependence, 57–58, 70, 95, 208;
  confident, 88, 94; fragile, 88–91, 94
Insight, 122–126. *See also* Image;
  Revelation
Institutional self, 73
Interaction, 61; generating
  development, 36–37. *See also*
  Community; Motion; Relation
Interdependence, 53, 58–61, 69, 70,
  95, 188, 195–196, 199, 201, 208
Interpersonal, as era in development,
  54–55, 208; Interpersonal Self, 73;
  Interpersonal stage, 54–55
Interpretation, moment in
  imagination, 127; in higher
  education, 159–161. *See also*
  Syllabus
Introjection of primary objects, 218
I-Thou relationship, 40

James, William, 107, 151–154
Jonestown suicides, 100
Joy, 51, 198, 201. *See also* Affect
Judaism. *See* Religion
Jung, Carl, 4, 50
Justice, 66–68, 108, 198, 200

Kahn, Mustapha, 234
Kant, Immanuel, 33, 101, 112–113,
  134, 225
Kaufman, Gordon, 212, 227, 236
Keen, Cheryl, x, 234
Keen, James P., x, 235
Kegan, Robert, x, 36–38, 39, 52, 54–
  55, 73, 82, 111, 215, 216, 217
Kenefelkamp, L. Lee, 217

Keniston, Kenneth, 78–82, 84, 85, 91,
  98, 168, 179, 180, 185, 221
Kernan, Alvin, 231
Kimmel, Douglas, 4
King, Martin Luther, Jr., 48
Kohlberg, Lawrence, 39, 40, 67, 73,
  101, 102, 206–207, 208, 209, 223–
  224, 231
Knowing, as composing, 112. *See also*
  Epistemology
Komarovsky, Mirra, 233

Lamont, Lansing, 233
Langer, Suzanne, 107, 124, 227–228
Late adolescence, 6. *See also* Young
  adult
Levine, Arthur, 180, 234
Levinson, Daniel, 97, 133
Levy, Frank, 181
Lifton, Robert, 131, 218, 229
Little, Sara, 213
Locus of authority, 85–86. *See also*
  Authority
Loder, James, ix, 117, 142, 224, 228
Loevinger, Jane, 216, 220
Lorde, Audre, 177
Loukes, Harold, 144
Love, 66, 68, 196, 200
Lynch, William F., 14, 22–23, 114

McGill, Arthur, 150
Malone, Nancy, 174, 232
Marstin, Ronald, 66–69
Marriage, 3, 56, 60, 133, 181, 185, 201
Masters, Edgar Lee, 43
Mature adult, 27, 69–70, 94, 155, 188,
  195
Maurin, Peter, 28
McDargh, John, 236
McFague, Sallie, 227
McGill, Arthur, 150
Mead, George Herbert, 33
Meaning, xii, xiv–xv, 9–27, 37, 109–
  111; in adulthood, 4–5; defined,
  13–19, 209
Meaning–making: activity of, 15–16,
  52; defined, 14
Meaninglessness, 16, 99. *See also*
  Furies; Suffering
Medea, 22–23
Men: moral reasoning in, 38–39;
  suicide of, 183

Mendelson, Everett, 143
Mentors, 86–88, 99–100, 139–140, 170–172, 195, 205; culture as mentor, 177–205; mentoring community, 89–91, 191, 200; original mentor, 221
Metaphor, 108–109, 111, 123, 186–187. *See also* Image
Michel, Richard C., 181
Mid-life, 58–59, 69, 98; of sixties generation, 192
Miles, Margaret, 235, 236
Missirian, Agnes, 233
Model, journey toward faith, 69–72, 95, 208
Modular, faith, 18, 186; imagination, 142–143, 158
Moral judgment, 38–39, 73, 49, 101–104, 113, 144–145, 203, 206–207, 208, 223–224
Moran, Gabriel, 215
Moratorium, 3, 75, 209
Moschella, Mary, x, 129–131
Motion, 37–38, 53, 56, 190, 191, 195; of affect, 61; of development, 38; as dialogue with promise, 26, 153–154; of faith, 26, 30, 40, 72; of life and Spirit, 116–117; of meaning-making, 63; as reality of universe, 40; of stages, 39. *See also* Development; Spirit; Suffering
Multi-systemic, 51, 207, 208

Neglects, in Piagetian theory, 36, 40; of imagination, 111–112
Network of belonging, 61–62, 89–90; deviation and, 66
Neugarten, Bernice L., 210
Newman, John Henry, 221
Niebuhr, H. Richard, 16, 17, 18–19, 125, 128, 129, 211, 212, 231
Niebuhr, Richard R., ix, 23–24, 213, 228, 236
Noam, Gil, 215, 216
Notes, 209–237
Novice adult, 133

Oakeshott, Michael, 229–230
Olmsted, Frederick Law, 29–30, 31, 41–42
Open to "other," form of community, 63, 66–69, 70, 95. *See also* Self and other
Over-against, characteristic, 79, 91–94

Palmer, Parker, 146–147
Palmer, Robert, 155
Parents, 2; young adults as, 198, 221
Parks, Sharon, 211, 219, 237
Passion, 23, 30, 97, 167-170, 189, 191, 195, 214, 131. *See also* Affect
Passover, 26
Pause, 23, 120–122, 227; in higher education, 145–147, 164
Perry, William G., ix, x, 41, 44–45, 47, 49, 50, 52, 82–83, 141, 148, 158, 209
Perspective Taking, 76, 208, 206–207, 215
Peters, R. S., 229–230
Physics, 5, 138, 154
Piaget, Jean, 32, 33–36, 39, 40, 52–53, 61, 110, 111–112
Pluralism, 185–187
Poetic imagination, 167–168
Polak, Fred, 233
Power, of relation. *See* Depenence; Promise
Praxis, imagination as, 161–165
Probing commitment, 82–84, 208. *See also* Ambivalence; Relation
Professor, 134–136, 145, 148, 157, 174, 175, 191; defined, 166; as spiritual guide, 165–173. *See also* Faculty; Mentors
Promise: characteristic of human, 107–108; faith as dialogue with, 26, 211; recompose at birth, 14–15, 211; of young adult, 75, 96–100; of young adult world, 187, 205
Psychology, 37, 61; defined, 31; object-relations school of, 218. *See also* Developmental psychology
Public, accountability to, 9, 21, 140–141, 144, 159, 165, 196, 204

Quakers, 84–85, 144, 167

Rankin, Robert, ix, 217
Reason, 112–116, 128, 135
Regression, 3, 73, 223
Relation: between self and world, 58; dependence as found in, 53; faith as triadic, 17; and human

development, 36–39; of self-other, subject-object, 36–37, 53; truth emerging in, 39, 59; of young adult to society, 80–83, 90, 94. *See also* Community; Dependence; Interaction

Relativism, 45, 47, 65, 101–104, 136–138, 155, 185, 208, 223–224; commitment in, 49–50. *See also* Unqualified relativism

Release of energy, as moment in imagination, 126–127; and higher education, 158–159

Religion, 10, 40, 66, 69, 114, 129, 161, 178, 201; defined, 124–126; Buddism, 71; Christianity, 12, 71, 155, 200; Hinduism, 20, 71; Judaism, 22, 97, 200; and pluralism, 185–186; and young adulthood, 197–204. *See also* Belief, Confucian Teaching; God; Revelation; Ritual; Sufi reflection; Theists

Religious language, 189, 197–198; of scriptures, 70–71, 174

Religiously committed schools, 202–203

Repatterning, 53, 126–127; and higher education, 158–159

Representations, 111–112. *See also* Image

Responsible, for one's own knowing, 56–58, 76–77; in moral reasoning, 38–39. *See also* Critical; Justice; Love; Service

Revelation, 125. *See also* Imagination

Rich, Adrienne, 164–165

Ricoeur, 51

Riesman, David, 236

Right distance, in process of imagination, 119

Rituals, 123; of adulthood, 2–3; of birth, 211; of faith, 10, 186, 191, 197, 200

Rizzuto, Ana-Maria, 218, 226, 236

Rogers, William, ix, 57, 209, 214, 218–219

Ruether, Rosemary, 155

Rugg, Harold, 227

Rupp, George, x, 136–137, 185–186, 217, 235

Russell, Letty, 235

Sarton, May, 171

Schleiermacher, Frederik, 218

Scholarship, 116, 136, 160, 229–230. *See also* Discipline

Self, 62, 37, 39, 56, 86, 87, 92, 109, 154; authority of, 57, 60; divided, 83, 98–99; form of, 208

Self-aware self, 76, 79–80, 103, 164, 208. *See also* Critical; Identity

Self-other relation, 36, 38, 53, 60, 190, 196

Self-selected class or group, 65–66, 70, 93, 95, 208

Selman, Robert, 40, 64, 67, 215, 216

Service to society, 30, 105, 140, 181, 182, 184, 195–196

Sexuality, 201

Shipwreck metaphor, 24–25, 26–27, 55, 198, 203; and higher education, 156–157; and culture, 186–187

Sixties generation, 179–180, 191–192

The Small Room (Sarton), 171

Smith, Wilfred Cantwell, 10, 11, 12, 16, 18, 20, 135–136, 190–191, 211, 212

Social awareness, bounds of, 64–70, 206–207

Sociology, 37, 61

Soul, 120–121, 122, 144, 157, 167; defined, 31

Spencer, Greg, 156

Spirit, 71, 115, 119, 122, 129, 166–168, 187, 189, 191. *See also* Faith; Imagination; Motion

Sraddha, 20

Stage, 32–33, 67, 75, 78–79, 82, 156; of composing truth, 41; of faith development, 40–41, 206–207, 208; motion of, 37–39

Strand image, 95–96, 216–217

Structure, xvi, 33, 34, 40–41, 45, 68, 100–106, 110. *See also* Content; Constructive-Developmental theory

Students, 134, 148, 202; experience of, 119, 143–144, 145, 149–150, 158–159, 170–172, 197; of lower academic ability, 217; graduate, 2, 129, 171, 172; undergraduate, 1, 74, 85, 172, 180

Subject-object, 36–39, 48–49, 229. *See also* Academic objectivity; Epistemology; Self-Other

Suffering, 51–52, 71, 130, 155, 157–158, 214; of childhood, 59; and faith, 21–27. *See also* Affect; Conscious conflict; Shipwreck
Sufi meditation, 190–191
Suicide, 100, 183–184, 214
Syllabus, 173–176
Symbolization, 107, 111, 124, 157, 206–207, 227–228. *See also* Imagination

Tacit system, 50, 206, 208
"Take Something Life A Star" (Frost), 52
"Teaching Language in Open Admissions" (Rich), 164–165
Technology, and culture, 79, 179–181, 184–185
Tested adult, 84, 88, 93, 94, 208
Theists: henotheism, 18, 231; monotheism, 18–19; polytheism, 17–18, 211–212. *See also* God
Theology, 37, 150, 185–186, 188, 202, 204
Theory and practice, 161. *See also* Praxis
Those like us, 64, 206
Those who count, 61, 66, 208
Tiemans, Timothy, xiii, 218
Tillich, Paul, 17
Tipton, Steven, 179–180
Transcendent, faith as, 13, 19, 22, 212
Transition, as young adulthood, 3, 73–75
Trust, 14, 19–21, 26, 30, 32, 58. *See also* Dependence
Truth: adequacy of, 42, 111–112, 123–124, 129, 134–139, 147–148, 160–161, 166, 167, 202–203; composing of, 38–39, 41, 45, 48–50, 71; empirical, xv, 134–135, 138; faith as, 19–21; in higher education, 8, 12–13, 158, 202; as relational, 38–39, 51, 59; relative nature of, 47, 71. *See also* Moral reasoning; Relativism; Revelation
Tu Wei-ming, 219
Two great yearnings, 63
Tyranny of the "they," 76

Ultimate: concern, 17, 53; environment, 14, 16–17; image of, 180–181; reality, xv, 16, 109–110, 135, 151, 177, 188. *See also* God; Faith
Unger, Roberto, 175
Unqualified relativism, 47–49, 65, 70, 137–138, 148

The Varieties of Religious Experience (James), 151
Vision, 28, 30, 96, 103, 108, 109, 131, 135, 136, 162–163, 175, 184, 196, 202, 204. *See also* Dream
Vocation, 133, 139; defined, 199; of higher education, 168; of religious community, 198–199
Vocationalism, 174, 181
Voice, 38–39
Vulnerability, of young adult, 75, 81, 85–91, 96–100, 145; to disappointment, 88; to erosion of social contract, 179–185; to financial dependence, 1, 5, 181–182, 194; to images and ideology, 68, 100, 105, 151–153; to mentoring leadership, xii, 86–88, 100; to own arrogance, 94; to pathology, 223; to relationship, 58, 65; of young adult world, 187, 205. *See also* Dependence

Wehr, Demaris, 170–171
Weinberg, Steven, 154–155
Welch, Sharon, 233, 235
Weyerhaeuser, William, 218
Wheelwright, Philip, 107–108, 118–119
When Dreams and Heroes Died (Levine), 180
White, Theodore, 168–169, 170, 179
Whitehead, Alfred North, 125, 188
Wilderness, 70–71
The Will to Believe (James), 153
Winnicott, D. W., 226–227
Wisdom, 30, 94, 139, 146, 166, 189, 195, 196, 208. *See also* Mature adult
Women, 1, 97, 185, 196, 215; moral reasoning of, 38–39; suicide of, 183

Woolf, Virginia, 121–122
World, concept of, 16

Young Adult, xii, 2, 27, 42, 50, 59, 73–
  106, 133, 139, 177–184; definition
  of, 77, 85, 109; emergence as "new"
  stage, 79–81; relation to society, 80–
  83, 94, 99; world as, 186–187
Youth, 85